Europe in the Media

A Comparison of Reporting, Representation,
and Rhetoric in National Media Systems
in Europe

The European Institute for the Media Series

 THE EUROPEAN INSTITUTE FOR THE MEDIA

This volume was sponsored by the European Cultural Foundation.

EUROPEAN

CULTURAL

FOUNDATION

CULTURE EUROPÉENNE FONDATION

FONDATION EUROPÉENNE DE LA CULTURE

Europe in the Media

A Comparison of Reporting, Representation,
and Rhetoric in National Media Systems in Europe

Deirdre Kevin
European Institute for the Media

LEA LAWRENCE ERLBAUM ASSOCIATES, PUBLISHERS
2003 Mahwah, New Jersey   London

Lawrence Erlbaum Associates, Inc., Publishers
10 Industrial Avenue
Mahwah, NJ 07430

Cover design by Kathryn Houghtaling Lacey

Library of Congress Cataloging-in-Publication Data

Kevin, Deirdre.
    Europe in the media : a comparison of reporting, representation, and rehetoric in national media systems in Europe / Deirdre Kevin (European Institute for the Media).
        p.   cm.
    Includes bibliographical references and index.
    ISBN 0-8058-4422-8
        1. Journalism—Europe. 2. Europe—Press coverage—Europe.
I. European Institute for the Media. II. Title.
PN5110 .K48 2002
079'.4—dc21
                                         2002023526
                                            CIP

Printed in the United States of America
10 9 8 7 6 5 4 3 2 1

This book is dedicated to my parents,
Tom and Mairead Kevin,
and to my family for their love and support.

Contents

For Lack of Affection: The Challenges for Europe in the Media and a European Public Sphere

Jo Groebel

European Institute for the Media

"I have a story in my head like a butterfly in a glass, and its untouchable beauty torments me." This sentence from an episode written by Leon de Winter on a tale read once and then gone also stands for Europe. We have an idea of our corner of the Earth, which somehow goes beyond history, the euro, politics, and everyday debates. We feel attached to our neighbours, we want peace, we feel mutual cultural roots. But we have no definite pictures, no myths, no media stories which would make the perceived fascination for Europe into a foundation for identity or at least for passionate interest.

When the towers of the World Trade Center collapsed on 11 September 2001 live for all to see, many Europeans temporarily became Americans. An attack on the Eiffel Tower, the Tower of London, or the Kremlin would make us into Frenchmen, Englishmen, or Russians. But even without this macabre scenario, we have no icon which would make us into Europeans. Europe is an abstract entity for most people, the result of sensible resolutions. It first becomes graphic when it stands for differences, differences between regions, peoples, and lifestyles.

However positive these differences can be viewed, without common cultural interests they do not provide a viable basis for political and military decisions for the coming months and years. These common interests must be gradually created by broad media-supported European publicity. Up to now such publicity has not existed outside of the spheres of politicians, intellectuals, and historians. Europe is still seen through national lenses. People know a French, a British, and a German Europe, but they do not know a European one. This is demonstrated by surveys amongst the population, and by analysis performed by the European Media Institute. It was also in this particular context that this book developed.

Among other things, Deirdre Kevin in her analysis demonstrates that press and television in the individual countries of Europe deal in quite different ways with the subject. It is not a central theme but when it is addressed then with few corresponding slants and directions. The German and French press tends to have a wide range of information and opinion about Europe whilst important sections of the British press often adopt a mainly negative approach. Television is more neutral but emphasises quite different subjects in connection with Europe. In Italy it is culture and multiculturalism, in Poland enlargement and the work of the Commission; the Dutch place emphasis on historical backgrounds, whilst in Germany and France it is everyday politics. Arte makes these two countries bilateral star pupils. The quality press devotes essays to Europe; there are some excellent European magazine programmes on the screen but for prime time television the main subjects are BSE, Commission scandals, the euro here and there, and flight corridors to Afghanistan.

Despite the same formats such as "Big Brother," common European interests in entertainment and TV film have even diminished. We watch fewer French, British, or Italian series. Since "Eurocops" there has been no real interest in co-productions addressing the subject. The cinema used to be the place for European yearnings, myths, and fantasies. According to analyses performed by the Strasbourg *Observatoire,* with the exception of the occasional individual success, there are ever fewer productions from other European countries nowadays. Pan-european media remain marginal. *The European* is no longer being published; "Euronews" has to fight not only for ratings but for cable spots. There are, of course, exceptions: the United Kingdom ran a midnight television show entitled "Eurotica" . . .

Since Europe hardly exists in the media, at least in the real mass media, it also hardly exists in the heads and emotions of the citizens. And because it does not occur here, it is also not a passionate subject in the media. It may appear exaggerated to expect a great passion, namely love, for a nation and for our corner of the Earth, as the former President of Germany, Gustav Heinemann, would suggest. But one subject of some delicacy is the majority of people's lack of affection for, or at least interest in, anything European. The unavoidable risks brought about by enlargement and possible military campaigns, but also the positive growing-together can only be mastered with the help of the population. This can crumble away at any time, as the Irish vote on the Nice treaty has shown, if Europe remains a politico-administrative process. PR campaigns are of no help. As long as the stories, pictures, and people are missing, the attractiveness for the mass media, and thus for the majority of citizens, will also be missing.

And yet there are stories that carry throughout Europe; literature has proved this to us. Cees Nooteboom, Zadie Smith, and Michel Houellebecq have local colour and yet they still hit the contemporary nerve everywhere. Their publishers did not even need much courage. Even if the audio-visual business is even more complex, the many good approaches for Europe which do exist in editorial departments need broader support.

Apropos Houellebecq. Presumably we really are moving within a transitional phase. In retrospect, numerous cultural phenomena and statements from the time before the attacks on the USA, social exhibitionism, l'art pour l'art violence, yuppy cynicism, could be read as indicators of climax and the start of the end of a phase of decadence at one and the same time. If the cards are reshuffled, if we seek a community of values once again, Europe will get a new chance because as a new entity it is innocent. The media cannot be expected to be what they are not: missionaries for Europe. But they are amplifiers, flow heaters for social developments, for the small beginnings. The wish of many to gain orientation, a cultural identity in complex times, can be satisfied by Europe. It is, after all, the root of that which made the United States strong, namely democracy, humanism, and enlightenment.

To strengthen these principles, we must now move together not only on a political and military level; we can also do so in the media. The means are there. A change of perspective, greater exchange of European series, now where some genres need new impulses and the ratings argument presents itself anew. Pressure on politicians to introduce the subject of Europe into schools. And: curiosity about our neighbours. The process which has made the USA strong and successful can also be put into motion in Europe parallel to transatlantic friendship, namely the welding of cultures in a melting pot to develop a new culture. The pictorial language of Hollywood was essential for this. We do not even run the risk of flattening out cultural differences. Because our everyday life still takes place in different regions. The borders are open. We have Schengen. What we now need is a communication Schengen. Stories serve as a link. We have neglected the European ones.

Let us refer to Gustav Heinemann once again. The things we love in a woman or man, the secrets, the facets, the buds—our corner of the Earth has them and, different to Germany, bears no historical burdens. Perhaps we might give Europe a try. We only need a few stories. The media could find them under the glass and let the butterfly fly away.

Preface

This book draws together the results of several research projects that examined media coverage of European political and cultural affairs and media representations of Europe. The work attempts to outline some of the important debates regarding European integration and also to describe the media landscape in which these debates are informed, reflected, and facilitated. The research sought to answer several questions, including the role of the media in the democratic process at the European level and the extent to which the media contributes to and reflects the process of European integration.

This research was developed at a time when the European Institute for the Media (EIM) was beginning to focus on some of the cultural implications of media development in Europe. Globalisation, with the integration of markets, the movement of people, and the opening of frontiers, is mirrored at the regional level in the form of 'Europeanisation,' a process additionally influenced and shaped by institutional and political cooperation between European countries. The subsequent changes in the nature of governance, and the interrelationship between the globalisation of business and international cooperation on the part of governments, serve to drive this process. At the same time, transport, travel, education, and communications have helped widen people's experience of the world, with the rapid integration of communication and media systems.

The text addresses debates and analyses from the fields of political science in relation to the process of European integration, EU policy-making, and public participation and opinion formation. It also outlines relevant media theory regarding the relationships between the media and democracy, and the media and identity formation. In this way, it provides a valuable link between these two separate fields of investigation in an area that is of increasing interest to academics, students, politicians, and journalists. The examination of the European media landscape is supplemented by recent data and statistics from a variety of research and analysis institutes concerned with media, film, and culture. The original data gathered by experts for the first part of the book is based on the news output of more than 50 media outlets in eight countries during two 1-week monitoring periods. The data from the second part of the book was collected and coded by experts with reference to the programming of more than twelve major broadcasters in six countries. This wide scope of comparative analysis allowed for an extremely interesting overview of the way that national media systems in France, Germany, Ireland, Italy, the Netherlands, Poland, Spain, Sweden, and the United Kingdom approach the issue of European integration.

ACKNOWLEDGMENTS

The research for this book was carried out in cooperation with European partners in nine countries who gathered data, provided background reports, and carried out interviews. I am especially grateful for the expertise, hard work, advice, and suggestions of the following people: Michael Palmer, Uwe Hasebrink, Hermann-Dieter Schroeder, Paschal Preston, Gianpietro Mazzoleni, Federico Boni, Leen d'Haenens, Thadeusz Kowalski, Maciej Mrozowski, Esteban Lopez-Escobar, Rosa Berganza, Lars Nord, Philip Schlesinger, Raymond Boyle, Gillian Doyle and Vince Campbell. Thanks to all the other people involved in the tedious task of coding news and television programmes, including Claudia Lampert, Roderick Flynn, Debbie Ging, Emma Miller, Kjm Jannsen, Sylvie Le Meut, Karine Grandpierre, Tamara Schlesinger, Hannah Schlesinger, Martin Macdonald and Will Dinan. The initial project, dealing with news coverage of European affairs, was supported by the European Cultural Foundation in Amsterdam. I would like to express my gratitude to the Foundation and to former Director-General Dr. Rudiger Stephan. The second part of the research was commissioned and supported by the German broadcaster Westdeutsche Rundfunk (WDR) in Köln as an original piece of research to serve as a basis for discussion at the WDR *Europaforum* in Brussels in November 2000. Professor Jo Groebel, director general of the EIM, presented the results at the conference, which focused on media coverage of European issues with the participation of EU and national politicians and journalists. At the WDR, thanks to Michael Radix, *Europaforum* organiser, and to the technicians who worked on the video clips for the conference.

At the EIM I completed the project organisation and analysis in consultation with Runar Woldt. Many thanks to Runar for his advice and support, to Jo Groebel and his predecessor Bernd-Peter Lange for their interest and support, and more recently to David Ward for his assistance and support in finalising the publication details and for general advice regarding the book. The news research was carried out with the assistance of Martina Pohl and Thorsten Faas, who spent many hours with me putting thousands of code sheets into SPSS. The television programme project was completed with the assistance of Anne van der Schoot. Help with proofreading and formatting was provided by Elena Muncey. Many thanks to the other EIM colleagues for continued support and friendship, especially Emmanuelle Machet, Gillian Mc-Cormack, Eleftheria Pertzinidou and Dušan Reljić all of whom also read parts of the text. I am also grateful for the valuable advice during the initial development of the project, provided by Professor Winfried Schulz and Professor Philip Schlesinger. Last, but not least, I would like to acknowledge the help and support of the people at Erlbaum publishers, especially Emily Wilkinson, Bonita D'Amil, and Debbie Ruel for their support and patience during the production process.

Introduction

According to much of the relevant literature, Europe is 'adrift,' being 'invented,' and 'rediscovered,' while there is an ongoing 'search' for a European identity. Such an identity is frequently discussed in the context of nationalism and globalisation, as well as from European perspectives (Delanty, 1995; Leonard, 1998; Mundy, 1998; Newhouse, 1997; Shore, 1993). There is a general consensus that the leaders of Europe can offer the people no definite direction and no overriding shape or plan for Europe in the new millennium. For politicians, the external influences of globalisation of markets, finance, and consumer culture are making the future difficult to control, while internal pressures regarding security, employment, and integration make the future difficult to predict.

It is widely agreed that the starting point for the current European identity crisis was the end of the cold war, which ended the concept of Europe defined as West in opposition to East. This also allowed for a resurgence of ethnic and nationalist tensions in Eastern Europe, most painfully borne out in the former Yugoslavia. This process continued with the Kosovo crisis, but examples of nationalist resurgence and ethnic tension are not confined to the 'new democracies.' The crisis involves not just these changes but also the political response to them.

Economic considerations may not strengthen the process of integration any further and may, without the development of a 'cultural' dimension to the European project, enhance divisions in European societies. This does not imply a cultural 'harmonisation' but rather a growing understanding of the cultural and political traditions that are shared between Europeans. Those traditions that are different are accepted as Europe's asset—a huge diversity of national and regional cultures. From a political point of view, the development of a European perspective alongside national and regional political

1

perspectives—not only in elite political circles but also in the wider society—
can contribute to the success of the project.

Definitions of Europe cannot logically be confined to specific political, cultural, or geographic descriptions. It would, perhaps, be appropriate to think
about 'Europeanness' on different levels. The integration of European Union
(EU) member states in the political and economic sense and the promotion of
European integration (political and cultural) by the EU is one level. A wider
view of Europe, which includes those countries just outside EU membership
and those in Eastern Europe and the trans-Caucasus states, represents another level. The word *Europe,* according to Boxhoorn (1996) 'has been debated
and defined time after time. It has been used—let us not forget—abused by
statesmen, politicians, clergymen, and ordinary citizens in order to achieve
various goals, and even now the word Europe is used in different meanings
and different contexts' (p. 133). The research presented here was devised with
a wide conception of 'Europe' in mind but is, to an extent, when dealing with
integration, forced into focusing on the EU and its continuous (slow-moving)
incorporation of the edges into the core.

In the midst of what could be considered largely economically determined
global trends, the European Union's political agendas, with the social project
of bringing people together, has its complications (not least the contradictory
problem of setting them apart as expressed in concerns regarding a 'Fortress
Europe'). The European Union has been described as the first attempt in history to build a zone of eternal peace, but at the turn of the century, European
integration faced many challenges including the implications of the enlargement of the European Union into central and eastern Europe. A further challenge involves the 'deepening' of European integration, with the launching of
full Economic and Monetary Union (EMU) and the development of a common
foreign and defence policy.

The process of 'Europeanisation'[1] has raised several questions about what
has been termed the *democratic deficit,* wherein the expansion of policy-making
powers at the European level, or the ceding of sovereignty by member states
to the supranational level, has not been accompanied by the development of a
clearly accountable governmental system.

With the difficulties over the ratification of the Maastricht Treaty[2] and
a perceived lowering of support for the European Union,[3] efforts have been

---

[1]This concept is further explored in chapter 1 but refers essentially to the impact that EU
legislation and regulation has on political and economic life at the national level.

[2]The Maastricht Treaty, known as the Treaty on European Union, was signed in 1992. The
main focus was to develop political and economic union, including the establishment of the single currency, and to develop a common foreign and security policy. Much of this was controversial, for example, the Danish and French referenda and the British debate on the treaty.

[3]Assessed regularly through Eurobarometers (see http://www.europa.eu.int/comm/dg10/
epo/polls.html)

made to increase the openness and transparency of policy processes and agendas. There have been some moves to reform the institutional balance of the Union in order to give more power to the European Parliament (EP), the only directly elected body of the EU. Although the EU is a supranational organisation and therefore in some way above or beyond the nation-state, its institutions are made up of member state representatives, whether elected or selected, and the ultimate forum for decision making remains the European Council/Council of Ministers, which represents the intergovernmental aspect of the EU. The problem, then, becomes one of a further distancing of the citizens from the policy-making process. This intergovernmental aspect has increased the executive power of the nation-states and their prime ministers and cabinets by allowing a certain element of 'sidelining' of the national parliamentary representatives in the integration process.

What becomes clear throughout the analysis presented here is the importance of elite and political influence on public perceptions and understanding of European issues. The initial Irish rejection of the Nice Treaty has been accounted for by a myriad of factors—the loss of structural funds, the issue of abortion, Irish military neutrality, and an added factor of voter apathy. A further important factor, however, was the public perception that the Irish government demanded a 'yes' response without clear discussion and debate and thus elicited a rebellious 'no.' Whatever the underlying reasons, the subsequent Forum on Europe—a travelling road show of consultation and debate—perhaps represents a rare example of EU citizens being consulted in such an extensive way. Given that in normal circumstances in most countries this is not possible, the reliance on information provision and debate, largely conducted through the media, constitutes the normal mode of citizen connection with the EU. Hence, the purpose of this research was to look at a wide range of media at particular periods in time in order to see what information is available that contributes to political participation in European democracy.

Perhaps another way of phrasing the question would be to consider how national cultures/nation-states, with their people, are reconciling the fact that the national government, the national representatives elected by the people, are no longer entirely or solely in control of the destiny of the nation-state. As policy making becomes Europeanised and different national political cultures adapt in different ways to this development, the question is raised as to how national citizens are engaged in this process.

The foundation of the EU was based on a contractual agreement between sovereign nation-states, which agreed to pool competences in particular areas. The development of the polity is elite-centred, and the extent to which the EU as a system of governance is legitimised by the support of a 'European Demos' is limited (Weiler, 1996). This distance further adds to the problem of a democratic deficit. What do people know, what do they think, and what do they want? How do they understand the impact that EU policymaking has on their lives, and how can they approve of, reject, or accept decisions?

A parallel development with the concern regarding public support is the increasing focus on the concept of 'European identity.' As a space forms in which economic, social, and communicative elements of life become more intertwined, it could be considered necessary that the people living within this space begin to identify with it, that is, to identify with people beyond the local or national environment. Such identification, it is assumed, would encourage people to participate politically, to support the integration agenda, and to be more welcoming or accepting of people from other cultures arriving in their homelands, as integration promotes the movement of people.

These processes, in a political sense, may help to legitimise the political and institutional developments at the European level while smoothing the social and cultural changes that Europeanisation brings about. In this cultural sense, one of the greater fears is the rise of nationalism, racism, and xenophobia. However, any narrow definitions of *European* may bring about a similar rise in xenophobia. Thus, *European identity*, a concept that is further explored in the context of this research, is frequently considered as a potential panacea for the challenges presented by integration.

Although travel, education, and personal experience, alongside more national historical links and experiences in other countries, impact on the perceptions that we have of our neighbours, the media play an important role through the reporting and representation of European cultural and political issues. Comparisons of news coverage across different national media systems has been a useful process for ascertaining common news agendas, information sources, and journalism practice, particularly in an increasingly globalised news environment. Such studies serve to highlight the similarities and differences between editorial policies, exemplify the extent to which globalisation takes place, point at the themes and problems that are shared between different cultures (or allocated equal 'news value'), and identify issues and concerns that are unique in every culture (Fiddick, 1990). Hence, cross-comparisons of news agendas particularly regarding common issues and themes, as is the case with European political and cultural affairs, prove useful tools in assessing changes in the informational role of the media.

The nature of media coverage of European Union politics has been of interest to academics particularly from the first European Parliament elections in 1979. Blumler (1983) edited a multiauthor collection of studies, carried out across Europe after the first European Parliament elections, investigating campaign frameworks, election involvement, messages, and perceptions in a cross-cultural dimension. It highlighted the common features of political communication across Europe and outlined distinct characteristics of the approaches to the elections in the different member states. The approach in all nine countries was largely to emulate the frameworks for coverage and broadcasting of national elections, which vary in tradition and practice across countries. The studies conducted by Leroy and Siune (1994) compared the role of television in the election campaigns in Denmark and Belgium (in 1979, 1984, and 1989). They wanted to assess whether differences in the approach of the broadcasting systems in the two countries had occurred due to changes in the structure of the mass media. They also examined whether the concepts of core and periphery were determinants in the methods of communicating European Community (EC) politics. Leroy and Siune (1994) distinguished the concepts of core and periphery as being attitudinal rather than geographical, reflecting the extent to which the member state (Belgium or Denmark) expresses a sense of belonging to the EC. In general these studies conclude that content remained nationally bound, but the development of a separate party system in Denmark did have the effect of increasing debate.

Previous studies indicate that a major characteristic of European election campaigns is the focus on domestic issues, and the election generally amounts to an indication of satisfaction with government performance (Bogdanor, 1989). The politicians have made little attempt to engage the citizen in debate about Europe and have allowed the campaigns to become a battleground over domestic issues. For the opposition parties, the elections represent an opportunity to claw back some support and test the preference of the electorate. More importantly, it is not made adequately clear to the electorate what the functions of the parliament are in a wider context, what the agenda of the national parties are in Europe, or how groups in the European Parliament are affiliated and how this relates to the lives of the average citizen. There has been little opportunity for a European public sphere to develop with European Parliament election campaigns being treated in the same way by broadcasters as national elections, the content and debates focusing on national issues, and the public learning little of the actualities of European governance. Many of these issues are further examined in chapter 4 in relation to the European Parliamentary election campaigns.

Another area of research interest has revolved around the media impact on referenda campaigns regarding EU membership or Treaty amendments. Analysis of the Danish 'no' vote in the first Maastricht referendum, and investigations into the change from 'no' to 'yes,' attempt to identify why there was opposition and whether the change implied an indecisive electorate or manipulation by the political elite (Siune, 1993; Siune, Svennson, & Tonsgaard, 1994; Svennson, 1994).

More recently, studies have begun to focus on the on-going coverage of European political and cultural news rather than on specific events such as elections and referenda. Although election campaign coverage provides a moment where debates are heightened, focus on more on-going issues maps changes in the development of a sphere of debate on European issues. It is generally useful to make cross-national comparisons as developments vary in different countries, implying an emergence of overlapping and concurring spheres of debate about Europe. Alongside this, there has been a development of research into media coverage of particular case studies of EU issues, especially scandals and crises such as the BSE crisis,[4] or the resignation of the Commission[5] (Meyer, 1999). One study of EMU coverage in four European countries focused on the agents and events that form the basis of EMU news coverage. The authors wanted to distinguish where discourses about EMU occurred in the context of politics, economics, or public opinion and also where the issue was of domestic or transnational concern comparing the UK, Germany, and France (Palmer, Law, & Middleton, 2000).

Several studies are more national in focus, such as Slaata's (1998) research into the Europeanisation of the Norwegian media, looking at institutional changes in news coverage but also focusing on the discourses in Norwegian media about European affairs. Similarly, and with some links to the research presented here, Robertson's (2000) work concentrates specifically on Swedish coverage of the European Parliamentary elections (Robertson, 2000) and Anderson and Weymouth (1999) examined the British press. Research angles are developing that attempt to explore the nature of any emerging European public sphere for debate as part of civil society at the supranational level. Crisis events or policy processes can be viewed through the communication processes of lobbying and policy influence (e.g., Miller & Schlesinger, 2000), through the public relations (PR) and information strategies of political actors, and through the activities of EU journalists (Morgan, 1995). Hence, this book fits in the framework of interest in this area but also provides an opportunity to examine specific political events, specific policy issues, and general discourses about, and representations of, Europe in a wide comparative framework. The research in this book was undertaken during a time when the communication industries and the media are undergoing continuous and rapid change. With the development of digital television and interactive media, it may, in the future, be more problematic to identify a distinct national communicative space. At present, it has been possible in each of the countries involved to identify important news broadcasts, influential newspapers, and programming types, which let us see what information the population has at its disposal regarding others in Europe, while also illustrating the important debates and perspectives of these particular nations.

The methodologies used in both research projects combine a mixture of quantitative and qualitative analysis. The news media was monitored during two 1-week periods in 1999—the first from May 17 through May 24 and the sec-

---

[4]The BSE (Bovine Spongiform Encephalopathy) crisis of March 1996 caused panic when the British government admitted the high levels of infection in the national beef herd. This raised questions regarding food production and the trade in food between EU member states.

[5]The European Commission resigned as a body in March 1999 following an investigation into fraud, mismanagement and nepotism.

ond coinciding with the last week of the June European Parliament election campaigns[6]—providing snapshots of coverage of European political and cultural affairs. Qualitative summaries of these periods with a background context and interviews with political and media actors were provided by experts in the eight countries, adding insight and enhancing the results of the quantitative analysis. Television programming was also examined during two periods, a 6-week overview in May and June of 2000, documenting the range of programmes, themes, and scheduling patterns in each country. This first phase was also considered exploratory in the sense of identifying potential programming for further analysis. The second period was limited to 2 weeks in September, during which a selection of programmes were coded and analysed with reference to themes, topics, actors, schedules, and formats.

Using a comparative approach, the study has attempted to shed some light on institutional changes in the media practice of European news coverage. It has looked at the impact of European news on national media and has tried to assess in which countries certain issues may be considered national or transnational, political or economic.

The process of European integration and the challenges for Europe require some initial examination. Chapter 1 provides a broad overview of the processes of integration and debates about Europe.

Chapter 2 places the research in the wider context of media developments in Europe, particularly with reference to transnational information flows and pan-European media. This discussion outlines the fragmented nature of the European media landscape within which European information is disseminated. Giving an overview of the type of work carried out in this area, the discussion moves on to outline some of the pros and cons of cross-national research.

The first part of this book concerns the news output of selected news media outlets in eight countries: in France, Germany, Italy, Ireland, Spain, Sweden, the Netherlands, and the UK (more than 30 press titles and the news broadcasts of 16 channels). The news media could not really be considered as having an obligation to promote or push the development of European integration or identification with Europe. Instead, we look at both how the news media reflect the development of European integration, and how they provide information on European political and cultural affairs. In this way, the role of the media in a democratic system is also considered with reference to the provision of information relevant to political decision making and participation, the provision of platforms for debate on European political and cultural issues, and the media's role as watchdog on the democratic process.

European political integration is largely, for the moment, more a question of EU politics as the EU represents a form of governance beyond the nation-

---

[6]The elections were held in the member states between June 10 and June 13 (The Netherlands, Denmark, and the UK on the 10th, Ireland on the 11th, all other members on the 13th).

state. Although this can still be viewed through EU policy structures such as the Common Foreign and Security Policy (CFSP), the war in Kosovo led to wider questions about European security architecture, and coverage of others in Europe. In terms of political identity and integration, the important areas of news reporting to be noted were policy issues such as CFSP, Economic and Monetary Union (EMU), and the Common Agricultural Policy (CAP). The coverage of Kosovo, immigration, human rights, and refugees were considered as wider European questions and were included to assess coverage of the movement of peoples in Europe whether for political or economic reasons. Unemployment and EU funds/budget were considered as issues connecting the European and the national sphere. Discourses and debates were examined, and the coverage of 'others' is mapped out to give a picture of the types of cultural identification that are occurring in a transnational way in news media.

Chapter 3 gives a general overview of all the coverage coded for the project, with comparisons between types of news outlets and also between the countries studied. Here we see the wide discrepancy as regards quantity of European news between countries, particularly when comparing Italy and Germany. The analysis also distinguishes between private and public broadcasters, national and regional press, and quality and tabloid newspapers.

The first area of news coverage, concerning the last week of the European Parliamentary election campaigns, is analysed in chapter 4. The European Parliament elections as a form of 'ritual' at the European level allowed some exploration of the media's informational role in the development of European citizenship through the discussions on policy issues and the coverage of campaigns in other EU countries.

The war in Kosovo dominated the news during both monitoring periods. We did not concern ourselves particularly with the propaganda battles, but rather looked at the way in which the discourses regarding the war connected with Europe and integration. The analysis in chapter 5 is more focused on discussions on European cooperation in the field of security and foreign policy in the context of the war.

In chapter 6, European economic issues and particularly news coverage of the EMU are analysed. In comparing the media from different countries, it became apparent that a common approach is developing, particularly in the 'Eurozone' countries.

The final area of analysis of the news in chapter 7 relates to cultural news in terms of the coverage of other cultures and information about the cultural output of others. This analysis also highlights the more 'important' European neighbours for each country, determined by frequency of reference and influenced by proximity, language, and events.

Chapter 8 places the results in the context of issues affecting the work of the media in reporting European news and is written with reference to interviews with media professionals and politicians. Problems such as information sources, the influence of 'national interests,' and the complexity of the policy-making processes are discussed.

The remaining chapters are based on research into nonfictional television programming about Europe in six European countries. The purpose of this research was to provide some original perspective on the nature of television coverage of European issues. In this instance, the focus is on types of informational television programming, limiting the project to two channels per country: the main public service and commercial channels. The research aimed to illustrate the themes and actors in the field of European informational programming and to look at types of programmes, formats, and scheduling decisions.

The project involved two phases. The first was more exploratory and provided, not an absolute, but rather a 'well informed' overview of television programming dealing with Europe, whereas the second phase focused only on a selection of programmes for analysis. Chapter 9, based on the initial period of study, reports on the overview of programmes during a 6-week period across a range of channels, genres and formats in each country.

Chapter 10, dealing with the second period of monitoring, looks more closely at themes and perspectives on Europe that emerged in several of the countries or were specific to certain countries. It distinguishes those countries where specific EU programming has emerged and those where innovative formats have developed that deal with some aspect of what is frequently considered a boring topic—Europe. Again, we look at the extent to which the media provides information and debate on European issues and also the extent to which the social and cultural aspects of Europeanisation and globalisation are examined.

The book concludes by drawing together the findings of the research and discussing the implications for the process of communicating European political and cultural issues. It summarises the extent to which different media or the media of different countries fulfil some role in the democratic system, and also the way in which the changing nature of political and social spaces is represented in the news and on television.

1

Europe and the European Union: The Dynamics of Integration

INTRODUCTION

This chapter describes the nature of integration in Europe with reference to the impetus for cooperation, and the current challenges to the process. The overall purpose of this work in investigating the nature of political communication and public debate regarding Europe is placed in an economic, political, and social context. A brief exploration of some of the expressions and concepts central to the issue of European integration is followed by an explanation of the workings of the European Union. The idea of European integration is outlined by examining different political science perspectives on why nation states agreed to pool competences and on how the dynamics work. Issues of citizenship, identity, and democratic participation are discussed with reference to information and opinion formation.

Several central concepts such as 'Europeanisation,' 'European identity,' 'European integration,' 'subsidiarity' and 'transparency' are referred to in this work and require some initial exploration. Attempting to find a definition of *Europe* itself presents the problem of differing geographical and ideological perspectives on its meaning. Ideological descriptions of Europe tend to focus on common basic beliefs and attitudes towards democracy and human rights. This has, in the past, influenced the geographical sense of Europe, with the division between east and west not simply concerned with physical borders but also with ideological and psychological borders. A further dilemma for the integration project is the identification of the final border—where does Europe, in a geographical sense, end? A particular example is the relationship with Russia, a country combining a geographical and cultural mixture of Europe and Asia.

Europeanisation

'Europe' is also frequently an expression that is interchangeable with the EU, not least in media coverage of European issues, and in political speeches, hence influencing public perceptions of Europe. Within the European Union (EU), 'Europeanisation' is considered in relation to the impact that EU legislation and regulation has on political and economic life at the national level (i.e., the way in which national politics and economics function). It also relates to the changing nature of overall economic activity and interest aggregation due to European association (i.e., new transnational alliances). In both cases, this Europeanisation reflects some positive implications of cooperation and sharing of information and expertise while at the same time being part of a larger process of globalisation. This expression is also used in relation to the idea of exporting European ideals to other parts of the world or, more particularly, other parts of Europe. One example is a quote from a former UK minister for Europe about the Europeanisation of standards in southeastern Europe:

> One year after the Kosovo crisis democracy is spreading throughout the region ... We want to see a new EU Balkan agenda to encourage this trend, one which will show the practical benefits of living up to European standards and ideals which will strengthen support amongst ordinary people in the region for what Chris Patten has described as the road to Europe.[1]

European integration is essentially a concept related to Europeanisation but incorporating the idea of 'ever closer union among the peoples of Europe'[2] in the Treaty of Rome. The preamble to the treaty, as signed by the leaders of the six founding members, expressed the overall aims of the integration project. The 'ever closer union' involved 'economic and social progress,' the 'improvement of the living and working conditions,' 'balanced trade and fair competition,' and 'abolition of restrictions on international trade.' They agreed to 'harmonious development by reducing the differences existing between the various regions,' to confirming the 'solidarity which binds Europe and the overseas countries,' and to 'pooling their resources to preserve and strengthen peace and liberty, and calling upon the other peoples of Europe who share

---

[1]Quote from Keith Vaz, former UK minister for Europe, Foreign and Commonwealth Office news item: 'The Europeanisation of South East Europe,' July 7, 2000, source: http://www. fco.gov.uk

[2]European Union (1992). Preamble to the Treaty Establishing the European Economic Community as Amended by Subsequent Treaties Rome, 25 March, 1957.

their ideal to join in their efforts.'[3] As such, the project of European integration involved the organisation of economic life, the promotion of trade and prosperity, and an element of redistribution of wealth.

Subsidiarity

The way in which the European Community (later the European Union) organised itself to pursue its objectives is explained here in more detail. Although the division of powers between the institutions was outlined, it was less clear where the division of competences between the European and national level lay. By the time of the negotiation of the Maastricht Treaty on European Union, it was considered necessary to enshrine the principle of *subsidiarity* in the treaties. The impetus apparently came from

> conservative British concerns about national sovereignty and the loss of state control, Christian Democratic/Catholic social philosophy concerning the importance of allowing lower units of authority to achieve their own ends, and German regional politics based on the constitutionally protected competences of the Länder. (de Búrca, 1999)

The EU's definition of *subsidiarity* states:

> The Community shall act within the limit of the powers conferred upon it by this Treaty and of the objectives assigned to it therein.[4] In areas which do not fall within its exclusive competence, the Community shall take action, in accordance with the principle of subsidiarity, only if and in so far as the objectives of the proposed action cannot be sufficiently achieved by the Member States and can therefore, by reason of the scale or effects of the proposed action, be better achieved by the Community.[5] Any action by the Community shall not go beyond what is necessary to achieve the objectives of this Treaty.

In more straightforward terms, the idea was that decisions would be taken as close as possible to the people. However, rather than a fixed list of competences for the national or supranational levels, the principle loosely relies on a judgement as to the scale and effects of action in a policy area. Hence, the subsidiarity issue still raises questions regarding EU activity in policy areas often considered at a national level to be only of national concern. The British press (certain sections) has reported on a range of issues it considers as interfering in national issues. The European Commission representation in the UK now has a website which it uses to counter what it calls 'Euromyths.'[6]

---

[3]Ibid.

[4]Article 3b of the Maastricht Treaty

[5]The Amsterdam Treaty: A Comprehensive Guide (1997), http://europa.eu.int/scadplus/leg/en/s50000.htm

[6]See Euromyths at http://www.cec.org.uk/press/myths

Openness, Transparency, and Information

As questions were raised about democracy, openness, and transparency at the European level, reforms were made to give the parliament more status with relation to decision making. Procedures were put in place to allow public access to documents and to create more 'transparency' in relation to decision making at the EU level. This included, for example, more access to the Council's documentation of policy negotiations although at the same time 'preserving the effectiveness of its decision-making process.'[7] When acting in a legislative role, the Council is required to be more open, but as negotiators, the intergovernmental aspect is protected.

As outlined in the introduction to this book, with the apparent opposition to further integration during the Maastricht Treaty debates, there was a realisation that the integration process, both in terms of goals and procedures, was functioning without the participation or support of the public. One perspective on this concerned the lack of citizen identification with this process and with EU institutions, and no 'sense of belonging' to a community beyond the local or national level. Subsequently, there were attempts to involve and inform the citizens with information campaigns such as the 'People First' campaign, information strategies on the Euro, the 'Building Europe Together' campaign that dealt with the Amsterdam treaty, and more recently, the 'Dialogue Europe' project. It is apparent that the EU recognises the need for popular consent, particularly as their future agenda includes both deeper political integration and expansion to the east. This expansion will undoubtedly have implications for the allocation of structural and regional funding, for the budget of the Common Agricultural Policy (CAP), and possibly for future investment and employment prospects.

The results of attempts by the EU institutions to inform and involve citizens can, on the one hand, be looked at through changing attitudes and opinions, the development of which are monitored by the EU through its use of Eurobarometer surveys. Frequent national polls are also commissioned in relation to particular policy issues, for example, attitudes to the single currency in the UK. Such polls cannot really predict electoral behaviour when it comes to elections and referenda. This is partly due to the complexity of national debates and attitudes towards EU membership being tied up with a range of other factors particular to the nation-state. Essentially, the ideas that shape these attitudes, combined with the reasoning behind such support, may stem from entirely different factors.

Another way in which the impact of 'openness' and attempts at informing and involving the citizen can be examined is through the dissemination process

---

[7]Article 207 (3) of the EC Treaty.

of the media. One major obstacle is the complexity of the process of policy making.

THE EUROPEAN UNION AND ITS FUNCTIONS

The main concerns of the founders of the European Economic Community (EEC) were: the control of the 'instruments of war' (with the original European Coal and Steel Community); the rebuilding of European economies; and, although not explicitly stated, the secure provision of food. After a situation of almost famine in parts of Europe during World War II, the development and protection of agriculture through the Common Agricultural Policy (CAP) was central to the integration agenda. The CAP has been problematic in its effects on overproduction and overdevelopment of agri-industries, has caused wide disparities in farm incomes, and externally has had a diverse effect on world food prices (i.e., causing a decrease in the income of farmers worldwide). Added to this, recent food scares and a growing distrust in the process of food production has further questioned the working of the CAP and also brought about a strong sense of connection between food production and national identity. The CAP has been reformed[8] but still generally consumes over half of the EU budget and remains a highly politicised aspect of EU policy making.

The Treaty of Rome (1957) gave the Parliament (which in the first instance was more a delegation of national representatives) initially just a consultative role, with the Commission proposing and the Council of Ministers disposing legislation. The Commission has three main roles, the first being the power of legislative initiative. Whereas in some areas the Commission shares the right to initiate legislation in general, the Council and Parliament must wait for a Commission proposal before they can legislate. The Commission is also described as the 'Guardian of the Treaty' with the role of enforcing Community law both against member states[9] and against enterprises, particularly in relation to competition. It also has an executive role in implementing some Community law and policies, but in line with the principle of subsidiarity, most implementation is the responsibility of the administrations at national, regional, or local levels in the member states. Currently, the president of the European Commission is selected by the governments of the member states and is approved by the European Parliament. The other members are designated by the 15 national governments in common accord with the incoming president. The larger member states nominate two Commissioners each and the smaller states one each, a situation that will change with the ratification of the Nice

---

[8]McShary reforms of 1988 and 1992, and Agenda 2000 reform proposals re enlargement.
[9]Article 226 of the EC Treaty.

Treaty. Finally, the president and the members are subject as a body to a vote of approval by the European Parliament.

The Council (officially the Council of the European Union, often called the Council of Ministers) consists of representatives of the member states at ministerial level. Originally the main legislative body, the Council now shares legislative power with the European Parliament on most subjects. Depending on the legal basis of the measure in question, the Council decides by unanimity (i.e., every member state has a veto), qualified majority, or simple majority. Each member state is allocated a certain number of votes by the Treaties: for example, Germany, France, Italy, and the UK have 10 votes each, compared with 8 for Spain, 5 for the Netherlands, and 2 for Luxembourg. At least 62 votes are required for a qualified majority. This system was intended to ensure that the larger countries could not out-vote the smaller ones, and led to the development of a vote-bargaining system. The Council meets in different compositions of national ministers, depending on the area. The Council's work is supported by the Committee of Permanent Representatives (COREPER). The European Council consists of the heads of state or government of the member states and the president of the Commission. The European Council normally meets twice a year, once under each of the 6-month rotating periods of presidency of the Council. The European Court of Justice (ECJ), aside from dealing with cases taken against member states and organisations in relation to the implementation of community law, has also become the arbitrator on interpretation of EU law with the frequent referral of cases from national courts. The European Central Bank, although not a Community institution as such, represents the supranational control of monetary policy for the members of the 'Euro-zone.'

The introduction of direct elections in 1979 helped to increase the legitimacy of the European Parliament, and subsequent treaties have extended the Parliament's influence in relation to amending and adopting legislation. The codecision procedure (implying an equal footing with the Council of Ministers on decision making) now applies to a wide range of issues such as the free movement of workers, consumer protection, education, culture, health, trans-European networks, employment, discrimination, and EU fraud prevention. The cooperation procedure previously applied to a large number of areas, but since the Amsterdam Treaty[10] the scope of this procedure has been reduced in favour of the codecision procedure and now applies only to certain aspects of economic and monetary union. Hence, the Parliament is now on equal footing with the Council concerning decision making in a range of policy areas particularly to do with free movement and social policy. Parliament's assent is required for important international agreements such as the accession of new

---

[10]The Amsterdam Treaty was signed in 1997 by the member states. One of the main points of the treaty was to increase the decision-making power of the European Parliament.

member states or association agreements with third countries, the organisation of the Structural and Cohesion Funds, and the tasks and powers of the European Central Bank (ECB).[11] Additionally, the Parliament must be consulted on the main aspects and basic choices relating to Common Foreign and Security Policy, and to policing and security.[12]

A further important aspect of the EP role in the European Union has been the involvement in appointing and approving the members of the Commission. The resignation of the Commission in 1999 undoubtedly compounded public perceptions of corruption at the European level and the idea of the EU 'gravy train.' It is difficult to assess whether the general public understood the role played by the European Parliament in this affair by exerting its powers over acceptance of the European Commission. Recent Eurobarometer data claims that 'EU citizens are now significantly more likely to express satisfaction with the way democracy works in the European Union (42%) than they were in spring 1998 (+7%)' (European Commission, 1999a). This change in opinion is interpreted by the Commission as a positive response to European Parliament's involvement in the protection of democratic interests at the EU level.[13]

From a media perspective, one senior BBC official noted that 'when they (the European Parliament) actually started to take some real decisions about the European Commission, they started to get coverage. I think when they start to make decisions that matter this is going to happen more and more.'[14] It is, however, likely that there remains a lack of public understanding concerning the division of powers at the EU level. Hence, any disgrace for one institution could have the effect of smearing the others, particularly in instances where 'Europe' in a generalising sense, or 'Brussels' in a diminishing sense, has become a catch-all expression for the European Union in many media outlets.[15]

The current make-up of the Commission (and the Parliament) and the weighting of votes in the Council have (after many years of deliberation) been reviewed with reference to future enlargement. A system originally designed for 6 members, which functions for 15, could not conceivably be workable for a community of up to 22 members. The institutional reform constitutes an important part of the Treaty of Nice. Part of the contentious debate over Nice is the fact that the national veto on legislation has been reduced to fewer areas of legislation due to the difficulty of obtaining unanimous agreement with so

---

[11]In European Commission (1999b), *Serving the European Union. A citizen's guide* (2nd ed.), Luxembourg, OPOCE, 1999 http://wwwdb.europarl.eu.int/dors/oeil/docs/FR212_doc_en.htm

[12]EC Treaty Title V, Article 21 and Title VI, Article 39.

[13]Anna Melich, European Commission representative, speaker at 'Transnational Communication in Europe' conference, Berlin, October 1999.

[14]BBC journalist interviewed for UK report.

[15]Journalists interviewed admit to a tendency to substitute 'Europe' and 'EU' in reporting.

many members. The influence of smaller countries will be reduced, as previously it was possible for countries to form alliances in the council of ministers when voting on issues and block the power of the bigger states. Now the larger countries will have a larger vote (to make up for the loss of a second commissioner), allowing the possibility for as few as three large member states to block any decision.

The policy-making process in the EU is complicated. Different policy areas are treated differently depending on the level of competence the EU has in these areas. For example, actions related to the development of the single market are core EU competences. Legislative initiatives are generally based on treaty principles, and proposals are developed through consultation, through the 'green paper' process involving the input of a wide range of experts, national committees, industry representatives, and often employee and consumer representatives. Depending on the basis for legislation, the EU can formulate a regulation that is directly applicable in all member states or a directive that outlines a required result to be achieved through implementation at the national level, or it can issue a recommendation, the principle aim of which should be achieved by the member states.

Again, depending on the basis for legislation, the involvement of the Parliament varies, as previously outlined, and a Parliamentary committee usually works on and reports on the proposal. Following rejections or amendments or adaptation, a piece of legislation will finally be voted on by the Council of Ministers. The Council has always had a tradition of bargaining on policy areas. Country representatives, notably from smaller countries, have built up alliances and worked through a system of trading votes, wherein countries often block or support initiatives that have little impact in their own countries, purely as an exchange for support from other representatives on more vital legislation.

By the time a new regulation or directive is introduced at the national level, the extent of influence on the substance of the legislation has frequently undergone a long process and the extent of, or indeed source of, influence is difficult to assess. Commission activities in a policy area are generally based on research and consultation, have been influenced behind the scenes by lobbyists and interest groups, are tempered by national preferences, and then bargained in the vote-swapping system of the Council of Ministers. Essentially, this complexity is a stumbling block for clear communication on how and why the EU has chosen to enact particular regulations or laws, and has made the work of journalists trying to follow the process extremely difficult. The system of voting in the Council of Ministers, although less secretive than previously, has also allowed national representatives to present themselves in the best light regarding community decisions. An unpopular decision can be blamed on the EU or other representatives, whereas a positive development is a triumph for the national government.

European Integration: Intergovernmentalism, Federalism and Neofunctionalism

Understanding the dynamics of European integration requires some insight into the reasons why so many policy issues are now decided at, and so much legislation now emanates from, the supranational level of the EU. Integration theories relating specifically to the EU as an emerging polity tend to define the nature of 'supranational governance' in Europe largely through examining negotiations of major treaties or the process of policy making in the EU.[16] Opinions differ as to whether developments in Europe are based on negotiations between nation-states acting purely in the national interest. The strongest proponents of this theory include Hoffman (1982), who stressed the important role of the nation-state and the power of national leaders and also the strong links that exist between the national and the Community policy-making processes. Moravcsik (1991) developed a theory of 'intergovernmental institutionalism.' He recognised the importance of supranational institutions but claimed that the main source of integration lies in the interests of the states. The intergovernmental school highlights the role of the nation-state in the process of integration but overlooks developments in transnational cooperation. Such a perspective was aided by the complementary interdependence theory, which stressed the need for cooperation and collaboration between states (Keohane & Nye, 1977). The benefits of such collaboration for nation-states in an era of globalisation is outlined by Milward (1992), who argued that without supranational cooperation, the nation-state would have been significantly weaker in the global political and economic arena. Similarly, Majone (1996) argued that EU membership has allowed member states the possibility of regulating a market that is increasingly global by transferring regulatory competence to the European level. The other side of the coin, as described by Scharpf (1997), is that national governments are constrained in their policy making by the need to negotiate with a variety of interests among other member states and are legally bound in many areas by their commitment to the European Union. An example is the hotly debated issue of economic policy in relation to the single currency. Furthermore, regarding the activities of national political actors, Mair claimed:

> European integration increasingly operates to constrain the freedom of movement of national governments, and hence encourages a hollowing out of competition among those parties with a governing aspiration. As such, it promotes a degree of consensus across the mainstream and an inevitable reduction in the range of policy alternatives available to voters. Second, by taking Europe itself out of national competition, and by working within a supranational structure that clearly lacks democratic accountability, party and political leaderships do

---

[16]For a discussion of the different approaches, see Sinnot, 1994.

little to counteract the notion of the irrelevance of conventional politics. (Mair, 2000, cited in Ladrech, 2002)

The issue of whether there is a real drive towards federalism or if federal developments are more a matter of function is addressed by the 'neofunctionalists.' Essentially, they claim that any process of cooperation has spill-over effects through regulation and jurisprudence that necessitate further moves towards integration. This theory of regional integration, more particularly European integration, developed in the late 1950s. Haas (1958) defined integration as the process whereby political actors in nation-states are persuaded to shift their loyalties, expectations, and political activities towards a new centre whose institutions possess or demand jurisdiction over the preexisting national states.

The work of the European Court of Justice (EJC) has been identified as central to such a spill-over process with the implementation of the treaties and other EU legislation being guarded, reinforced, and defined by the court (Burley & Mattli, 1993; Weiler, 1993). This included numerous individual cases relating to workers rights and social policy. On a wider European level, the European Court of Human Rights (ECHR) has been accessed by interest groups in response to inaction or injustice at the nation-state level, leading to an increase in networks and cross-national cooperation. These schools of thought can, in a sense, be directly linked to the different institutions, as with spill-over and the ECJ. The perspective, which sees cooperation as a negotiation between nation-states, is more relevant to the work of the Council of the European Union, particularly as this is the forum for negotiating institutional reform and EU treaties. Alongside the idea of functional spill-over, as just described, there is also what is described as political spill-over. This refers to the transference of loyalties from the national to the supranational level of political elites, and includes a range of actors in the policy community, for example, lobbyists.

Although the ideological basis for uniting Europe as a means of preventing war remains an important context for cooperation, the main driving force to date behind European integration has been economic. A major incentive for cooperation between nation-states at the European level has been the necessary reaction to the globalisation of markets and finance. In the context of globalisation, the liberalisation of finance markets and capital has also brought about a weakening of the ability of national governments to influence national economies. Aside from this, there are certain policy areas that naturally require a wider cooperation, such as international crime, or environmental policy wherein the industrial activities of one nation-state can have an adverse impact on the environment of its neighbours.

A less functionalist perspective on the process of integration relates to such common goals, which require a perspective beyond national interests. In outlining a theory of deliberative democracy in relation to the European Union, Eriksen and Fossum (2000) emphasised the development of cooperation, which cannot be considered solely as a battle of conflicting interests. They described the workings of the EU as involving a variety of actors who pursue common goals and work together in establishing workable solutions. The very process of negotiation and cooperation can also, to some extent, serve to alter the perspectives of the actors. Even within this less mechanical approach to the dynamics of integration, there is a need to ensure the rationality of decision making through addressing both the democratic and the communicative deficit of the EU: 'The critical questions to ensure rational outcomes, public accountability, and popular authorisation of a mode of governance, then, revolve around the central tenets of public freedom; the nature, scope and composition of representative bodies; and the quality of debate' (Eriksen & Fossum 2000, p. 259).

European integration has, outside of the direct activities of the EU, taken on its own momentum. Recent attempts at reviving the economic integration process included the establishment of the single market, the liberation of financial markets, and the launching of a single European currency. These developments have had a major impact on the business community, prompting mergers and alliances between firms. Economic regulation has promoted integration and pan-European cooperation in the form of lobbying, interest representation, and policy consultation. Part of the process of creating a single market has necessitated financial aid to some areas and regions to develop infrastructure in order to ensure a level playing field. The idea of a level playing field has also required harmonisation of standards of work, production, safety, etc. and a mutual recognition of qualifications and standards.

Social legislation in the EU has not been subject to the same legislative drive. It is largely due to the pressure of individuals or interest groups pursuing cases based on principles of the treaties that the EU has expanded its jurisprudence in this area. The strong business lobbies at both national and supranational levels work hard to prevent moves towards higher levels of social protection and employment rights where these are conceived as having a negative impact on economic goals.

The focus on subsidiarity, combined with the need for regional lobbying has brought about a system of multilevel governance, cooperation, and aggregation of interests. Hence, business and other interest groups position themselves at all levels of government in order to maximise influence over legislation and to be forewarned about change (Gardner, 1991; Greenwood & Ronit, 1994; Marks, 1995; Mazey & Richardson, 1993).

Related to subsidiarity and the principle of implementing change at the lowest possible level is the development of regionalism. Discussions of integration in Europe also necessitate looking at the level of what might be considered disintegration in Europe (Davidson, 1997; Schmidt, 1997). While the break-up of the Soviet Union has brought about the re-emergence of ethnic and national political forces in the East, EU funding and promotion of regional development has partly led to regional assertion throughout EU member states. The form of devolution of competences to the regions or nations within the nation-states differs from country to country, but it is apparent that in most cases the process is on-going.

Some nation-states may fear that:

> If the process is followed to its logical conclusion the sub-division of Europe could be endless, a recipe for constant local conflict not dissimilar to the feuding between petty statelets in the seventh and eight centuries (and) for nations like Scotland and Catalunya the vision of independence within Europe is the answer to many inconvenient questions. The responsibilities which the strengthened European Union would deal with are those which they do not want and cannot take on themselves in any case—macro-economics, free trade, international crime prevention, foreign affairs and external defence. For France, Spain, Italy, England and Sweden, however, these are precisely the responsibilities which they hold most dear and which give them a status in world affairs which they will not lightly relinquish. (Mundy, 1998, p. 53)

Although this vision of 'feuding' may be slightly pessimistic, it is true that the shape of Europe, how people organise their lives, how they are governed, with whom they trade goods, cooperate, and share resources, receive information, and share cultural interests is continuously developing. This is also reflected in a different kind of regionalism, regions that cross borders but join peoples in particular areas that make sense geographically. There is even reference to 'super-regions' based on areas of industrial wealth, one described as stretching from Barcelona, through Southern France, and into Northern Italy (Newhouse, 1997). 'European regions are linking themselves directly to the global economy. Instead of working through national capitals, they are exploiting global trade patterns, the information highway, the free movement of capital, and the ease of high-speed travel' (p. 24).

Regions and 'stateless nations' hence add another dimension of governance within Europe and further complicate the process of European integration. On the other hand, 'this new regionalism puts value on the diversity and differences of identities in Europe, and seeks to sustain the variety of cultural heritages, regional and national' (Morley & Robbins, 1995, p. 17).

EUROPEAN IDENTITY

With a complicated multilevel system of governance and representation, and the contradictory pulls of globalisation and 'localisation,' it is important for people to be able to identify, and identify with, the relevant sphere of influence in relation to various aspects of their lives, whether that sphere be regional, national, European, or global. Identity is already multilevel based on family, local and regional community, and nation, and to an extent there already exists a further level of European identity. The concept of identity is complex and not something that can be considered fixed or stable but rather as an ongoing project (Giddens, 1991).

From the outset, it is necessary to consider the *value* of the concept of a 'European identity' and question what the features of 'Europeanness' might be. There are some frequently cited common values—respect for human rights, rule of law, tolerance, common traditions based on democratic institutions, a free and pluralistic media, and Public Service Broadcasting—that provide a basis for elements of common political and civic culture. There are several reasons why this concept has become part of the language of European integration.

Boxhoorn's (1996) analysis of the use of the term *European identity* in EU treaties and texts concluded that such a concept was deemed more relevant to the collective approach of the union as a whole to external issues, namely common foreign policy. He claimed that:

> References to identity in the internal meaning, however, to the 'essence' or 'substance' of the Union are not to be found. Instead, it seems as if the EU civil servants have substituted such expressions as 'European dimension' and 'European awareness', almost as if taken from a thesaurus. (p. 139)

Despite the lack of explicit reference to European identity, there appear to be more implicit approaches to encouraging collective identification with the EU. Although the caution over the use of the term may be political and related to any perceived threat to national identities, the motivations behind such encouragement are fairly obvious.

For the political and economic actors, there are certain challenges facing the EU that must be communicated to the public: the integration of 'business Europe' to compete with the US and Asia; the implementation, acceptance, and success of a single currency; and the expansion of the EU. These developments naturally aid the globalisation of business and the expansion into new markets. The success of business for most only makes sense at the national level (how is our economy doing) or at the individual level (how do I benefit). Hence, such an agenda requires skilful dissemination at the national level in relation to the benefits of integration. On a less cynical note, business success can be translated into jobs, prosperity, and progress.

The single currency, introduced in January 1999, affects national economic policy and demands low inflation even in the event of localised economic shocks. On the one hand, it could be argued that this might intensify the elements of national bias in media treatment of these issues and increase the levels of xenophobic and anti-immigrant rhetoric (the 'other' within and outside the nation-state). It has been claimed, on the other hand, that the introduction of the single currency will precipitate the construction of a European public sphere, as not all nationalities will have representation at the ECB and therefore decisions will not be so 'politicised' via the national press.[17]

For some, namely politicians, the process requires public acceptance, which in turn presents the challenge of increasing public understanding of and participation in the political process at the European level (through elections, information campaigns, education, and/or public opinion).

Linked to these political and economic challenges are further cultural and social challenges. From a more social point of view, the integration project aims to spread the benefits of economic integration (through social cohesion or regional development funding). This involves a redistribution of wealth previously only understood at a national level, that is, the willingness to pay tax for the benefit of one's fellow countryman. Such willingness to support other Europeans therefore requires a sense of identification with others in Europe.

The enlargement of the EU and the integration and movement of 'new Europeans' also involves a redistribution of wealth and an identification with others. Expanding EU membership is also considered necessary to stabilise new democracies and spread 'European ideals' throughout the continent. Further deepening of the Union will require the loss of national competence and sovereignty in a growing number of areas. The low levels of participation in European elections and understanding of European governance suggest that the development of some form of European political identity could be an important part of engaging people in the process of governance at the EU level and help to overcome the democratic deficit. New membership will mean more new nationalities moving freely within the EU boundaries. Fostering understanding may have a role to play in attempting to quell racial hatred by helping people understand other cultures, beginning with those that live side-by-side in the nation-state.

Citizenship and Democracy

The concept of a 'European identity' could therefore be considered as relating to issues of citizenship and democracy. In relation to individual rights and responsibilities, the actuality of European integration needs to be recognised, that is, that governance at the European level has an actual effect on people's lives (the nature of work, social benefits) and has an impact on lifestyles and consumption. For these reasons, a better understanding of the process should allow for greater participation and debate wherein people can reject or accept integration on the basis of facts.

---

[17]Peter Pex, MEP, chairman of EP Committee for Culture, Youth, Education and the Media, speaking at the conference 'Media Literacy as a topic of Civil and Political Education in Europe,' Granada, December, 1998.

Explorations into 'European identity' occur in the fields of legal, political, philosophical, and cultural studies and are useful for comparing the normative arguments with what can be achieved though institutional development and cultural awareness. Integrating these discussions about citizenship and political and cultural identity helps to establish what a European identity could in reality entail. There are differing perceptions of this identity that already exist in the minds of academics, in the declarations of politicians, in the language and traditions of the media, and in the minds of people.

Discussions on political identity, or identification with political institutions and democratic processes, are largely focused at the national level and tied up with the idea of a common history, nationalism, with the founding of nation-states, and the development of a vernacular used in the media and education. In relation to Europe, different debates occur at the same time in terms of the development of a type of legal or political identity. A lot of the fear that exists in the face of an emerging European identity reflects the idea that identity is a singular rather then a multifaceted concept and that national identities as well as national sovereignty are threatened. Such arguments are often tied up with symbols of identity such as a national currency.

These arguments are frequently reflected in elite debates on European policy issues at the national level. There is the dilemma of constructing some form of 'European security identity' between states with very different foreign policy outlooks in relation to both traditional allies and postcolonial links. There are different expressions of identity in the discourse relating to Economic and Monetary Union (EMU). One relevant study (Risse, Engelmann, Knopf, & Roscher, 1998) conducted in Britain, France, and Germany examined elite political discourse about the single currency and provided interesting insights into national identity, collective identities, and the 'Europeanisation' of national identity. They argued that the divisions over EMU appear to have little to do with economic arguments or geopolitical interests and are really based on 'identity politics.' Looking at the debates between the political parties, they concluded that 'the controversies among political elites in these countries as well as the variation in attitudes can be explained by differences in the construction of collective identities and their relationship to the European order' (p. 4). According to their study, for British elites Europe is considered the 'other' and integration is considered a threat to British constitutional and parliamentary traditions. In Germany, *European identity* is defined against the 'other,' which is German nationalism. Being a 'good European' implies being a 'good German' (reflecting the focus on a European Germany rather than a German Europe). The authors claimed that the reunification of Germany brought about a 'Europeanisation' of French identity, combining a fear of loss of influence on the world political stage and a belief in the importance of the influence of French democratic traditions on the development of Europe. National identities persist and accordingly, even the motivation for feeling European varies in different countries.

Europeans are being defined institutionally by the EU in terms of European citizenship, which grants or limits (depending on your perspective) belonging to those with national citizenship within the member-state countries.[18] Current debates on cultural identity and citizenship appear split between those who wish to establish what common cultural traditions could form a basis for European identity, and those who argue for the separation of culture from citizenship. The US model is mentioned as an example of citizenship leading to identification but not incorporating a common culture.

Weiler (1996) argued that Article 8 of the EC Treaty, in bestowing European citizenship to the nationals of the member-states, can be interpreted as having separated nationality and citizenship; hence, a recognition of different nationalities implying a 'closer union of the peoples of Europe' rather than the development of a European people. In 1996 the estimated number of third country nonnationals living in the EU was 9 million, a group without citizenship rights at either level of governance (European Commission, 1996). This may lead to a narrow exclusive belonging along ethnic and religious lines, largely a White Christian belonging. Delanty (1995) outlined the dangers of such a narrow concept of citizenship as reflected in the problems of immigration politics. He claimed:

> Citizenship is being disengaged from universal rights and is being subordinated to the particularism of nationality. Citizenship should not be a means by which Europe defines its identity as a white bourgeois nationalism. This is the danger today, that citizenship is being reduced to the national chauvinism of the advanced nations. In this regression, Europeans are consumers, recipients of welfare, tourists. (p. 162)

Delanty further claimed that much of the basis for debate over European integration is not confined to issues of sovereignty:

> It is rather that Europe as a discursive strategy, is the focus for articulating a variety of political standpoints which are increasingly tending to coalesce in opposition to immigrants. In the discourse of Europe, mutually opposed groups can find in the single entity a focal point for the pursuit of their projects. The very concept of a European Union makes little sense if something is not going to be excluded. (p. 157)

It is important to consider how this affects that which is understood by both 'insiders' and 'outsiders' as the criteria for 'Europeanness.' It is necessary to widen the perspective of European belonging, particularly towards the east and especially to the areas where there is still conflict. Although membership of the EU may not be imminent, at least there could be signifiers through action and information, which shows a wide definition of European identity in order to help 'remove people from the Europe of the past' (Fischer, 1999). The same argument comes from the field of constitutional law, as

---

[18]Article 8 of the EC Treaty.

Bauböck concluded from his analysis of potential European citizenship that the recognition of other nationalities is vital:

> This means recognising rather than ignoring the particular collective identities of the many sub-national and transnational minorities and uncovering their histories submerged by segregationist and assimilationist nationalisms . . . A pluralistic conception will also find it easier to keep the Union open for territorial enlargement and for the integration of immigrants coming from outside. (Bauböck, 1997:online)

In other words, if these people are not drawn in, what are the implications of them being left outside? Galtung prophesied that the development of a European Union that is predominantly western and Christian will eventually cause the development of a Russian Orthodox union and a Turkish Islamic union (Galtung, 1993). These will form in opposition to or as a reaction to such an exclusive EU, and the recent conflicts in the new states of the former Yugoslavia has highlighted these emerging divisions.

European identity, if it is to develop, must be linked to citizenship, both rights and duties. It could not really be considered adequate that common cultural beliefs are sought out that could be propagated and developed in order to encourage cultural sameness. The aim should not be to create a new level of nationalism at the European level of governance. The relationship between citizenship and identity is important in this regard. The Commission's Agenda 2000[19] included a proposal for the creation of a common bill of basic rights for all citizens of the European Union. The further development of the Charter of Human Rights, and debates regarding citizenship, will undoubtedly be a central focus of concern for the EU in the coming years.

Debate, Public Opinion, and Political Participation

To date, the levels of public participation in the democratic process at the EU level has not been very satisfactory. From an EU average voter turnout for the European Parliamentary elections of 63% in 1979 to an average of 49.4% in 1999, the level of participation has steadily decreased.[20] However, any concern over these levels should be counterbalanced by considering the general trend in low participation in elections at the national level in the EU (excepting countries where voting is compulsory). For example, the national turnout in the UK general election of 2001, at approximately 59%, was the lowest since 1918,[21] although still a great deal higher than the 24% who voted in the 1999 European Parliamentary elections.

---

[19]See Europa website: http://europa.eu.int/comm/agenda2000/index_en.htm.

[20]Figures from the UK Office of the European Parliament Online: http://www.europarl.org.uk/guide/textonly/Gelecttx.htm

[21]http://www.electoralreform.org.uk/sep/publications/briefings/election2001.htm#chap2

A problem generally associated with this is the lack of political parties at the European level, aside from transnational political groupings in the parliament. One country where a distinctive dual party system has emerged is Denmark, while parties such as the Referendum Party in the UK contest issues of European integration at the national level. Despite this, there have been developments within national political parties in response to the changing nature of governance:

> The overarching process of responses by parties is labelled Europeanisation, manifested in a variety of possible actions. These responses may include organisational changes repositioning the role of their EP delegation; programmatic developments signalling a more sophisticated attention to the influence of the EU in domestic policy-making; increased factionalism or even new party formation; an additional dimension in party-government relations; or new linkages with European actors beyond the national political system. (Ladrech, 2002, p. 19)

Opposition to the entire process of European integration, or to the nature of European integration, is expressed through individuals, factions of political parties, specific political parties, and other organisations, most of which have a presence on the Internet.[22] From a brief survey of Web presence of Eurosceptic groups, it is possible to make some generalisations regarding the nature of opposition. The issues of concern for these groups are varied but the most common themes are antifederalism, fear of loss of sovereignty, and the promotion of European cooperation between independent European sovereign nation-states. In this sense, the entire institutional architecture as well as the perceived direction of the development of the EU is questioned. Other forms of opposition include antiglobalisation and anti-Europeanisation with arguments regarding threats to the environment, increasing divisions between the rich and poor in Europe, and the impact of large trading blocs on the world market and the quality of life in poorer countries.

More specifically, groups may focus on a particular aspect of policy making, such as the environment, agriculture, fishing, or natural resources, that is either of particular national interest or a shared regional or transnational interest. These organisations are mainly British, many Danish, (more recently) Irish, and some Norwegian, Italian, Swedish, and French. An interesting development is the Europeanisation of Euroscepticism with the example of The European Alliance of EU-critical Movements (TEAM), an organisation bringing together groups from 13 European countries including Poland and Slovenia.[23] Similarly, the British 'Keep the Pound' campaign has its web site translated into French, German, Italian, Spanish, Danish, and Portuguese. A

---

[22]A sample of Eurosceptic websites includes: www.eurosceptic.com/ www.euro-sceptic.org www.eurocritic.demon.co.uk and www.euroscep.dircon.co.uk

[23]http://www.ljudmila.org/team/

further common thread running through the concerns expressed by the variety of groups and individuals is the idea that somehow national identities and cultures are directly threatened by European integration.

The European Union has been monitoring public opinion since 1970, with the first survey, *Europeans and European Unification,* published in 1973. The use of Eurobarometer data, and analysis of research using this data, emphasises the impact of the media on people's information on, and opinions regarding Europe. Data gathered about the correlation between media usage and attitudes towards Europe or 'feeling European' remain ambiguous. Regular surveys in the context of the Eurobarometer show that people with a higher level of media consumption tend to feel better informed and express a more positive attitude towards a European identity. However, people using print media tend above average to express more negative attitudes to membership of the EU. Obviously, the correlation between usage of (different) media, opinions about European institutions, and European identity is a very complicated one, also linked to factors such as education. The arguments about education, information, and European integration are largely based on the concept of cosmopolitanism.

Ingleharts's (1970) examination of the links between cognitive mobilisation and what he terms the *cosmopolitanisation of values* has given rise to a whole stream of studies exploring the relationship between levels of education, exposure to mass media, political involvement, and attitudes to the European Union:

> Cosmopolitanism presupposes that we abandon our inherited national or cultural prejudices in order to connect from above with the peculiarities of other cultures and societies. In our view, it requires a potential for judgement in a strong sense: that we may both be ready and able to stand back from our social reality and values and at the same time approach 'the other' 'empathetically'. It calls for the fostering of empathy and detachment, for more than passive or 'negative' tolerance. (del Aguila & Vallespín, 1995, p. 102)

Inglehart's (1970) study showed that higher levels of cognitive mobilisation and a tendency towards postmaterialist values generally inspired positive attitudes to European integration. He claimed that rising levels of exposure to formal education and mass communication tend to favour integration at the European level. Janssen (1991) challenged Inglehart's assertions, stressed the importance of the content of messages of political communication, and questioned how appropriate the EC was as a focus of postmaterialist values.

The work mentioned earlier (Risse et al., 1998) concerning identity politics and the single currency suggested a differing basis for elite attitudes to identity in some member states. Similarly, another study, which examines whether attitudes are based on nationality, political affiliation, or sociodemographic factors, found national characteristics to European identity formation (Delfem & Pampel, 1996). This work looked at sources of individual support for European unification among citizens of the EC countries. The sources relate to both country of citizenship and social characteristics that link citizens across different countries. In summary, the researchers found that although age did not affect attitudes, gender did, in that men were generally more positive about European integration, and increasing education levels also led to positive effects.

In terms of political orientation, there were conflicting interests for right- and left-wing affiliates. The support of free trade outweighed the tendency for conservative anti-EU feelings. For those on the left, the economic concerns over free trade outweighed left 'postmaterialist' values, which would be more pro-European. This is perhaps an indication of how economic integration has stifled true debate on political and social integration. Essentially, the differences between countries emerged as more important than individual differences. Delfem and Pampel (1996) also concluded that:

> These trends indicate that conditions of confusion over sources of authority and decision-making may facilitate a continued identification with individual countries. In the absence of a developed European public sphere, particularly with respect to the media (Gerhards, 1993) politically relevant identities remain mediated through familiar forms of association rooted in diverse national histories and cultures. (p. 138)

They further concluded that:

> The legitimization of the EC is not secured, not only because anti-European citizens do not support unification, but also because pro-Europeans do so out of concerns related to their own countries. Both anti-Europeans and pro-Europeans are nationals, not Europeans. (Delfem & Pampel 1996, p. 138)

This suggests that it is not just the elite and politicians who have remained focused on economic factors. We could assume such a focus may result from political messages received by citizens, which are largely disseminated through the media. Other research examining attitudes to Europe and levels of knowledge has pointed out some anomalies regarding knowledge and support. Eurobarometer data allows an assessment of both subjective and objective levels of knowledge. Regarding the support for the Maastricht treaty, we can look at some examples of this. For example, in Ireland, data from Eurobarometer surveys in 1992, revealed a high level of positive perception of the Maastricht summit, coupled with the majority of respondents who felt they had a medium to high level of understanding of the issues (EMU, political union, common defence, social chapter) involved. On the other hand, when asked to mention some of the key themes addressed by the treaty, the level of salience of these issues was extremely low (Kevin, 1995). In some cases respondents are more honest about their lack of understanding but not, it would seem, aware of the contradiction in having negative or positive opinions based on little or no information. By mid-1998, 66% of UK respondents claimed to be against EMU, but only 13% felt they were well informed about EMU. Of Irish respondents, only 17% felt well informed, although 69% were in favour (in Italy the figures are 17% feeling well informed and 79% in favour).[24] The conclusion again must be that attitudes are strongly influenced by politicians and the elite, and by means of arguments presented in terms of economic loss or gain. Gehrke's (1998) findings were similar in relation to public attitudes measured during EU referendum campaigns and questioned the extent to which Europeans were in any way focused on a 'shared destiny' rather than simply economic perspectives.

CULTURAL INTEGRATION AND CULTURAL IDENTITY

Over time a political identity may emerge that is based on citizenship and identification with democratic institutions and political culture at the EU level. In Europe there are many common elements of political culture, and overlapping these similarities are the differences, many of them cultural in another sense, the differences in language, religion, history and traditions, and way of life.

In reference to culture there are, as Schlesinger described,

> two distinct senses of 'culture': (a) a culture broadly understood as a way of life, broadly shared values, practices and beliefs of a social group: and (b) culture narrowly understood as the production of artefacts that may become commodities traded in the marketplace. (Schlesinger, 1997, pp. 371–372)

His distinction allows a consideration of, on the one hand, those elements of culture that may be common between Europeans, aside from traditional aspects that are more particular to distinct groups, and on the other hand, the cultural output that may be enjoyed across different groups.

The current approach of the EU to cultural policy is a promotion of 'a community of cultures' as outlined by former Commissioner Oreja:

> The first thing we need to overcome is misunderstanding. I would not identify with those who are keen to define and construct a European cultural identity for all the people of Europe. Identity is something that is felt, not imposed. In any case I prefer to talk of a 'community of cultures' which Europe represents rather than of European culture. In the same vein, I prefer to talk of the shared cultural aspirations that bring regions, countries and the community together rather than of a European cultural policy. (The) basis of our cultural project for Europe: to show Europe what unites them, and to show them the strength of their common cultural roots, despite the wide variety of cultures that Europe has produced (and to) highlight the common characteristics of Europe's cul-

---

[24]Eurobarometer data published in The Economist: *Europe's new currency: gambling on the Euro,* January 2, 1999.

tural heritage, to promote artistic creation by links and cultural exchanges, to respect the diversity of our cultures, these are the objectives which I believe will enable us to clear up the misunderstandings which persist between our fifteen countries and to allow culture to play the role it should in European integration. (Oreja, 1997)

Accordingly, the two meanings of culture are not really separated here, but recognition is given to the plurality of cultures that exist within the Union, if the expression 'variety of cultures that Europe has produced' is not interpreted as excluding people of non-European origin. The EU has encouraged exchange, cooperation, and the patronage of cultural output, which is in itself an old European tradition. Where elements of common cultural identity have emerged, such development has been aided through travel, tourism, student exchange, cooperation in the areas of art and culture, and what we learn of others through both experience and mediated information. In this way, people's sense of 'Europeanness' is often dependent on personal experience, personal contact, places visited or languages studied.

Languages

Central to this 'organic' integration is the question of languages in Europe. The Europe of diversity has required recognition and protection for the variety of languages used in the EU. The reality of Europe reveals a different development in the strengthening of languages. The extent to which multilingualism increases appears to be related to the growing business and political elite in Europe. The top four languages used by Erasmus students in their courses abroad were, in the years ending 1991 and 1999, respectively: English 41% and 44%, French 22% and 18%, German 15% and 15%, and Spanish 10% and 8%. Not much changed statistically in these 10 years, with English being the most popular second language of European students.

The preference for acquiring English is also borne out in relation to preferred sites of study. The highest numbers of universities (percentage that took the opportunity to become involved in the scheme) that acted as hosts to students were in the UK (66%) and Ireland (61%), whereas it was lowest in Greece (23%). The EU study revealed that in the academic year 1997–1998, estimated student numbers show that students in business studies (24%) and languages (19%) were more strongly represented (European Commission, 2000).

According to Eurostat figures, in schools in the 15 EU member states, over 92% of secondary school students are studying English as a second language, compared to only 28% of students studying French, 20% German, and 1% Russian. In central and southern Europe, English is also popular in secondary schools. Among the candidate countries for EU membership, the percentage of secondary students studying English was generally in the 74–100 percentage range. An exception is Hungary, where German is popular. Here, only 55% of students are studying English. The popularity of English is described as being beneficial to both US business operating in Europe and to European businesses competing against the United States in other foreign markets, notably in Asia, where English is already the accepted common business language.[25]

Based on EU opinion surveys, it appears that English is the first foreign language most used by Europeans (70% in Sweden, 66% in Denmark, and 47% in Finland, with an EU-15 average of 33%). French is second (19% in Italy, 17% in the United Kingdom, 14% in Portugal, and 10% in Spain and Ireland, with an EU-15 average of 10%), and German third (28% in the Netherlands and 18% in Denmark, with an EU-15 average of 4%). Spanish is the fourth language of choice (3% in France and the United Kingdom, with an EU-15 average of 2%) (European Commission, 2001).

For some, English is considered as a practical solution to the complexity of languages in an expanding Europe, but for others (particularly the French) its dominance is considered a threat to national languages and identity. In a more global sense, a further survey on languages preferred by the business elite reveals that Russian and Chinese follow English as the top languages.

Travel and Tourism Between European Countries

Tourism and travel patterns may perhaps illustrate other links between places, although geographical proximity can imply more movement between certain countries, for example in Scandinavia or the British Isles. For certain countries, the choice of destination may be limited by visa requirements or by costs. Concerning criteria for holiday destinations in EU member states, the most important were listed as scenery, climate, cost of travel, cost of accommodation, and historical interest (European Commission, 1998). Just less than 20% mentioned criteria such as meeting people, visiting friends, or the proximity to home as being important. Language was suggested by less than 10% as a criterion for selecting a holiday destination. There was no reference in this survey to ease of travel or any other restrictions, which may be more relevant to travellers in central and eastern European countries. Linguistic and ethnic links also appear to play an important role particularly in relation to Diasporas, which is perhaps more pronounced in southeastern Europe.[26]

---

[25]From: 'Mon Dieu! English Set to Become Second Language for Europe' in *Europe Business News,* May 21, 2001. [On-line] http://www.europebusinessnews.com/Feature/Feature.cfm?content=795

[26]These issues are further explored in an EIM pilot study by Deirdre Kevin regarding Communication Flows in Europe.

Other Cultural Exchange

Youth culture, music, film, sport, computer games, and new media technology form a meeting point of different cultures, but this commonality applies on a global and not just European level. It is difficult to see how such youth culture can have a distinct European rather than a global flavour. Sport is frequently cited as an example of a cultural meeting point. The commercialisation of sport, particularly in relation to media coverage rights and the Bosman ruling,[27] has allowed a Europeanisation or indeed a globalisation of national football leagues, wherein fans may support a team in each of several national leagues, and heroes in local teams can come from all parts of Europe and beyond. The European and World Cup championships, based on national teams, allow us to return to a more nationalistic tribalism. For a minority, this is expressed in violence and hooliganism, but for many, such events are the sites of friendly exchange and integration.

The Commission has, in the past, been accused of taking too narrow an approach to the idea of a cultural identity, and there is a need to alleviate fears of an exclusive membership. As Shore (1993) pointed out, 'Identity formation is an ambiguous and dualistic process involving the manipulation of boundaries and the mobilisation of difference for strategies of inclusion and exclusion' (p. 781). Although there is some recognition of the need to reach out to other cultures, it is not stated that those other cultures already exist within Europe, or more specifically within the EU. 'There is a dialogue between European and other cultures . . . We are no longer talking about integration, but about co-operation designed to contribute to the flourishing of European cultures and better understanding between different peoples' (Oreja, 1997). As Mundy (1998) concluded, the main challenge to the European Union, and indeed to national leaders, is to try

> to recognise, as so many member states are loathe to do, that it (Europe) is made up not just of native citizens of itself but of people who have arrived in Europe from all over the world for a variety of legitimate and honourable reasons (and) to fail to win their allegiance will be just as dangerous to the future cohesion of the continent as it would be to alienate a powerful Member State.' (p. 53)

'European identity' can thus be considered to have two separate but interconnected elements of political and cultural identification. Collective identities require 'another' against which they are defined and this is an aspect of

---

[27]Jean-Marc Bosman, a Belgian footballer, wished to transfer to a French club when his contract ended with his Belgian club. The transfer fee offered was not considered high enough by his club. He took his case to the European Court of Justice on the grounds of free movement. He won his case and won the right, for all EU players, to a free transfer at the end of their contracts within the EU. The ruling also implied that the number of non-national EU players on a team in a national league could no longer be restricted. Case C-415/93 Bosman.

European identity that, as pointed out earlier, could serve to divide rather than unify people if too narrowly defined.

> Arguments for the importance of postnational identity would claim that national citizenship will continue to influence European attitudes but will decline over time as forces of globalization promotes postnational identity over national identity. Arguments for national identity predict that if change occurs, it will involve the rising importance of national identity as the reality of the European Community draws closer and the potential for economic and political conflict within the EC increases. (Delfem & Pampel, 1996, p. 126)

CONCLUSION

The development and nature of European integration, as apparent in academic and political debates and discussions, is complex. Also, the extent to which a cultural or social integration, leading to a common identity, has evolved is difficult to assess. What is apparent from the debates is a concern with having a narrow definition of Europeans. As regards those countries, namely EU and prospective EU member states, the major problem is one of democratic participation in the supranational level of governance. In this case, there is obviously some role for the media in contributing to the improvement of information, debate, and participation. The form that this may take or the media that may be most appropriate to the task is investigated in the following chapters.

2

The Media
and European Integration

INTRODUCTION

This chapter first explores the role of the media with reference to the discussions from chapter 1 regarding democracy, legitimacy, and public participation at the EU level. Next it outlines discussions regarding the media and identity. Then the current situation concerning the audiovisual landscape in Europe with reference to Pan-European media, the film industry, and programme exchange is considered, leading to a discussion on the European public space and the need to concentrate on the output of national media systems.

The Media and Democracy

There are several ways of thinking about the media and the process of European integration, European democracy, and identity formation. The media function to provide information, education, and entertainment. The media can also, through representation and analysis, influence people's perceptions of the world, provide a space as part of education information, and break down (or strengthen) boundaries between people.

The principles of public service broadcasting, journalism ethics, and issues of press freedom that are intended to influence the practice of media outlets are put forward as the guidelines that ensure a functioning democratic role for the media. The 'canons of journalism' as outlined by McQuail (1992, p. 38) are responsibility, freedom of the press, independence from vested interest, truth and accuracy, impartiality, and fair play. The remits of public service broadcasters are based on criteria considered to be of public interest and may vary somewhat between countries. Essentially, they generally include, as a minimum, ideas such as impartiality, accuracy, fairness, pluralism and diversity, and respect for privacy, taste, and decency.

Although this framework represents a normative ideal for media practice frequently considered to exist in Western liberal democracies and held up as best practice to developing democracies, there are many factors that hinder the ideal functioning of the media. Subsequently, there is a huge range of academic investigation and debate into a range of influencing factors, just briefly mentioned here. Increased competition for readers and viewers has been considered as undermining the seriousness of media outlets leading to the trivialisation of news. Issues of cross-media ownership and market concentration raise questions regarding the pluralism of representation, ideas and opinions, and the variety of content available. The influence of ownership on content and editorial policy and hence on political decision making and public opinion is also a concern, especially where the media corporation has an economic interest in the development of national (or supranational) economic or foreign policy (as examined by Herman & Chomsky, 1988).

Government and political or business influence on media content is complicated by their important role as sources for news outlets. A relationship of reciprocal exchange is developed wherein the journalist has access to reliable, usable information and the politicians have controlled access to their target audiences (Gandy, 1982). However, the extent of influence through the more recent development of 'spin-doctor' tactics on behalf of political actors and the sophistication of public relation activities questions the nature of this relationship.

Despite these problems, the media remain important elements of the public sphere in which people may discuss, debate, or negotiate the democratic process and important policy issues. The media are the most important information sources that feed into this exercise of citizenship, and are expected to provide a forum for the debate of these issues that is balanced and representative. Through the practice of investigative journalism, the media also carry out a role of watchdog on the activities of the state and political actors.

The Media and Identity

The influence of the media on identity formation is most often examined at the national (or regional) level and considered as complementary to education and (taught/oral) history. Discussions of media influence on national identity formation focus on the way in which both education and the development of print strengthened the boundaries of national cultural identity (Anderson, 1983; Gellner, 1983). The central discussions of Gellner and Anderson suggest that identity lies somewhere between an artificial construction and 'an imagined' bonding between peoples. In relation to national identity, or Anderson's imagined bonding, Gellner described the media as 'boundary makers.' In this sense, media contribution to national/regional/ethnic identity includes the use of common language/languages, the representation of history in documenting the past, and the telling of stories with films, soap operas, and fiction, reinforcing community ties with cultural references. News broadcasts also play an important role, presenting national agendas and important issues of the day and also outlining the national perspective on world events. Other events and rituals such as elections, royal or state weddings and funerals, and sport and competitive events featuring national teams or clubs are a further element of this process. 'Preferential access for such matters (including international sporting events), especially by way of special television coverage may, other things being equal, be taken as a sign of active engagement by the media with the national culture' (McQuail, 1992, p. 298).

In arguing against the idea that media influence identity formation, Waisbord (1998), for example, questioned this concept on the grounds of the existence of regional or local identity formation within the nation-state. His argument ignored the power of the media affecting regional, ethnic, or minority identities by the very act of addressing and serving the majority culture within a state. As Barker (1999) noted, globalisation (and post colonisation) has already influenced the make-up of the nation-state, implying that 'few states have ethnically homogenous populations' (p. 67). If media activity does not produce positive results, from the perspective of the nation-state or dominant culture, this cannot imply that there is *no* influence on identity formation. Similarly, the potential for negative impact of media coverage should not be overlooked, particularly in terms of reporting foreign news or information about other people and cultures. With reference to some of the issues discussed in chapter 1, any media efforts to represent 'Europeanness' would have to incorporate the reality of the varieties of people (not just of European origin) living in Europe.

The way in which the media may influence the development of a European identity is more problematic for many of the reasons mentioned in chapter 1 and also in terms of transposing the traditional influences of national media on national identification to the European level. National news media, as mentioned above, have traditionally played a role in 'framing the nation' through a combination of the mode of address to a defined group, and outlining the news agenda relevant to the nation-state. Given the lack of pan-European media outlets beyond those that serve business and the political elite, there is no defined group of Europeans that is addressed in any collective fashion in relation to European economic and cultural issues.

Although news media cannot really play a proactive role in the promotion of European identity or integration, it is possible to examine how the media contribute to identification with Europe through their information, education, and entertainment functions. The development of a European public space that is distinct from a national one should allow for more pragmatic debate on policies and developments, as 'citizens have no effective means of debating European decisions and influencing the decision-making processes' (Habermas, 1992, p. 9). This space could be pan-European, part of the national public sphere, expressed through regional media, or more likely a mixture of all levels.

A final point should be added regarding the two lines of inquiry in this study: media and democratic participation, and media and identity formation. Although they may in some sense be considered to be different areas of focus, there are many overlaps and links between the two. In the first instance, I have linked citizenship to political identification with a system of governance, developed via information and opinion formation, and expressed through political participation. A second issue, as pointed out in chapter 1, the work of Risse et al. (1998) on the Europeanisation of national identities as perceived through the discourses of political actors regarding EMU, has shown that the development of European perspectives is strongly influenced by national perceptions and identities. The sense of what 'Europeanness' is depends largely upon your starting point. Finally, Schlesinger's (2001) analysis of communication theories of nationalism suggests that the coinciding of a social communication system (shared self-expression and understanding) and the space of political communication (or public sphere) at the national level cannot be so easily or quickly transposed to the supranational level. Hence, the issues of identity, contesting identities, and citizenship are intertwined and influence not just the agendas of political actors, but also the shape of communicative activities regarding policies and democratic decisions.

THE EUROPEAN AUDIOVISUAL LANDSCAPE

Before addressing the issue of Europe in the national media systems, this section examines the nature of the European public space and revisits the issue of cultural exchange that, in chapter 1, looked at languages and travel. The role of the media in national democracies has already been outlined. Furthermore the media, television in particular, are considered in many countries to act as a promoter of national and regional identities, and specific regulations are in force to ensure that broadcasters fulfil certain cultural obligations (Machet & Robillard, 1997). In relation to the developing transnational and supranational polity, we can question whether there might be an emergent European public space that can fulfil some of these roles.

Pan-European Media

After the emergence of satellite television in the early 1980s, European institutions such as the European Parliament and the European Commission expressed expectations regarding the cross-cultural functions of television. It was hoped that as more Europeans were able to receive television programmes from other countries (cross-border flow) or share the same programmes as people in other parts of Europe (pan-European television), this would boost the process of European integration. In 1980 the European Parliament initiated the idea of developing a Pan-European public service space in cooperation with national broadcasters and the European Broadcasting Union (EBU). The idea was to combine a sharing of national programming with specific programming related to European Community/Union issues, and hence tackle the democratic deficit by providing a common platform for discussion of policies. The subsequent attempt by four national broadcasters to cooperate with *Europa TV* in 1986 was unsuccessful due largely to financial difficulties and the limited transmission possibilities, the difficulty of developing a 'European audience' (Collins, 1998), and also essentially the refusal of some of the larger public service broadcasters in the community to become involved (Ward, 2001). The other EBU initiative—Euronews—is discussed shortly.

Meanwhile, the focus of European media policy has also shifted from a cultural towards a market-oriented approach (Schlesinger, 1996). Initiatives such as the EC directive 'Television Without Frontiers' and the MEDIA programme were created to develop a pan-European audiovisual market and to strengthen the production sector (Collins, 1994). Concern has been expressed regarding the implications of a market-driven approach to transnational communication on the development of a European public space because of the impact of commercialisation of public service broadcasting (Venturelli, 1993). According to Hamelink (1993), these 'European moguls are increasingly in command and unlikely to have a human rights mission. Their mission is entertainment, or as an ultimate concession info-tainment. Media audiences are not perceived as citizens; they are targeted as markets and consumers' (p. 9).

The extent to which EU policies have undermined public service broadcasting was questioned by Ward (2001), based on his analysis of EU decisions on competition and state aid and the promotion of the audiovisual industry. He concluded that the EU has 'found a novel method to achieve a level playing field for commercial broadcasters as well as extending the right of Member States to implement and sustain policies, in support of democratic communication through the provision of state aid' (p. 143).

Although the development of pan-European media for the purposes of cultural integration has not been particularly successful, commercial and technological factors in the media industry have helped shape particular media outlets such as Euronews (Machill, 1998). Among these changes was the acquisition of 49% of the stake in Euronews by ITN, a news provider seeking further distribution possibilities. More recently, Euronews claimed that this commercial partnership helped to stabilise finances in order for the channel to fulfil the public service role central to its foundation:

The vision of the original EBU members was to provide European viewers with a news channel that would reflect the perspectives and common interests of Europeans—a channel covering European and international news events from a European perspective in the languages of Europe. . . . Although the shareholding structure of Euronews has altered to incorporate a commercial partner, this vision has not changed over the years. (Wheatley, 2000, p. 44)

It is apparent, however, that the business and international press have encouraged the emergence of a European public space, but it is a space of commercial and political information, largely conducted through English and serving the policy and business community of Europe (Schlesinger & Kevin, 2000). Additionally, the authors stated that despite a lack of success in developing a public sphere through policy initiatives:

> it is the very existence of the emergent Euro-polity that has created the conditions for a transnational, elite media to develop. To the extent that pan-European media have begun to emerge in the press and in television—and these are still rare birds indeed—market-seeking behaviour has been the driving force rather than the search for the new public imagined in normative theory. (Schlesinger & Kevin 2000, p. 229)

This is further clarified when looking at what is obviously considered the target market for many of these outlets based on market research. In many cases the population sample itself is revealing. The European Marketing Surveys (EMS; 2000) survey men and women who are described as the main income earners in the top 20% of households in each country. The respondents are more likely to be male (68%) than female (32%). More than half are between 25 and 44 years old, and more than half have at least a university degree or equivalent professional qualification. Most EMS respondents are considered to be 'opinion formers' through both their professional and their private activities, for example in addressing conferences, sitting on industry or professional committees, or advising government (European Marketing Survey, 2000). The subjects of these surveys (largely carried out for advertising and marketing purposes), preselected as a wealthier, more influential section of society, further indicate the type of readership of pan-European titles.

Undoubtedly, certain print outlets have identified an elite European group who operate in business and politics at a transnational level, and hence these outlets form part of a sphere of debate on developments at this level. The fact that their marketing advertising (Fry, 1998), and readership analysis focuses entirely on this elite implies that these publications do not view themselves as having any role in the development of a wider public sphere in Europe.

There is an overall impression that the print media and broadcast channels perform different roles at the European level. The former tend to serve a business elite and thus in a sense report on, or contribute to, some aspects of a European public sphere, especially the political and economic actors most directly concerned with EU legislation and regulation. The latter, television, has proved more successful in the area of entertainment. News channels such as Euronews (mentioned earlier), CNN, and Sky News compete as global news providers. However, much of the development of these channels is driven by competition. For example, CNN has had an influence on global communication and the establishment or development of other transnational TV news channels such as BBC World and Euronews. Such news channels are often considered to contribute to a global public sphere and hence encourage transnational political action (Volkner, 1999). However, the issue of whose 'global news agenda' becomes dominant is still problematic. Euronews claims to have as a central aim the establishment of some kind of European news agenda, a European perspective on news rather than a national. The extent to which this multilingual approach, which limits a certain amount of creativity as regards reports and analysis, can provide this common platform remains to be seen.

The most successful pan-European channels are undoubtedly sports and music TV channels. Pan-European media constitute a particular sector of media development that cannot largely be considered as a European alternative to national media systems and that have a limited role in the process of European integration. On one level, the entertainment, sport, and music channels reflect global tastes, but even here the trend is towards localising channels like MTV and Eurosport. According to the *Television 2000 Report* (IP/CLT-UFA, 2000) the pan-European television (PETV) market is described as maturing in the context of changing technologies and distribution systems, particularly with the increase in access to digital satellite distribution. Trends in the market include increased 'localisation,' with tailor-made local channels, and also a multiplication of niche services. The report cites, for example, MTV, which in 2000 launched French, Polish, and Spanish versions alongside the British, German, Nordic, Russian, and Italian services. Eurosport now broadcasts in more than 16 languages and Discovery Europe in 12. Hence, global channels still require a 'local feel' in order to be successful.

As a European cultural channel, ARTE appears to have developed its distribution channels. More than 70% of German households have the technical ability to receive the cultural channel ARTE with cable, or with satellite connections with Astra, or with the digital packages of ARD or Canalsatellite. In France 90% of French households can receive ARTE, with terrestrial, cable, or satellite connections. It is also available in Belgium, Switzerland, Austria, and the Netherlands in various cable packages. In Spain, selections from ARTE programming are offered on the second terrestrial channel. In Poland 20%, and in Finland 32%, of households can receive ARTE over satellite, and programmes will soon be offered on more cable networks. ARTE will also be launched on particular cable packages in Denmark, Luxembourg, Estonia,

Hungary, Romania, Lithuania, Slovenia, and Norway.[1] As a cultural channel, ARTE is probably on the way to becoming truly pan-European, at least in terms of distribution, if not viewing figures.

Other examples of cultural pan-European channels include the German language 3SAT, a cross-border channel established cooperatively by the German, Austrian, and Swiss TV channels with almost half of broadcast time devoted to cultural reports and programmes. Similarly, the French TV5 is a French-language channel with programming from Belgian, Canadian, French, and Swiss TV stations and is available around the world on satellite and cable.

While discussing the development of pan-European media, it is also useful to consider the potential impact of regional media. It is suggested that if Europe is diversity, then regional TV can supply the diversity wherein politics, economics, culture, and society need to be discussed with relation to the interests of the region (Thomas & Lopez, 1998). Alongside this focus, programming and promotion of regional television could also involve cooperation with other regions and cultures, including sharing cultural programmes as an aid to communication and understanding. A recently developed initiative from the EBU called 'Night Trade' involves the cooperation of seven national European broadcasters in just such an exchange of programmes 'dedicated to promoting cultural diversity' and planning to 'surprise audiences from Italy to Finland, from Ireland to Poland, with programs they would not normally see.'[2]

Television in Europe: Cross-Border Channel Reception and Programme Exchange

The extent to which such cultural exchange occurs can be looked at in terms of the reception of the broadcasting and production output of other countries. Looking at geographical coverage of the European channels reveals that it is mainly the larger countries (i.e. Germany, Spain, France, and Great Britain) that broadcast to smaller neighbours.[3] For the most part, language is an important factor, particularly in multilingual communities such as Belgium, or between same-language countries constituting mainly bilateral flows of information. There are some channels specifically directed at particular audiences, as is the case with the German channels for Austria and Switzerland. Several Swedish channels are directed at Norway, Sweden, and Denmark. More than 50% of the Irish audience has access to all the British channels, and there is a claimed potential audience for the Austrian public service channels in Austria's central European neighbouring countries. There are a large number of

---

[1]Source: ARTE website: http://faq.arte.fr/faq/dtext/index.html

[2]'European broadcasters establish programming alliance' from European Journalism Centre news 28/02/00. Source: http://www.freedomforum.org/news/2000/02/2000-02-25-16.asp

[3]Sources: Statistical Yearbook 2000, European Audiovisual observatory; *Television Business International Yearbook*, 2001, InformaMedia Group, London.

television channels licensed in the UK, including the headquarters of some American channels. Many European channels broadcast from the UK to home, often due to a more relaxed system of licensing.

One major aspect of programme exchange is the influence of culture and taste:

> When comparing television in Europe with that of the USA and Japan, we have to point out that in fact there is no one, homogenous European TV market. There are significant cultural differences between West and East, North and South. British viewers prefer soaps and dramas. Germans like crime series and TV movies. French viewers are fond of TV movies and mini-series. The Spanish prefer to watch comedy series. The Swedes appreciate lifestyle magazines. (IP/ CLT-UFA, 1999, p. 34)

Additionally, a recent study (David Graham and Associates, 1999) for the UK department of Media Culture and Sport discovered in their interviews with various European television channels that certain aspects of British drama and fiction are not deemed suitable for some continental audiences:

> *British stuff is so 'realistic'. It doesn't necessarily mean that it is violent, but it is dark, drugs, sex—not always graphic violence, but just perverse. We rejected Prime Suspect because of that.* (M6 Television, France)

> *Television should be about entertainment and escapism. We do not want to watch a programme that deals with the same problems that you faced in the day.* (Canale 5, Italy[4])

Differences in formats, in terms of length of individual programmes and series length, can inhibit the potential to sell programmes abroad. This has been the case particularly for British producers, as a certain harmonisation has occurred in other countries as regards length of evening programmes in the entertainment genre. A further problem is the tendency to slot foreign programming as 'filler material' rather than featuring it during prime time, again an indication of the preference for nationally produced television programmes.

As regards television fiction, there is a high tendency for broadcasters to broadcast national fiction. The recent Eurofiction report claims that national fiction gained ground in most of the major EU countries and developed in terms of forms of production, growth in output, and audiences (Buonanno, 2000).

The fiction most appreciated by the audience is that which is most identifiable, that is, with more direct cultural links to the nation or region. The patterns in the importation of television fiction in European countries can be characterised by a dominance of American products, particularly as these

---

[4]Quoted in: David Graham and Associates, 1999.

statistics from the European Audiovisual Observatory (EAO; 2000b) include feature films. US fiction constituted 71% of all imported fiction shown on the major television channels in the EU (minus Luxembourg, plus Norway and Switzerland).

There are examples of programmes that have managed to cross boundaries and become successful in other countries. The more significant genres seem to be that of children's programming or animation. One example is the award-winning show Teletubbies, a successful TV export with viewers in 120 countries.[5]

Aside from the dominance of US products, the patterns of importation seem to broadly follow linguistic lines. German products comprise 12% of Austrian imports and almost 6% of Swiss, whereas French products are significant in Belgium and Switzerland. British fiction comprises 21% of Irish imports and also does well in the Scandinavian countries and the Netherlands, where English language skills are well developed. 'The Swedish and Dutch markets have been strong followers of UK television for many years, and the number of English speakers is a definite advantage for UK distributors over their European rivals' (David Graham and Associates, 1999, p. 17).

The situation with the film industry, based on recent statistics, is more extreme as there is no dominance of national products in national cinemas. The market in Europe is very fragmented, and so far the real winners are American productions. Audience figures have risen since the early 1990s, particularly since the development of multiplex cinemas, and the market is strongly dominated by US films. In 1999, 71% of all films shown within the European Union came from the US, whereas European films were only able to reach a share of 5.6% in the US market. The total market share in the EU consists of the aforementioned 71% of US films, 17% of national films in the domestic market, and 11% to 12% of European films in the nondomestic market. European films are also most successful in their home markets.[6]

Co-Productions for Film and Television

The figures for percentages of imported European fiction that are co-productions are quite high for many European countries, particularly Great Britain with 51%, and Spain and France both having 31% (EAO, 2000b). According to another study from the EAO (2000a), the UK and Spain are involved in international fiction co-production on a very small scale. For Austria, Germany, Switzerland, Belgium, and Italy, co-productions represent between one quarter and one third of imported European fiction. Germany and France are

---

[5]Teletubbies team up with McDonald's, Thursday, 13 January, 2000, 12:45 GMT Source: http://news.bbc.co.uk/hi/english/entertainment/newsid_601000/601858.stm

[6]Sources: European Audiovisual Observatory Statistical Yearbook 2000, Eurimages, Europa Cinemas, Lumiere.

involved in quite a lot of co-productions. However, most of these (75%) in Germany tend to be with German-speaking countries. 'This way of working has a well-established institutional and cultural background and is used especially by the ARD and ZDF public channels. The other channels do not show the same affinity for this kind of international collaboration' (EAO, 2000a, p. 47).

Over a third of ZDF fiction (total) involves co-production between German-speaking countries. The French pattern is similar, with the most common partnerships being between French-speaking countries. For the British, cooperation within Europe is uncommon, the exception being with Ireland (mainly carried out by the BBC channels). Co-production is quite common in Italy, amounting to a third of the value of all fiction. The private channels (Mediaset) are more open to this. The tendency towards co-production varies greatly and can have an impact on the development of the production industry overall. As the 1997 Eurofiction highlighted, of the domestic fiction series and films shown in Germany, France, and Italy (19%, 31%, and 40% respectively) were international co-productions.

Co-productions in film in each country contribute to just a small share of the overall production and are most common in France, Germany, and Spain. The reason for this relative caution in co-production is based on various factors. The first relates to the fact that the European film market is made up of 15 separate industries that primarily want to secure their interests and carefully control the distribution of their subsidies. On the other hand, production costs in Europe (based on the relatively small audiences) have risen while the distributors' investment in financing has declined.[7]

Nevertheless, various European initiatives such as *Eurimages,* set up by the Council of Europe (COE), or *Europa Cinemas*[8] support the production and distribution of European films.[9] In the year 2000, *Eurimages* supported 44 film co-productions. In order to receive *Eurimages'* support, the co-producers must involve at least two member states of the COE. Film support was carried out under two separate schemes. The first supports only films with a good potential for circulation within the European Union and generally involves some of the bigger players (from the larger countries). The second involves films that reflect cultural diversity and generally involves cooperation between smaller countries. The fact that European distributors are not able to enter the European market initially gives the American distributors the opportunity to benefit from this weakness. Obviously, the fragmentation due to languages and different market structures prevents a 'European industry' from attaining the economies of scale that their American counterparts can achieve and exploit.

---

[7]Sources: European Audiovisual Observatory Statistical Yearbook 2000, Eurimages, Europa Cinemas, Lumiere.

[8]Supported by the MEDIA Programme of the European Union, Euromed Audiovisual, Eurimages, Council of Europe, CNC and French Ministry of Foreign Affairs.

[9]*http://culture.coe.fr/Eurimages* http://www.europa-cinemas.org

Television largely remains a national medium, with the strongest common feature of European audiences being the popularity of American movies and American TV series. The extent to which foreign channels are actually viewed in other countries is difficult to ascertain. Co-productions appear to work well within linguistic communities and have the overall effect of enhancing the industry at home. The broadcasters and producers of Germany, France, and Italy have made more progress in this area than their British counterparts.

What has probably been more successful is the exchange of formats between European countries and with the United States. Formats provide a tried and tested programme with prior experience of promotion in the original country, are generally innovative, and can be adapted to conform to local tastes and traditions (de Mol, 2001). The extent to which television and television programmes can play some role in integration in Europe is limited by the fact that fiction and entertainment are the more important genres that cross borders. Entertainment formats for games shows and reality TV shows are more easily transferred and offer little in the way of cultural understanding aside from a general interest in the humiliation of others and the potential of becoming a millionaire. Additionally, the levels of trade and success are affected by language, taste, and viewing habits. The challenge is to produce fiction or film that can deal with common themes and issues of human interest that appeal across cultures.

COMPARING REPRESENTATIONS OF EUROPE IN THE NATIONAL MEDIA SYSTEMS

The work presented in the following chapters has, in a comparative way, attempted to glean some idea about institutional changes in media practice in covering European news. It has looked at the impact of European news on national media and the Europeanisation of the national agenda, and it has tried to assess in which countries certain issues may be considered national or transnational, political or economic. Discourses and debates are examined, and the coverage of 'others' is mapped out to give a picture of the types of cultural information available in news media.

Given the fragmentation of the media landscape in Europe, cross-national comparison of media coverage and representations of political or cultural issues is an extremely useful, if not essential, exercise when dealing with transnational or global issues. Although the empirical information provides solid data relating to coverage by amount, placement prominence, or themes, qualitative information from national experts involved in data gathering provides a better insight into journalistic traditions and debates about particular issues. It is important at the outset to outline the complexities of attempting to examine the treatment of similar content and issues across a wide range of systems and traditions.

Patterns in Media Consumption

The importance of different media varies between countries in terms of readership and audience figures. Recent statistics confirm a north–south divide as regards typical media consumption especially in relation to newspapers. The Italians and Spanish watch the most TV in Europe at just over 4 hours a day (3 is the European average), with an average of 3½ in Britain. By comparison, the proportion of people reading national daily newspapers has grown during this period in Germany (recording the highest overall figure in Europe in 1999, 39.1, compared with less than half this, 18, in 1989). In 1989 Britain had Europe's highest national daily newspaper circulation figures per 100 of population (40.5); in 1999 that figure was down to 31.4.[10] Having a balance in the study between print and broadcasting outlets and between news and nonfiction television programmes helps to counterweight these differences.

Media Systems: Broadcasting

The number of channels and the nature of competition in broadcasting can vary widely between countries, for example, the highly competitive and fragmented German market and the impact on the British market of technological and ownership issues. The German media market, with about 82 million people, is the biggest in Europe and is concentrated on national, German-language media. In contrast to countries like Belgium, Switzerland, or the Netherlands, foreign television programmes do not reach a substantial level in market share. The free television market in Germany is the most competitive in Europe. Due to high cable (57%) and satellite (30%) distribution, most German households can receive around 25 national channels. As a consequence, the audience market is quite fragmented; in recent years the market leaders (1998: ARD; 1999: RTL) reached a share of no more than around 16%. The process of audience fragmentation is of particular importance with regard to current affairs and political journalism. Some channels strategically design their news programmes for specific target groups, as, for example, RTL II with young people. Here the assumed preferences of the target group achieve more weight in the process of news selection than, for example, the public relevance of the specific event. Although there is no general trend towards tabloid journalism across all channels and programmes, such a trend seems to be obvious with regard to specific target groups, particularly young people.[11]

---

[10]Data from: 2001 European Marketing Pocket Book quoted in Cozens (2001).

[11]Information and statistics from the German report for the study.

Currently, the biggest challenges to the British media are being posed by new technology. In the television sector, competition continues to intensify due to the growing penetration of cable and satellite, and the launch of digital terrestrial and satellite broadcasting in 1998 escalated this competition. Traditional print-based media, meanwhile, are increasingly exploring new electronic delivery platforms and are having to assess to what extent these new delivery techniques represent an opportunity or a threat. A more relaxed regulatory environment, after the 1996 Broadcasting Act, led to further consolidation of ownership both within and across the traditional sectors of the media. Against this trend towards more concentrated ownership in the UK, it should be noted that public service broadcasting has an enduring popularity with the public.[12] At the time of publication, the new Draft Communications Bill in the UK (May 2002) appears likely to further loosen restrictions on media ownership in the UK.

Competition, and the increase of commercial channels, has had a major impact on public service broadcasters, who have had to redefine or 'justify' their role in the national media landscape. Liberalisation of markets and competition have also allowed for commercial channels to question the 'privileged position' of public service as regards public funding (Woldt, Dreis, Gerber, & Konert, 1998).

Indeed, the very tradition of public service can vary widely, and although all of these broadcasters now face similar pressures in the market, many have only recently had to face commercial competition from within national borders. An example is Ireland, where the first commercial channel (TV3) only began broadcasting in 1998. Hence, although our selection of channels for monitoring during the study required consistency in the sense of having one public service and one commercial channel, we also had to bear in mind the different landscapes in which these channels operate. (A full list of the channels monitored in the study on news can be seen in Appendix I).

Television Formats, Production, and Scheduling

Comparisons of the approach of national broadcasters to the challenge of dealing with European and European Union issues in television programming must also take into account different broadcasting traditions regarding formats, production and scheduling. Later chapters examine types of programmes in six European countries. Some of the aforementioned issues regarding public service broadcasting and different media landscapes also apply in relation to programming. The traditional formats of programmes vary in relation to length and the development of an overall broadcasting schedule. Programme formats, for example in relation to current affairs, can also vary; one such case

---

[12]Information and statistics from the UK report for the study.

is the tradition of magazine-type shows in Germany or France, which are not typical of British television. However, an important aspect of the research dealing with television programmes on Europe was precisely that of identifying the different formats and approaches in different countries.

Media Systems: Printed Press

The printed press in each country also operates within different systems and traditions. For the purposes of the research, we wanted a relatively broad view of what we termed *quality* and influential press coverage of European affairs. Aside from this, we added some regional titles and also some tabloids for a wider view of coverage and also a comparative aspect of regional news agendas in this area. However, regional titles play different roles in their respective countries. A characteristic of the German newspaper market is the dominance of regional newspapers and the existence of very few national newspapers. The latter reach a smaller section of the population, but because they are regarded as 'quality papers' and are read by many opinion leaders, their contribution to the public debate is nevertheless an important one.

Similarly, with regard to Sweden, it is necessary to stress the importance of regional and local newspapers. Even if the overall trend here is also towards a decline in subscriptions, local papers still have a large audience and play an important role in the local political process. Most Swedish households subscribe to a local newspaper, whereas the biggest national dailies are becoming increasingly elite papers and the national tabloids have had substantial problems in keeping their audience.

There is also a growing development in Germany and Sweden in the provision of free press publications. The critics, including publishers of traditional newspapers, emphasise that it might be difficult for these newspapers to avoid having a dependency on the advertising industry and a strong trend towards tabloid issues. The most remarkable single change on the newspaper market in Sweden was the introduction some years ago of the tabloid *Metro,* a free newspaper in Stockholm distributed in the subway system and a commercial success story.

Despite the diversity in printed press traditions, the selection of three major dailies in each country supplemented by regional and/or tabloid titles (over 30 in all) provided an excellent snapshot of the information available to people on European issues and of the important debates in each country.

Traditions of Political Affiliation in the Press and European News

A study of news, particularly press coverage of political issues, must take into consideration any possible political bias traditionally associated with the news outlet. Subsequently, newspapers can be selected in order to represent a wide range of political viewpoints within each country. As regards the EU, both left and right ideologies have, in many countries, been divided over membership. Socialist and left-leaning parties have generally welcomed the social policies and concern for workers' rights at the European level while being suspicious of the impact of free trade. The right, on the other hand, embraces the liberalisation of markets but questions the need for deeper integration or EU interference in national political and social issues. Categorising newspapers in terms of political affiliation or left–right bias is not as straightforward as it may have been in the past. Such allegiances are becoming less relevant due to both the centralising of political ideologies and the impact of market forces having a greater influence on newspaper content. These developments are relevant to each of the countries in the study even for countries like Sweden, where a tradition of links exists between media outlets and political organisations. 'The partisan press in Sweden has almost disappeared, even on opinion pages, and market-driven journalism has to a large extent replaced politicised reporting.'[13]

Such categories are not really relevant for the main Irish newspapers. Although traditionally Irish newspapers have had a fairly clear party political orientation, this has become blurred in recent years, and it is no longer possible to identify links between individual papers and individual parties. In any case, since the foundation of the state, Irish politics has been characterised by an overwhelming adoption on the part of individual parties of centrist positions—this absence of any substantial ideological differences between parties is reflected in the relative neutrality of the Irish dailies.[14]

In the UK, although there are no formal links between political parties and national newspapers, partisanship has settled into clear-cut patterns since World War II, with a definite slant in favour of the right wing for most of that period. From the mid-1990s onwards, however, the Conservatives began to lose their traditional newspaper support, and the Party's position on Europe was central to this. By the 1997 general election, outright support for the Conservative Party was difficult to find, *The Sun* having openly switched support to Labour and *The Times* urging readers to vote only for Eurosceptic Conservatives. The Labour government thus inherited a press that is both ostensibly supportive of the party but also, in some sectors at least, still ardently Eurosceptic. Confusion in 1997 over government policy on joining the European Single Currency, and Oscar Lafontaine's comments about tax harmonisation in 1998 ('the most dangerous man in Europe,' according to *The Sun* at the time) demonstrated that support for Labour had not diminished opposition to Europe within the British press.'[15]

---

[13] Swedish report.
[14] Irish report.
[15] UK report.

In Spain, *El País* always backed the Spanish PSOE (Socialist Party of the Spanish Workers) and the governments headed by the former Spanish Prime Minister Felipe González. *El Mundo,* in spite of having a young newsroom politically situated in the left, has opposed González, due to corruption. *ABC* has traditionally been in a more conservative stance, criticising the PSOE governments and supporting the PP (Partido Popular) candidates. However, as is the case with the Spanish political parties, all three newspapers are supportive of European integration, despite the relative popular indifference revealed in surveys and polls.[16]

Many of the outlets can still be described as more traditionally right-wing or conservative, particularly *FAZ, ABC, The Times,* and *Le Figaro,* whereas others can be seen as more left-wing, such as *Le Monde, The Guardian, Süddeutsche Zeitung,* and *El País.* On the whole, it was expected that the selection of newspapers (see Appendix for the full list of press outlets), including regional, would provide a balance of views regarding Europe, the EU, and other aspects of integration.

A EUROPEAN PUBLIC SPHERE?

So has a European public space 'distinct from the national' emerged? It would appear that for the vast majority of the population no, such a space does not exist. The prior analysis of the European media landscape highlights the lack of a common frame-work in which people receive information and news or programming about Europe, and the subsequent necessity to focus on national media systems. An overriding factor in this is the diversity of languages. Despite the preference for English as a second language for many Europeans, for the moment it remains chiefly a language of business, a point further supported by the overwhelming participation of business students in Erasmus schemes. Aside from perhaps the people of Switzerland, Luxembourg, and the Netherlands, the majority of people in European countries could not be considered bilingual or multilingual in a real or practical sense. Instead, the citizens' economic, political, and social interests are represented at the European level and within the EU polity by national representatives and national organisations, often with transnational and multinational links. Habermas' (1962/ 1989) description of the public sphere never assumed a system open to all, but the added distance of the citizen from the EU political community, coupled with the unequal access of business over social interests, imply a greater focus on the people as consumers rather than citizens. Whereas political or interest group actors are served by identifiable transnational media, the subsequent discussions and debates that are available for citizen engagement

---

[16]Spanish report.

remain within the national public sphere. This development of a 'sphere of different publics' (Schlesinger & Kevin, 2000), or overlapping public spheres, is for the most part dependent on the output of the national media.

This chapter linked some of the central questions regarding democratic development in the EU and issues of information, participation, and opinion formation from chapter 1 with the role of the media. It also linked the questions of European identity and cultural exchange with aspects of media output and the media's informational educational and entertainment functions.

A description of the overall European media landscape indicated the obstacles to examining the issue of European news and programming with reference to Pan-European broadcasting or transnational exchange. Finally, the need to focus on the output and activities of national media systems, bearing in mind some of the major differences and traditions that exist in European countries, was outlined. The following chapters present the results of the examination of news media and television programmes dealing with Europe.

3

Overview of European News Coverage

INTRODUCTION

For the purposes of this research, *Europe* is understood in the wider sense and European news (all coverage coded) thus has been defined as including not only EU political and economic news but all political, economic, and cultural news dealing with Europe or people residing in Europe. For each country in the study, this does not include self-reference or national news unless connected to Europe or to other countries. The emergence of some form of European political identity can be reflected in media debates and discussions of political issues. Although this cannot be a measure of the extent to which Europeans incorporate such aspects of EU politics and decision-making processes in their daily lives, it demonstrates the role the media play in the informational and educational components of European citizenship. This political element was examined through media coverage of specific topics with reference to the research questions.

The reflection of cultural integration or the way in which the news media contribute to this integration is viewed in two ways. First we looked at news coverage of other peoples and countries in Europe, dealing with the idea of the increased knowledge and understanding of other cultures and other ways of life. Then we looked at cultural news from other people in the sense of culture as 'product,' the aspects of other peoples' cultural output that we learn about through the media.

Prior to looking at more specific coverage of political and cultural issues, this chapter gives a general overview of European news during the two 1-week periods of monitoring. The partners in each country who coded news stories were asked to identify relevant articles and news stories as being those referring to: Europe/European; those referring to the EU; all articles dealing with the political, cultural, and abstract topics detailed on the code sheets; and news about other countries and cultures in Europe. Many stories dealing with Europe were not about the EU and the term *Europe* was not coded unless specifically referred to (although in theory it could be assumed that all coded stories were by definition 'European'). For this reason, the majority of the news items are either coded with reference to Europe, EU, or both, but some stories have neither reference as they may deal with, for example, film production in France.

With each reference, coders were asked to state whether the topic was the *main* focus of the news item, *secondary,* or merely a *minor* reference. They were also asked, in their judgement, to decide whether the *tone* of the article was *positive, negative,* or *neutral,* not as an indication of the nature of the news but the nature of its coverage by the writer/presenter. Finally, they were asked to assess whether the story was presented from a *national, European,* or *neutral perspective.* This was intended to show where the news and debates about Europe had become Europeanised and also which issues remained dominated by a national perspective. The issues of tone and rhetoric are dealt with in later chapters dealing with specific topics and policies.

This chapter focuses more on the quantitative aspect of the news during the two periods with cross-country comparisons, comparisons between outlets, and between types of coverage. Based on data analysis (using statistical software), the following outlines the dominant stories, the sections of news outlets that deal with Europe, and the presence of issues and topics central to the project.

EUROPEAN NEWS IN THE NATIONAL MEDIA OUTLETS

The media outlets that were selected for monitoring in the study are outlined in Appendix I. Here we look at the distribution of European news, as defined for the research, throughout different types of news outlets (see Table 3.1). Coverage of Europe on television and in newspapers is treated separately for most aspects of analysis. The categories used in coding the types of news outlets were:

- Public service broadcasting television news programmes: TV PSB
- Commercial/private television news programmes: TV comm.
- National daily quality newspapers: Press Q.
- Regional newspapers: Regional

TABLE 3.1
Total Number of European News Stories by Outlet Type

	Public Service Television	Commercial Television	Quality National Press	Regional Press	Popular Press	Tabloid
May week	268	225	3410	793	60	449
Average per outlet	33.5	28	180	132	20	150
June week	322	323	3759	902	91	558
Average per outlet	40	40	198	150	30	186

- Popular daily newspapers (often tabloid format): Popular
- Tabloid newspapers more in the style of *The Sun* and *Bild:* Tabloid

Unsurprisingly, the amount of news items or articles in the press hugely outweighed that of television news and the 'quality press' outweighed all other newspaper types in terms of quantity of coverage of European news.

The overall amount of coverage increased during the second period, most likely due to the European Parliamentary elections, a topic of particular interest in this study. The amount of news items on all outlet types is very similar for both periods.

Television

When comparing the concentration of news in different outlets, in different countries, a similar overall pattern emerges, but some differences are reflected in the coverage of European news and perhaps in the interpretation of European news.

Table 3.2 illustrates television news coverage that was coded in both periods in each country. The table displays the total number of news items coded for television news and includes short, medium, and long items. For all comparisons of news outlets, the total quantity of news items is the quantitative measure but totals are discussed with reference to any major difference in patterns regarding the relative size of items.

All news programmes are broadcast everyday in each country but are not exactly of equal length. The Spanish television news outlets certainly have more news items that feature a European aspect than any other country, although these broadcasts are dominated by short and medium-length items.

The pattern is similar in both types of television outlet. In Germany, the lengths of items are similar in both types of outlets and dominated by short and medium news items, as the broadcasts are quite short. For France and Ireland, commercial news is characterised by the large amount of short items, with the public channel RTE having longer items related to Europe than its

TABLE 3.2
European News Stories on Television

	May Period		June Period	
	Public Service	Commercial Television	Public Service	Commercial Television
France	33	51	47	65
Germany	41	38	42	45
Ireland	28	44	26	60
Italy	16	14	21	18
Netherlands	13	11	18	25
Spain	86	51	96	73
Sweden	10	7	12	10
United Kingdom	13	9	23	27

French equivalent. Sweden, Italy, the UK, and the Netherlands had the least number of news items relevant to the study, but the items on UK and Dutch television were frequently longer, implying at least more in-depth coverage than the other two.

Quality (National) Press

For the purpose of looking at overall quantities of newspaper coverage of European news, the types of newspaper outlet have been separated. Table 3.3 details the number of articles relevant to the study in quality, national papers, as coded in each country.

The obvious observation to be made here is the large quantitative difference in coverage of Europe between the German sample and the rest (a similar pattern is apparent in the regional press).

This occurs despite the fact that in the German sample, we are dealing with two titles (*FAZ* and *SZ*), whereas in the Italian, Spanish, and French samples, three quality national papers were monitored. This may be an issue of selection of articles and might be due to a lower threshold when relevance had to be coded. However, it is more likely that the two German quality newspapers (*FAZ* and *SZ*) actually provide more European coverage than the media analysed in other countries. Also, a bigger sample size implies that there are many short articles, including just pure sports or business news, without any in-depth coverage.[1] In the case of German newspaper articles, almost 60% were short items and around 35% of the articles were medium or average sized.[2]

---

[1]German report.

[2]A count was made of the second week only as both periods displayed very similar patterns as regards amounts of coverage in different outlets in different countries.

TABLE 3.3
European News Stories in the Quality Press

	May Period	Average per Title	June Period	Average per Title
France	265	88	387	129
Germany	1589	794	1563	781
Ireland	422	211	522	261
Italy	68	23	104	35
Netherlands	114	57	142	71
Spain	646	215	726	242
Sweden	114	114	179	179
United Kingdom	192	96	136	68

The next large samples are Spain, France, and Ireland. In the Spanish case, almost half of the news items were short, 20% were medium, and around 30% coded as long or very long. The French balance was approximately 40/40/20, and in the Irish case 10/50/40 implying, in the latter case, that the articles coded were predominantly medium and long.

As is clear from the average number of stories per title, the country with least coverage is Italy (with three titles monitored). The Italian, Dutch, and British articles are primarily medium, then long, whereas the Swedish articles are predominantly short and medium. Despite the differences in article size, the press outlets in Italy and, to a lesser extent, the Netherlands have a lower level of 'European news' coverage than in the other countries.

These differences, although based on the project's selection criteria for European news, must to some extent reflect different interpretations at the individual level as to what qualifies as 'European' and can be considered as a cultural factor that impacts slightly on the overall results. This should be borne in mind in the context of further quantitative analysis. On the whole, it must be concluded that a European element permeates a great deal of German news, perhaps implying a stronger Europeanisation of German political and cultural life, at least as it is reflected in these quality press outlets. For the four countries with least coverage, various explanations can be offered, which will be looked at in more detail in the more qualitative reflection on news coverage of specific topics. These range from issues of quality in the Italian press influenced by market pressures and ownership, to national news agendas as in the case of the Netherlands where the big story was the resignation of the Dutch cabinet, to the traditional isolationist attitude of British elite debates as regards Europe.

Regional Press

Many of these patterns are repeated in relation to the regional press; one example of each was monitored in six of the countries (see Table 3.4). Although

TABLE 3.4
European News Stories in the Regional Press, One Title per Country

	France	Germany	Ireland	Netherlands	Spain	United Kingdom
May	26	315	206	41	121	84
June	38	343	241	63	144	73

categorised as regional papers, there are some differences that should be pointed out before comparing the amount of coverage in each. *The Herald* in Scotland (previously the *Glasgow Herald*) is considered a national paper in the Scottish context, and both *The Herald* and the Edinburgh-based *Scotsman* worked towards positioning themselves strongly in this space in the run up to devolution. In a UK context, *The Herald* is considered a regional paper. *The Examiner* in Ireland (formerly the *Cork Examiner*) relaunched itself as a national paper after the collapse of the *Irish Press,* and its readership extends beyond its home county.

The French title *Ouest France* is more strictly regional but has the largest readership of any of the French newspaper outlets. The Spanish title *Diario de Navarra* (13th in terms of circulation among the Spanish dailies) is also a more straightforward regional title. It is published in Pamplona, the capital of Navarra and the region with the highest rate of newspaper readership in the country.[3] In The Netherlands, *De Gelderlander* has the highest circulation of the 45 regional papers. The German *Westdeutsche Zeitung* (*WZ*) has the greatest readership of all the regional titles, and although the two papers in the more national category (*FAZ* and *SZ*) are in a sense regionally based, the content and focus of *WZ* is far more regional in nature.[4]

Despite this description of the *Westdeutsche Zeitung* as being more regionally focused than the *FAZ* or *SZ*, the number of news articles coded as relevant to the study is again greater than that of its counterparts in the other countries, although not far ahead of the Irish title. The relative size of the articles in the *WZ* is more or less balanced across small, medium, and large, whereas *The Examiner* in both periods tends towards medium and long articles.

For both the French and German titles, there is an increase in long articles during the second period of monitoring (coinciding with the last week of the European Parliamentary election campaigns), implying a greater overall increase in coverage for both than is apparent from the table. In both periods, the French paper tends towards more medium and long articles, so its Euro-

---

[3] Spanish report.
[4] German report.

TABLE 3.5
European News Stories in the Popular Press and the Tabloid Press

	Germany	Ireland	United Kingdom	Netherlands	Sweden
May tabloid	147	58	23		
June tabloid	223	56	25		
May popular				27	26
June popular				53	36

pean coverage is probably more in-depth than it appears. The *Herald* is one of the few titles with decreased coverage during the election period. This is explained by the proximity of these elections to the first Scottish Parliament elections with the lack of coverage illustrating an 'element of election fatigue'[5] at this time. However, in comparison to the other regional titles, specific coverage of the elections is quite high (see chapter 4).

Popular Press and Tabloids

This section takes a brief look at the other types of newspapers monitored for the project (see Table 3.5). In both Sweden and the Netherlands, a newspaper was selected that, although tabloid in format, could not be directly compared with *The Sun* and *Bild*.

The Swedish *Expressen,* published since 1944, is one example whose introduction into the newspaper arena, with its nonpartisan reporting and man-in-the-street point of view, has been central to the modernisation of Swedish newspapers.[6] Subsequently, it is characterised as a popular paper although more serious and closer to the quality press outlets than the tabloids mentioned before. Similarly, in the Netherlands *De Telegraaf* is characterised as a popular newspaper. The other titles in this chart are *The Sun, Bild,* and the Irish version of the UK outlet *The Star.*

According to the Irish report for the project, *The Star* is technically an English paper with Ireland-specific content, but in contrast to other UK-based 'Irish' newspapers, the Irish content is relatively high (up to 50%) and goes beyond tokenism.

The other two titles, *The Sun,* with an average daily circulation of 3.7 million, and *Bild,* with an average daily circulation of 4.4 million copies, are the two best-selling newspapers in Europe. They provide an interesting comparison of populist tabloid outlets, which is useful regarding specific topic and policy coverage analysis.

---

[5]UK report.
[6]Swedish report.

WHERE EUROPEAN NEWS APPEARS
IN NEWS OUTLETS

Continuing with a wide definition of European news based on the whole sample coded in the project, this section looks at the positioning of the news in the media outlets. This relates directly to the question regarding the impact of European news on the national agenda.

European Stories in the Broadcast News Agenda

The idea of news broken into specific sections is more relevant to newspapers, but for the coding of European news on television (Table 3.6), the following categories were used:

- Main headline
- Short headline
- Foreign World news
- Sport
- Culture/art/literature
- Comment
- Other

Categories such as politics, business, and home news were very rarely coded, so they have been put together as 'other' for the comparison that follows. The categories allow us to identify to what extent European news constituted the first item in the news bulletin under 'main headline.'

Both periods were dominated by the Kosovo crisis, which accounts for the large proportion of headline news. In the second period, this increase is possibly due in part to the election campaigns. The PSB channels show more of a propensity for headlining European news than the commercial channels, whereas sports coverage has greater prominence on the commercial news programmes.

TABLE 3.6
European News Stories on Television by Section of Broadcast

	Main Head	Short Head	World/ Foreign	Analysis/ Comm	Feature/ Special	Sport	Culture/ Art	Other
PSB May	83	90	27	2	11	28	14	13
Comm May	40	75	22	0	12	44	21	11
PSB June	122	67	52	0	20	18	12	31
Comm June	86	81	33	15	7	57	4	35

European News in the Press:
Sections of Newspapers

The following, more detailed, categories were used for coding news in different newspaper outlets:

- Front page news
- Feature/special section
- World/Foreign
- Europe
- Home/National
- Comment/opinion/analysis
- Politics
- Business/economy/finance (later merged)
- Sport
- Culture/art/film
- Society/life
- Other

The categories were intended to show, among other things, where European news in general was given prominence in the papers and the extent to which Europe was a foreign or national issue.

Table 3.7 compares all papers in the sample; any significant differences between outlet types or countries are referred to later. News about Europe in a general sense, and the EU in particular, appears in all areas of news outlets.

The various interpretations and debates regarding concepts like Europe, integration, and so forth, as outlined earlier, reveal that there are 'many Europes' that impact on the news agenda.

TABLE 3.7
European News Stories by Section of Newspaper

	Front Page	World/ Foreign	Home/ National	Politics	Business Economy	Comm/ Opinion/ Analysis
May	240	584	483	377	521	165
June	344	588	423	443	613	266

	Feature	Europe	Society/ Life	Culture/ Art/Film	Sport	Other
May	676	105	52	480	812	161
June	637	364	154	410	908	160

This table shows where all aspects of news about Europe and others in Europe occur in the press. For the study, we specifically asked that this wide range of news be examined for reference to European political and cultural issues.

Coverage in the sport section is dominant, although this area of news was coded in varying amounts in the different countries and cannot be directly compared across different countries. Aside from this, the news was coded most often in 'feature/special' sections, 'world and foreign' news, 'economic, business and financial' news and 'home and national' news. The level of coverage appearing in the 'home and national' news sections of media outlets reflects the impact of European political and cultural news affairs on national affairs. (This is developed later in more detail in relation to coverage of the EU.)

Political and cultural sections are not so far behind, but there is quite a low level of coded material in the 'comment, opinion, analysis' sections of news outlets. This changes during the second period coinciding with the election campaigns. It is also apparent that few press outlets carry a particular section entitled 'Europe.' As a section of a newspaper outlet, this is most frequently coded in *Le Figaro*, *The Irish Times*, *Süddeutsche Zeitung*, and *El Mundo*. According to the Spanish national report:

> *El Mundo* is the only national newspaper having a daily section dedicated to European information which is entitled 'Europe.' The existence of this section implies, from our point of view, the recognition of a European public sphere, which is different from the foreign news section and the acceptance of Europe as a political reality. While other Spanish newspapers have separate sections dedicated to international and national affairs we could ask why they do not have a similar 'European' section. This serves to highlight the different levels of governance (national, European and foreign) and appears to contribute to an increase in European information in the newspaper.[7]

Indeed, the presence of a dedicated section on European news does imply a development of a sphere of debate regarding Europe and also a sense that Europe is a constant issue on the news agenda. Although this trend is only apparent in a few outlets, in the second period of monitoring, during the election campaigns, there was an increase in coverage coded under this section due to newspapers producing extra supplements and features. Coverage of sporting issues in Europe certainly outweighs news about culture, film, art, and literature, implying that sport is a more important, more visible European phenomenon.

Similar patterns of coverage are apparent in the second monitoring period. However, in this instance more references appear in what is termed the 'main news, headline, or front page' section of the news outlets due to both the European Parliamentary elections and the Kosovo peace discussions.

---

[7] Spanish national report.

THE EUROPEAN UNION IN EUROPEAN MEDIA OUTLETS

This section focuses on the appearance of references to the European Union in the news and where this appeared in news outlets. The same categories as before were used but much less variety of categorisation was required.

The European Union on Television News

For the television coverage particularly, references to the EU were largely either headline news or shorter news items, with some items coded as foreign or domestic. The only major observable difference between both periods is the increase in headline news on public service channels and the overall increase in references on the commercial channels. Table 3.8 illustrates the news coverage on television.

The European Union in the Press

For press coverage, a wider variety of categorisation was used, and EU references appeared in articles in the sections outlined in Table 3.9. Not surprisingly, coverage in all sections increases dramatically in the second period due to the last week of the European Parliamentary election campaigns. In both monitoring periods, the EU is most frequently referred to in the context of 'features' or 'special' articles.

In contrast to the overall coverage, there are more references under politics and also more coverage in the 'national/home' sections, but there is still relatively little comment or opinion on EU issues. In the first period, this type of coverage only occurs in the quality national and regional press.

The amount of coverage in the 'commentary/opinion' section increases in the second period during the end of the election campaigns; many of the articles that appear under 'features' apply to special supplements and sections produced during the election campaigns and the Kosovo peace process. Refer-

TABLE 3.8
The European Union on Television News

	Main Headline	Short Headline	World/ Foreign	Home/ National	Feature	Other
PSB May	18	18	1	1	6	1
Comm May	8	6	0	0	8	1
PSB June	26	10	1	0	7	8
Comm June	10	19	3	2	2	17

TABLE 3.9
The European Union in the Press

	Front Page	Feature/ Special	World/ Foreign	Home/ National	Europe
May	40	142	72	122	23
June	92	224	114	125	133

	Comment/ Opinion/ Analysis	Politics	Business/ Economy	Other
May	22	31	30	42
June	75	175	139	115

ences under 'culture' and 'sport' are greatly reduced (here merged with 'other') compared to overall coverage, leaving the EU as mainly a political and economic issue.

In both monitoring periods, there are fewer 'front page/headline' references to the EU, implying that top stories and headlines regarding European news, particularly during the June monitoring, had more to do with the Kosovo peace talks than with the European Parliamentary election campaigns.

The placement of European news in national newspapers, and the categorisation of this for the purposes of this project, is no doubt, influenced by the newspaper traditions in each country. Table 3.10 summarises the patterns in each country as regards categorisation of EU news. It shows in which countries the press gave prominent (front-page) attention to the EU, and also where EU news is focused within papers.

The fact that French, Irish, and Italian newspapers more frequently categorise EU issues under 'home news' reflects, in one sense, the traditional lay-out of the newspapers, and also raises the question as to whether 'home news' is Europeanised or EU news is nationalised, that is, focused on domestic interests. On the other hand, categorisation in the Dutch press places EU news mainly in the 'foreign/world' section. The majority of EU-related news in Sweden and the UK is treated under either 'feature/special' sections or in the 'politics' section of the newspapers. These two countries happen to be the more Eurosceptic in the study, and this could be reflected in the categorisation of EU news as a special or separate issue while also a highly political one. It should be pointed out that in the case of Sweden, a concurrent study, focusing on Swedish media and having a wider remit of outlets monitored, concluded that Swedish media coverage of EU issues was predominantly an issue of 'domestic' news while also being centred in 'politics' sections (Robertson, 2000).

The difference in the categorisation of EU news as 'domestic' rather than foreign, in Robertson (2000), is probably due to the wider selection of outlets rather than a focus on quality press. As regards the EU becoming front-page news in the period of the final week of election campaigning, this only really occurred in France and Germany, and to a lesser extent in Italy.

TABLE 3.10
The European Union in the National Press:
Sections of News and Prominence of Coverage

Countries	Period 1: May	Period 2: June Last Week of EP Campaigns
EU Focused in 'Home/National' News		
France Increase in prominence of EU references in second period and extra 'Europe' sections	No front page coverage News in 'Features' 'Home' and 'Politics' sections Few articles under 'Europe,' most likely in Le Monde	Lots of front page coverage Most under 'Europe' (extra sections for elections) and 'comment/opinion,' 'World,' 'business' and 'home'
Ireland No major changes in prominence of EU references but extra 'Europe' sections	Some front page coverage Coverage mainly under 'home news' and 'features/ specials' Some under 'foreign' 'Europe' sections and 'politics'	Some front page coverage Mainly covered in 'Home news' and 'politics' and 'features' Fairly good coverage under 'world' and 'Europe' sections
Italy No major changes in prominence of EU references but extra 'Europe' sections	Lots of 'front page' coverage Mainly 'home news,' 'politics' and 'features'	Some 'front page' news Additional 'Europe' sections also 'features,' 'home news' and 'world news'
EU Focused in 'World/Foreign' News Sections		
The Netherlands No major changes in prominence of EU references	Very little front page Mainly in 'World foreign,' and 'business/economy' Some 'features' and 'politics'	Some front page coverage Mainly in 'World foreign' Then 'commentary,' 'business,' 'features' and 'home news'
EU News Spread Across Newspaper		
Spain No major changes in prominence of EU references	No front page coverage News in 'World,' 'Home,' Europe, Business and features	No front page coverage In 'commentary' and 'society/life' section Some in 'Europe,' 'Foreign' and 'Business'

(Continued)

TABLE 3.10 (*continued*)

Countries	Period 1: May	Period 2: June Last Week of EP Campaigns
EU Mainly Under Business and Politics		
Germany Increase in prominence of EU references in second period and extra 'Europe' sections	Some front page coverage Majority under Business/ economy and politics Home news more than foreign Little under 'Europe' Lots of features and commentary	Lots of front page coverage Majority under business/ economy and politics More under 'Europe' (extra sections for elections) Lots of features and commentary
EU as Mainly 'Feature/Special' and 'Political'		
Sweden No major changes in prominence of EU references	Little front page Mainly Features and politics Also home news and world news	No front page Mainly features, politics and Home news
UK No major changes in prominence of EU references	No front page coverage Mainly covered under features, commentary and politics Some home news and business	Little front page coverage Mainly features, commentary Then politics, business and additional 'Europe' coverage

STORIES AND TOPICS
THAT DOMINATED THE NEWS

We have looked at where news appears in media outlets; now we examine the relevant dominant stories during the monitoring period. Focusing on just 2 weeks of the sample of European news, the project gives an overview of the news agenda during this period. The following looks at overall coverage in the eight countries, bearing in mind that each team selected three or four newspapers and the two main television channels for both periods. This is not, therefore, a quantitative representation of all news on Europe within these countries. However, as the national partners were asked to choose several outlets that are influential and 'set the agenda,' one can assume that this presents a reasonable picture of what coverage was like in general during this time.

The 10 most prominent topics (political, cultural, and abstract) of relevance to the project during both periods are seen in Table 3.11, based on the total number of references to each topic from the entire coding process in all eight countries. The figures represent the overall number of coded articles, and the dominant stories during this time may have varied between countries. The numbers in brackets represent the number of news items where these topics were coded as the main topic of the news item. As regards all topics coded under 'main topic,' both groups of 10 represent the top 10 topics, although the order changes slightly. The total number of references gives an indication of the importance of these issues across the news agenda, whereas the count of those coded as main stories (in brackets) shows a more focused picture of the dominant themes.

It is apparent that the crisis in Kosovo dominated the news and that 'Europe' and the 'EU' are two of the most frequently coded terms. Due to the wide remit of the project, the focus was on a range of issues that received varying attention in the different countries. For example, the coverage of sport is particularly large, but the amount of coding carried out in this area varied greatly between countries, is less easily comparable, and is later excluded from analysis.

Aside from the coverage of sport, Kosovo is a top issue in both periods in terms of total references and also in terms of being the main topic of news items.

The large number of references to Europe reflects the overall focus of the project. The fact that only a third of these references constituted a main topic implies that Europe is more often an underlying theme in news than a central issue. Coverage of the EU increases during the second period as, obviously,

TABLE 3.11
Topics Receiving Most Frequent Reference Based on Data Analysis

	1	2	3	4	5
1st Period	Kosovo 1403 (983)	Sport 931 (891)	Europe 862 (250)	EU 782 (332)	Art/lit/music 601 (524)
	6	7	8	9	10
	Political Culture 766 (365)	Refugees 398 (195)	Economic Integration 356 (148)	EMU 246 (131)	European Elections 165 (110)
	1	2	3	4	5
2nd Period	Kosovo 1415 (864)	EU 1326 (476)	Europe 1215 (408)	Sport 1064 (1014)	Elections 912 (706)
	6	7	8	9	10
	Political culture 766 (506)	Art/lit 566 (447)	EMU 450 (230)	Economic Integration 437 (191)	Refugees 436 (138)

does reference to the European Parliamentary elections, the majority of election references constituting the main topic of discussion in these articles.

For the EU, another major issue during the second period was the dioxin scare, which would also account for increased coverage.

Political and Economic Topics in the News

Whereas the next chapter deals in more detail with specific topics and events and their coverage during both periods, this section looks briefly at the topics covered on television and in the press. These topics include the main EU-related policy areas that were considered relevant and also wider issues such as immigration, the Kosovo crisis, refugees, human rights, etc.

Table 3.12 outlines television coverage of political and economic topics, with Kosovo and the refugee crisis being the most important stories. Aside from election coverage, the only topic that increased in coverage was the Common Agricultural Policy. In the first period, this was only an issue in Ireland, The Netherlands, and Spain.

Coverage of the EP election campaigns was also somewhat overshadowed by the dioxin scandal in Belgium. Although this issue was not coded as a variable in the monitoring process, its impact is reflected in the large increase of references to the Common Agricultural Policy (CAP). During the second period, agriculture was also an issue in Spain, with the 'flax case' relating to subsidy corruption. The focus on CAP, dioxin, and the flax case is more apparent in television coverage, as it represents a more newsworthy issue, falling under the category of 'crisis/scandal.'

Human rights as a topic only occurred on ARTE, on the Spanish public channel, and on the commercial channels of France and Sweden.

EMU was covered on television only in Sweden and the UK during the first period, but also on ARTE and Italian Public Service television during the second.

TABLE 3.12
Political and Economic Topics on Television News

	European Elections	Expansion	Immigration	CFSP	Kosovo	Refugees
May period	10	4	4	33	204	77
June period	122	3	1	21	234	88

	EMU	Human Rights	Unemployment	Funding	CAP
May period	5	7	9	7	5
June period	12	10	11	6	58

TABLE 3.13
Political and Economic Topics in the Press

	European Elections	Expansion	Immigration	CFSP	Kosovo	Refugees
May period	152	64	19	104	1197	321
June period	766	92	28	265	1160	350

	EMU	Human Rights	Unemployment	Funding	CAP
May period	239	88	54	128	105
June period	424	101	83	138	164

The patterns of press coverage (see Table 3.13) are almost identical for both periods, with the greatest increase in articles relating to the elections, CFSP, and EMU. Although not depicted in the table, the coverage of EMU in the press is highest in Germany, followed by the UK, Sweden, and France, then Ireland and Spain. Dutch coverage increases in the second period. CFSP is given an almost equal coverage in France, Germany, Ireland, Italy, Spain, and Sweden in the first period. During the second period, coverage of CFSP in the German, Swedish, and French press far outweighs the others, with a good deal of references in the Dutch and Spanish press.

Abstract Topics in the News

Overall, the coverage of or reference to more abstract issues such as European integration, citizenship, or identity is very sparse throughout all the outlets in the eight countries. ARTE (as a 'European' channel) has more frequent references to these concepts, and the references to 'Europe,' the 'EU,' and 'European integration' were more inclined to have a 'European' rhetoric. European identity as an expression occurred only in the quality press in the first period mainly in France and Germany, with a few references in Italy, the Netherlands, Spain, and Sweden. In the second period, references were also evident on ARTE and on Spanish and Italian PSB television. European integration, where it appeared, more often on ARTE or Swedish television, was generally covered from a European perspective. 'European integration' did appear in the press in all eight countries but mostly in France and Germany.

During the election period, European citizenship was only mentioned on ARTE and Italian, Spanish, and Swedish television (few references in all) and in a largely balanced or positive tone with a neutral or European perspective in the presentation of the news items. It was discussed in the quality press mainly in Germany, France, and Spain.

CONCLUSION

The European news coded for this project is heavily dominated in a quantitative sense by the German media, with the least amount of news being coded in Italy. To a small degree, the differences between the countries in terms of quantity rests partly on interpretation of criteria and partly on the individual level of decision making as to what constitutes European news. However, the overall quantitative differences reflect the varying levels of national debate and the extent of the Europeanisation of national political and cultural issues.

The majority of this news is in the quality (national) press, although some differences in agenda can be noted between television and the press—for example, the emphasis on agricultural issues in relation to the dioxin scandal. This provided a more interesting television news item than, for example, EMU and CFSP, which were important in the press agendas.

All coverage increased during the second period and in general, although there may be more focus on regional issues such as funding and agriculture, the regional press reflects their national counterparts in each country, giving coverage to more 'European' issues. Although *The Herald* in the UK was considered to have less coverage of the elections in comparison to the other UK papers, due to the proximity of Scottish elections, it still featured more news than the other regional titles. *The Herald* also paid more attention to CFSP debates during the Kosovo crisis than the other UK media outlets in the project.

The most frequently coded topics were Kosovo, news about sport and culture (although this varied greatly between countries), the EU, Europe in a general sense, and the European elections. European news, due to the wide remit of the project, is spread across a wide section of the news outlet, particularly in the case of newspapers. Comparison of the countries reveals different tendencies for categorising EU news in particular, with the majority of news being, for example, in the 'foreign' section (the Netherlands) or the 'home' section in Ireland, Italy, and France. It is not entirely clear whether or not one should consider the appearance of EU news mainly in the 'home/national' section as an indication of Europeanisation of national political and cultural news and debates. This may also represent the extent to which European news is viewed primarily in a domestic setting with the focus on national interests.

Coverage of some of the more abstract topics coded for the project (i.e., European identity, integration, citizenship) is infrequent and occurs mainly in the French and German media and on ARTE.

4

News Coverage of the European Parliamentary Election Campaigns

INTRODUCTION

The final week of the European Parliamentary election campaigns in each country provided an opportunity to examine the media coverage of and media debates concerning a political event at a level above the nation-state. These last elections of the century left an uncertain view of the future of European citizenship. Low turnouts, apathy, and a lack of media debate on EU policies raise the question of when this supranational level of governance will be balanced by public participation, and what role the media might play in this development. Other major studies (Blumler, 1983; Leroy & Siune, 1994) on the structure of European Parliamentary election campaigns and their coverage in the media (referred to in chapter 2) examined campaign frameworks, election involvement, messages, and perceptions in a cross-cultural dimension. In the context of this research, the focus was on the coverage of the elections but with a wider reference to other issues and debates. The coding of news items and articles allowed for a quantitative assessment of news coverage and frequency of reference to particular topics, and a qualitative overview of coverage by national experts facilitated the comparison of national debates. Although the elections represent a process of political participation outside the national sphere, there is no corresponding common sphere of debate that can be examined in relation to this exercise of citizenship. Comparing the activity in the various national spheres highlights some of the distinct national ideas

TABLE 4.1
European Parliamentary Elections News and Debates, June Monitoring
Period, Total Number of News Stories and Number of References to Topics

	Total Articles	EMU	CFSP	Jobs	EU Expansion	CAP
France	263	18	20	17	2	4
Germany	147	17	9	4	9	14
Ireland	71	2	5	0	4	1
Italy	75	2	1	3	0	2
Netherlands	47	9	2	1	0	4
Spain	114	18	4	5	2	14
Sweden	156	34	39	9	13	20
United Kingdom	99	39	1	0	0	0

	Funding	European Integration	European Political Culture	European Citizenship	European Identity
France	1	30	26	22	14
Germany	8	13	30	12	15
Ireland	3	3	3	2	0
Italy	0	6	6	4	4
Netherlands	8	12	7	0	1
Spain	9	8	2	11	6
Sweden	13	14	78	12	3
United Kingdom	1	11	24	0	1

and debates about European Union membership while also bringing to the
fore some common concerns and debates that reflect growing political and
economic integration. Alongside this, the extent to which the electronic and
press media carried out a role in the process of electoral participation at the
European level is assessed in the various countries.

OVERVIEW OF MEDIA COVERAGE

The following is a brief overview of election coverage. In the first period, there
were already quite a lot of references to the elections in the UK, Sweden, and
Ireland, with fewer in France, Germany, and Spain. Patterns were similar to
the second period (outlined in Tables 4.1 and 4.2), with the focus in the UK
being on the single currency and the Swedish and Spanish media covering
a wide range of issues. Overall, there was not so much news about the campaigns and so this analysis focuses on the last week and deals with the data
from this monitoring period only.

Table 4.1 looks at all election news items during the second week of monitoring; Tables 4.2 and 4.3 focus separately on television and press coverage of the elections and other relevant topics. Table 4.1 includes both television and newspapers, which reflects the entire picture of the election information available in the outlets monitored. These items were cross-referenced (using crosstabs) with a selection of topics relating to EU policy areas, and also to some of the more abstract topics. As the chart includes the total, we can see to what extent election coverage actually dealt with policy issues. Many of these cross-referenced topics may have appeared in the same news item.

The cross-referenced items do not add up to the total number of election items; in fact, in some cases they constitute a very small percentage of coverage. It can be assumed that the other news items dealt with different issues or were more focused on the actual campaigns, personalities, etc. This aspect of the coverage is explored in more detail later with reference to the qualitative summaries of the national reports.

Although the overall amount of coverage coded for this project in Germany far outweighed that of any other country, it is the French media outlets that gave the most attention to the European elections. It is also reasonable to say that the Swedish, German, and French media display a wide range of discussion of EU policies and European themes in their coverage. In proportional terms, the coverage in the other countries may not be as lacking in depth as is apparent from Table 4.1, although both the Irish and the Italian media coverage of EU policies and related topics in the context of election coverage seem sparse. The campaigns of Irish MEP candidates were described as being tangential to the EU, wherein the EU was coded as receiving only a secondary reference in the majority of stories about the European elections.[1]

The CAP was not widely referred to in the context of the EP elections but surfaced in Spain, Sweden, and Germany, whereas in France and Sweden unemployment was discussed in this context. During the second period of media monitoring, there was an overall increase in the amount of coverage of the CAP that is not reflected here. As the coverage did not occur in the context of news items dealing with the elections, we assume that it was primarily discussed in connection with the dioxin scandal (not, therefore, linked in a major way to the European Parliament).

The expansion of the EU toward eastern Europe was not a major election issue but was given more consideration in Germany and Sweden (probably for geographical reasons). This issue was also relevant in Ireland, possibly because of the potential loss or transference of structural funds to new members. Common foreign policy hardly surfaced in the UK media (see also chapter 5) in relation to the EU elections but was a relatively important issue in the Swedish media.

---

[1] Irish report.

In the UK media, almost half of all articles relating to the elections made reference to the single currency, indicating the way in which this issue continues to remain central to any debates about the EU in the UK. The EMU also appears quite prominently in the Swedish media. In the other countries the single currency is, in proportion to overall election coverage, a minor issue, perhaps indicating its acceptance as a *fait accompli*.

The topic 'European political culture' was included in the coding of news items in order to reflect debates about the political processes at the European level both in relation to the electoral process of the European Parliament and to any discussions of the other institutions, particularly the Commission. Although the actual expression 'European political culture' may not have occurred, the coders did identify news items that raised these issues. Reference to this aspect of the elections occurs most frequently in the UK and Swedish media, but the coverage is not negative, and it is neutral in the UK and balanced and 'European' in Sweden. For the Swedish media (particularly television), this involved a comparison between European and Swedish political culture. In the context of the 2 weeks of monitoring, there does not appear to be a high degree of critical discussion of 'European political culture,' with references being predominantly balanced and neutral and many references coded as occurring within a 'European' perspective.

Television

For the purposes of examining television and the press separately, I have not in this case cross-referenced election news items with the other topics but rather included the elections as one topic among a variety of relevant political and abstract topics. So the figures for each topic represent all the news coverage of these topics.

Table 4.2 compares the different countries in the study, with ARTE included but separated from the French and German data.

Overall, there are fewer news items and less variety in the range of topics even though this table deals with all news relevant to policy issues and to the elections. Once again the French television outlets gave the most attention to the European elections. On both German television channels monitored, the European elections received practically no coverage (one news item on each) during the last week of the campaigns when the news focused on Kosovo and the dioxin scandal, with reference to CFSP and the CAP.

Compared to German press coverage and the television coverage of the other countries, this is rather surprising. The Swedish television channels and ARTE, and to some extent the French channels, displayed a wider range of discussion of EU policies and European themes at this time. Aside from election news, EMU was the only topic in this selection discussed on UK television. The CAP was the main issue dealt with in France, Italy, the Netherlands, and

TABLE 4.2
Elections and Related News on Television

	EU Election News	CFSP	EMU	CAP	EU Expansion	European Citizenship	Funding
ARTE	9	1	1	4	1	4	1
France	35	8	0	17	1	0	0
Germany	2	2	0	1	0	0	0
Ireland	16	2	0	0	0	0	1
Italy	16	2	3	13	0	2	0
Netherlands	6	2	0	14	0	0	0
Spain	25	1	0	6	0	3	0
Sweden	18	5	4	3	1	4	4
United Kingdom	11	0	4	0	0	0	0

TABLE 4.3
Press Coverage of Elections and Related Topics

	Elections	European Citizenship	Expansion	Funding	CFSP	EMU	Jobs	CAP
France	204	42	11	23	43	49	26	23
Germany	146	18	31	34	101	126	24	42
Ireland	81	2	9	8	9	40	0	9
Italy	59	2	1	0	9	9	6	21
Netherlands	42	1	0	17	6	38	6	21
Spain	89	14	24	24	26	58	7	22
Sweden	138	11	13	29	66	39	13	24
United Kingdom	88	3	3	3	5	65	1	1

Spain. Both Spanish channels had a separate block of campaign news, which started and finished with special music and images clearly identifying election information.

Press

The quantity of press coverage of the elections and related topics is outlined in Table 4.3. Again, these topics are not cross-referenced with articles about the elections but provide a picture of the overall information available about EU policy issues (and also areas of national interest such as funding and unemployment) that was available during this week.

In quantitative terms, the French, followed by the German and Spanish press, provide the most coverage of the election and the German, French, Swedish, and Spanish press appear to have more coverage of other policy issues.

EMU is quite an important issue in all countries (particularly the UK) due to fluctuations against the dollar. It is primarily in the UK and Sweden, and to a lesser degree France and Germany, that this issue is more politicised by being directly linked with the election campaigns (as seen in Table 4.1). In reference to more 'national' concerns, we can see that unemployment was not an issue in Ireland, and that funding and the EU budget are no longer central to British debates about the EU. The funding of the EU was certainly part of the debate in Germany, Spain, Sweden, and France. In Germany, both the Christian Democratic Union (CDU) and the Social Democrats addressed the issue of 'fairness,' in the context of the German contribution to the EU budget, in their campaigns.

Election Coverage and Debates in the Regional Press

The amount of coverage given to the European elections and relevant topics in the regional press in six countries is outlined in Table 4.4. The regional papers selected in France, Germany, and the UK paid more attention to the European elections, with *The Herald* mirroring the importance of EMU in the British press while apparently providing some balanced coverage of the single currency issue. Also according to the UK report for the study, *The Herald* tended to adopt a distinctively Scottish perspective, assessing events and arguments related to the European elections in terms of their implications for Scotland and, especially, for Scotland's newly established Parliament.

Topics that one would assume are relevant to a regional paper include funding, CAP, and unemployment. The CAP and funding are both widely reported in the Irish, Dutch, and Spanish titles, with funding and unemployment being quite important in *Ouest France*.

The more 'European' topics are reasonably well dealt with in the regional titles, and this reflects a pattern similar to press coverage as a whole. Of a total of five news items referring to CFSP in the British outlets monitored during the June period (in the first monitoring period there were none), three

TABLE 4.4
Election News and Related Topics in the Regional Press

	Elections	EMU	CAP	CFSP	Expansion	Funding	Jobs	Citizenship
Ouest France	25	7	0	0	3	5	4	6
Westd. Z	27	10	1	1	2	1	0	0
Examiner	10	12	7	2	3	5	0	1
De Gelderlander	11	7	7	0	0	4	1	1
Diario de Navarra	11	5	3	4	9	5	0	1
The Herald	28	17	1	3	1	1	1	1

appeared in *The Herald.* This could imply a slightly different focus on the security debate at this time in Scotland as opposed to the rest of the UK media.

EMU is an important topic in all the regional titles and has more coverage in *The Examiner* than the European elections. Questions relating to European citizenship are most prominent in the French regional newspaper, as is the case with the other French newspapers. In relation to the quantity of articles featured, the Spanish title *Diario de Navarra* and the Irish *Examiner* appear to cover most comprehensively the policy issues relevant to the elections.

COVERAGE OF OTHER MEMBER STATES IN THE CONTEXT OF EUROPEAN ELECTION COVERAGE

A further indicator of the extent to which the coverage of the elections takes a European view can be seen in the reference to the other member states. Table 4.5 outlines the percentage of election coverage in each country (total of television and press news items cross-referenced with member states) that refers to the other EU members. Beside each country is the figure representing the total number of countries referred to (14 or fewer) in the election news items.

The countries divide into two groups wherein the top three have little news (as a percentage of overall coverage) about events in other countries connected to the elections, whereas the bottom four have a large percentage (between one quarter and one third) of news items referring to the other member states. Within these groups, there is a distinction between how many other member states are included in election coverage. Although Italy included other member states in much of the election coverage, reference was made to only six countries. Conversely, the Irish and German media, while not referring regularly to other EU countries, have more or less mentioned all of them (this is discussed later in reference to the national reports). In the German case, this is surprising given the overall range of news that refers to Europe or other Europeans.

TABLE 4.5
Percentage of Election News That Deals With Other Member States
and Number of Member States Mentioned in News

United Kingdom	5%	6
Germany	8%	14
Ireland	10%	13
Netherlands	24%	11
Italy	25.3%	6
France	30%	14
Spain	34%	14
Sweden	34.5%	14

A further relevant point is that despite the disinterest displayed in the UK media outlets when reporting on other member states, the UK was the most frequently mentioned EU member in France, Germany, Ireland, and Italy. It was also the second most relevant country for Spain and Sweden. The Netherlands was the only exception, with the media showing more interest in its neighbours Germany, France, and Belgium. Germany and France also continuously appear in the top three countries mentioned by the media in each country. The Swedish and French press monitored in the study provide more comprehensive coverage of the elections in terms of policy issues linked to European election news items and in relation to the extent to which reference is made to other member states.

A YEAR OF CONFLICT AND CRISIS

With respect to electoral participation, certain events of 1999 undoubtedly had an influence on the attitudes of the public towards the EU. The resignation of the Commission compounded public perceptions regarding corruption at the European level and the idea of the EU 'gravy train.' It is difficult to assess whether the general public understood the role played by the European Parliament in this affair by exerting its powers in relation to the acceptance of the European Commission. Recent Eurobarometer data suggests that 'EU citizens are now significantly more likely to express satisfaction with the way democracy works in the European Union (42%) than they were in spring 1998 (+7).'[2] This change in opinion is interpreted by the Commission as a positive response to the European Parliament's involvement in the protection of democratic interests at the EU level.[3] From a media perspective, one senior BBC official noted that 'when they (the European Parliament) actually start to take some real decisions about the European Commission, they begin to get coverage. I think when they start to make decisions that matter this is going to happen more and more.'[4] However, it is likely that there remains a lack of public understanding of the division of powers at the EU level. The development of political decision making and economic influence at this level has not been accompanied by a development of civic participation on the part of the citizen. The Kosovo crisis and the subsequent peace talks overshadowed much of the campaign period. The extent to which European security issues and the role of the EU in conflicts in Europe were integrated into national debates on Kosovo varied from country to country (see chapter 5).

---

[2]Eurobarometer 51 [FR-EN-DE] July 1999, European Union Publication Office.

[3]Anna Melich, European Commission representative, speaker at 'Transnational Communication in Europe' conference, Berlin.

[4]From UK report: Interview with BBC official.

A further issue, which dominated the final week of campaigning, was the dioxin scandal in Belgium. This led to discussions in the media of EU regulation of food production and a re-emergence of a lack of trust regarding food production beyond national borders, which was most apparent during the BSE crisis of March 1996. By and large, the references to Belgium during this time were considered balanced and neutral, but quite a lot of negative news coverage (between a third and a half of references) occurred in France, Italy, Spain, and Ireland, with the German and British media more neutral. The Italian report for the study describes the nature of the news from Belgium as having a clear us/them rhetoric, which interestingly switched during the subsequent Coca-Cola crisis to an issue with a more global flavour, addressing the blaming discourse towards the American model of globalisation and to American imperialism.

Within national boundaries, there were also other events that influenced the news agenda during this period. Although the dioxin affair was of major importance in all countries, in the Netherlands the main story was the Dutch cabinet crisis. This dominated political discussion and overshadowed the European campaigns. In Spain the European elections coincided with regional government and mayoral elections, causing a decrease in interest in the European elections. Consequently, European issues were not clearly differentiated from national ones in the candidates' discourse. In other words, one could say that European issues were 'nationalised' by candidates in attacking opponents. For example, the Socialist party (PSOE) tried to involve the Popular Party (PP) candidate in a case of corruption concerning EU agricultural funding (known as the 'flax case'), and the PP accused the PSOE ex-Ministers of not having correctly negotiated the integration of Spain in the European Union. This struggle was emphasised during the June period, making flax the key topic of the campaign.

THE NATURE OF EUROPEAN PARLIAMENTARY ELECTION COVERAGE

Coverage of elections throughout the member states has traditionally reflected the campaign strategies of political actors, characterised by a focus on domestic issues. Electoral behaviour generally amounts to a type of referendum on the incumbent government. Based on the monitoring of one week in May at the launch of the national campaigns and one week in June at the end of the election campaigns, the recent elections appear to reflect similar tendencies. As Table 4.1 illustrates, the majority of coverage in each country did not deal with many of the central policy issues at the EU level, implying coverage focused on the campaigns, personalities, and domestic issues.

Such agenda setting involves a reciprocal process between politicians and journalists, so it is necessary to take into account the influence of politicians when assessing media coverage. For example, in Spain the coverage of the elections is described as not having been 'an occasion to discuss Union problems or to reinforce European citizenship, but to talk about domestic issues and to measure the popularity of the two main parties, PP and PSOE.'[5] Political corruption was also a relevant issue in the strategy of the campaign reflected by the mass media.

The pattern was similar in Italy, with a focus on internal political games and strategies, with little attention being paid to European policies. This was particularly apparent in the press, with the exception of *Il Sole 24 Ore,* the only outlet reporting the main European policies and directives, although focusing on economics. In Ireland some of the candidates explicitly 'stated that the elections should be treated as an opportunity for the electorate to express their opinions as to the performance of the present national government.'[6]

Likewise, in Britain, particularly in the quality press, the elections focused on the divisions within the two main parties over European issues. Riddell, writing in *The Times,*[7] noted how Europe was an important issue within the ranks of the Conservative Party, yet was considered relatively unimportant among the wider electorate, where issues such as health and education were viewed as priorities.

The data analysis suggests that Spanish media coverage was more comprehensive than that of their British, Italian, or Irish counterparts. The Spanish report refers to issues that received special attention in the press including economic integration and the Euro, CAP, unemployment, social policy, CFSP, and the 'democratic deficit,' but indicates an absence of discussion about political integration.

Dutch media coverage concentrated on reimbursements of fictitious expenses, the expected low attendance rate of the elections, and interviews with prominent Dutch members of the European Parliament. *NRC Handelsblad* (June 5) included a special appendix dedicated solely to the European Union. Overall, the last week was characterised by a low amount of news with little attention paid to 'visions of Europe in the various party platforms.'[8]

Further description of the Irish campaign claims that 'virtually every Irish party (with the possible exception of the Green) adopted a standard Irish campaigning approach—clientelist and localist. Candidates stressed what they could do for their European constituency (e.g., better roads, more jobs, etc.) rather than their stance on more explicitly 'European' issues. As a consequence, in the first monitoring period, coverage of the European Parliamentary elections failed to engender much media coverage of specific European issues such as Agenda 2000, EU eastern expansion, common foreign policy,

---

[5]Spanish report.
[6]Irish report.
[7]'A choice of intimacy or separation,' by P. Riddell, 17 May 1999, *The Times,* p. 20.
[8]Dutch report.

etc. Given that these were not campaign issues in Ireland, this is hardly surprising.[9] Apparently, this situation has improved somewhat in Sweden compared to the last EU elections (their first), and there was more of a focus on
EU issues rather than on the earlier arguments about EU membership. This
is indeed reflected in the coverage (as illustrated earlier) wherein Swedish
coverage (both television and press) provided a fairly wide debate of EU policies. Although the elections thus provided a platform for national political
issues and rivalries, there were certain EU policies that came to the fore in the
national campaigns.

WHERE THE EU IMPACTS ON THE NATIONAL SPHERE

It is not too surprising that the EU election campaign in the UK provoked
lively debate. Both the Conservative and the Labour parties are divided over
the issue of European integration with the Labour government being, in general, more in favour of closer integration. Although Prime Minister Tony Blair
requested that the elections should not be used as a referendum on EU membership or EMU, it was only to be expected that these issues would be subject
to some emotive journalism. As pointed out earlier, EMU was referred to in
almost 50% of all the election coverage. Rupert Murdoch's UK newspapers expressed opposition not just to the Euro but to the concept of the EU elections
in general. *The Times* focused on the Euro as an important election issue. One
columnist (in a more subtle sense) advocated abstention as the best use of the
vote; *The Sun* was more explicit in its suggestions for '10 (alternative) uses for
a load of Euro ballot (papers)' including using them as confetti or as draught
excluders.[10]

In contrast to its daily counterpart, the *Sunday Times* (Scottish edition), on
June 6, reported more positively on the European parliamentary elections and
it made a direct appeal to voters to take part in these. Similarly, the Westdeutsche Allgemeine Zeitung (WAZ) offered a series about the German parties
and their campaigns, another series about individual candidates, and on June
12 included a commentary with the title 'Vote!' dealing with the low participation in other countries and arguing for the importance of the European Parliament. On the day before the elections, despite previous criticism, *Bild* presented an article on the bottom of the front page entitled 'European elections:
Why they are so important for us.'[11] In this short article, basic information
was given on the number of people entitled to vote and on the competencies

---

[9] Irish report.
[10] UK report.
[11] *Bild,* June 12, 1999, cited in German report.

of the European Parliament. There is no clear indication as to whether the 'us' in the headline refers to Germans or Europeans.

During the Irish campaigns, two issues did appear that touched on a more European perspective although both, by their nature, can still be considered central to issues of national interest. The first concerns enlargement of the EU, which is particularly relevant to Ireland because of structural funds. In relation to this, several newspaper articles[12] explicitly stated that the European Parliament (and thus Irish MEPs) would have the power to determine, to a large measure, the degree of enlargement. Although the press outlined the implications for the country of this development, there was no attempt to outline the candidates' positions on this issue, thus not really fulfilling the responsibility to assist the citizen in making informed choices. Another issue was the question of Ireland's possible membership in NATO's Partnership for Peace, more a global issue than a European one, but useful for candidates opposing the government stance.[13]

A wider European issue appeared in the Italian media in relation to the emergence of a common European Left political programme, based on Blair's 'Third Way,' presented as the new political identity of the left European governments, but noting divisions in the proposal of an alternative way by French politicians. This allowed for a potentially more 'European' debate as regards political culture and common trends in European governance. Similarly, in the German media

> this discussion took place on the national as well as the European level. The Green Party, the trade unions, as well as some members of Schröder's party, the SPD, argued against this paper which was criticised as neo-liberal without providing any idea about how to organise social security and employment. On the European level, Lionel Jospin, the French Prime Minister, criticised the paper for the same reason.[14]

In relation to this perspective, it is interesting to note how the international press responded to the results of the 1999 elections. Most stories focused on the defeat of the European left, or the success of the European (centre) right.[15] This illustrates the way in which the EU is, from the outside, considered as a single political entity with opposing blocs of political ideology. This is an aspect of EU politics seldom reflected in the national sphere due in some respects to a lack of debate about cross-national alliances and the party structure within the EP.

---

[12]*The Examiner* 8/6/99, p. 5, cited in Irish report.

[13]Irish report.

[14]German report.

[15]Cited in French report. Based on Reuters news stories.

COMMENTARY ON CAMPAIGNS AT HOME

There were some further interesting characteristics of coverage of the election campaigns. The first involved the tendency towards media commentary on media coverage and political debates. Much of the discussion in the UK revolved around the lack of debate, the fact that central issues were not being discussed, and the likelihood of a low turnout in the elections.[16] Similar commentary on the lack of debate occurred on TG1 in Italy. The discussion on voter abstention also appeared in the Italian press, and most media outlets reflected the lack of interest in the elections after the first three polls in the UK, the Netherlands, and Denmark.

The Irish media regularly refer to confusion on the part of voters as to the relevance of the elections in their lives. One TV3 vox pop feature on the European elections made it clear that most people were completely unable to see the relevance of the elections or indeed of their MEPs. The possibility that the media themselves might be to some extent to blame for this was never broached, let alone seriously discussed. There is at least a case for suggesting that the Irish media failed to point out the very real impact the overall results of the election across Europe might have for the lives of their readers/audience.[17]

Another trend, one that can be seen as a type of personalisation of the campaigns, involved what might be described as novelty candidates who were given media attention in other countries. In Italy TG5 reports underlined the 'pop' aspects of the elections dealing with 'bizarre' candidates from the spheres of show business or sport. Similarly, in Ireland the ex-Eurovision winning candidate Rosemary Scanlon attracted a good deal of media attention. European journalists regularly express the difficulty that they have in convincing national editors of the importance of EU news stories. The attempt to brighten the news with more interesting or personalised angles merely reflects the trend at the national level due to the commercialisation of media outlets. 'It is always an enormous task to cover the news in an attractive way. Otherwise readers just lose interest. It is perhaps strange to say but thanks to crises, fraud, etc., the interest in Europe has somehow increased.'[18]

This type of candidature did not occur in the Spanish elections but, on a different note, the Spanish media aroused interest in the two main opposing candidates in the election who happened to be female. In this instance, the media displayed their skill at trivialisation of a political process. One example dealt with Loyola de Palacio (Popular Party and Commissioner in the EU) with commentary on her image and lack of make-up.[19] The Swedish media devoted

[16] UK report.

[17] Irish report.

[18] Dutch journalist.

[19] *Diario de Navarra*, 6 June 1999, p. 8., cited in Spanish report.

some coverage to the first 'Swedish' mayor in Harwich, England, Ann Evander, who ran as a candidate in the UK elections.

A further theme relating to candidates in the national campaigns emerged in the German media and could be considered as a type of criticism of 'European political culture.' Whereas other countries indicated an overabundance of novelty candidates, a contrary complaint in the German media was the lack of familiarity with candidates. On June 10, the *SZ* published a long report on the campaign in Germany,[20] including an interview with the former president of the European Parliament, Klaus Hänsch (SPD), emphasising the lack of public awareness of candidates. Part of this problem lay in the campaigning strategies wherein most of the posters and advertisements did not show the candidates, but rather general slogans, some of them critical of the European Union. One example was an advertisement of the Social Democrats showing two identical cucumbers with the message that instead of regulating irrelevant details, Brussels should deal with the basic problems of unemployment and social security.[21]

Some slightly more cynical commentary on the candidates occurred in a commentary where a correspondent criticised the election campaign from a citizen's perspective, of not knowing the candidates. Using quotes from a German TV comedy, *Bild* referred to the abovementioned critique about not sending the very best people to Brussels. The European Parliament is called a 'reception camp for the remaining stock of political parties,' and the elections are criticised as 'legalised deportation with full pay.'[22]

Criticism of candidates also appeared in the UK press, in particular a story concerning allegations of expenses fiddling of a Labour MEP: 'Euro MP in £1.5m Expenses Probe.'[23] The story implied that EU expenses were even covering payment of a gardener and, with its references to expense 'fiddling' and the 'gravy train,' reinforced the negative image of overpaid Euro MPs enjoying a lavish life style at the taxpayer's expense. A further issue of contention related to the actual electoral process as reformed by the Labour Government. This introduced an element of proportional representation but included a system whereby candidates were presented in a 'list system.' In an editorial, *The Times* attacked the closed list system of voting, noting what it saw as the very real differences on Europe that existed between the pro-European Liberal Democrats, the slightly less enthusiastic Labour government, and the anti-Euro Conservative Party. They urged that 'voters who care about Europe should read these manifestos and discover that even if they cannot choose

---

[20]'Gherkins instead of faces. Trying to attract voters is not easy for Members of the European Parliament—almost nobody knows who they are and what they do.' (SZ, June 10, 1999).

[21]German report.

[22]Ibid: *Bild,* June 8 and 9.

[23]*The Sun,* May 20, quoted in UK report.

their MEP, that does not mean that the forthcoming election, however depressingly undemocratic its form, offers them no choice at all.'[24]

There was occasional commentary on the European elections in the UK papers. *The Guardian* columnist Hugo Young wrote two pieces during the week (Thursday 20, Friday 21, May). Both *The Times* and *The Guardian* simply restated already well-known (among broadsheet readers at least) pro- and anti-Euro positions. The launch of the parties' manifestos attracted attention in all the papers; however, the overall tenor of reporting was factual and low key.[25]

Although the European Parliament's UK Office had previously detected a shift and slight softening in the previous predominantly anti-Europe stance of the London-based media, they also recognised that part of their job involved attempting to influence the tenor of European Parliament stories. 'In many respects it's fire fighting, because the editors and many of the journalists have their own agenda anyway. So they will write their own story and then come for confirmation, denial or information.'[26]

COMMENTARY ON CAMPAIGNS IN OTHER COUNTRIES

Reporting on the campaigns in other countries, the German *FAZ* offered a series of stories with portraits of European countries each day.[27] With reference to the campaign in France, they emphasised the dominating inner political perspective claiming that in France, Europe hardly happens. The article on the United Kingdom and Ireland dealt with the British debate on the pros and cons of participation in the EMU. In the Netherlands, articles were identified that indicated the Dutch parties' concern about the low interest in the elections among the Dutch population. Reports on Spain, Denmark, Sweden, and Finland followed. A similar overview of the campaigns in other countries was published by the *SZ* on June 10, 1999. The main article was headlined: 'Europe's underestimated power. The weary election campaign shows that citizens and politicians are almost not interested in the European Parliament—unjustly.' On June 12, the day before the election, the *SZ* published another full page on the elections with reports about the campaigns in different German regions.[28]

---

[24] 18 May: 'Manifestos for Europe': Criticism was made of the closed list system suggesting that this contributed to the lack of identification people felt with the process.

[25] From UK report.

[26] European Parliament office representative, UK.

[27] *FAZ*, June 7–10, 1999.

[28] German report.

Spanish coverage of the elections was mainly grouped with coverage of local and regional elections (*El País* and *ABC*) and in *El Mundo,* they were in the 'national' section. An additional section called 'European elections' (in *ABC* and *El País*) and 'Europe' (in *El Mundo*) was dedicated to news related to European campaigns in other countries. *El País* also included interviews with relevant political personalities and features on different issues.[29]

The French report details election coverage on *Le Monde*'s Internet site, which summarised the campaigns in each of the 15 member states. These stories were all sourced from the Agence France-Presse (AFP) and included the following:

• The European elections of June 13 meet with general indifference in Germany where people are far more concerned about the Kosovo conflict than a European Parliament about which most Germans are virtually ignorant.

• Known as the champions of "Euro optimism," the Italians are nonetheless experiencing a European election campaign centred on domestic issues, possibly because local by-elections, municipal, and provincial elections are also being held on the same day.

• Tony Blair's Labourites have to conduct a difficult balancing act in the European elections: how to campaign and limit the number of probable lost seats, without getting involved in the vexed issue of a single currency.

• The dioxin-infested chicken scandal, which has led to two ministerial resignations, has transformed the Belgian election campaign: hitherto this was lacklustre and its European dimension had been completely eclipsed by the parliamentary and regional elections held the same day.

• A record low turnout in the Netherlands is likely to mark Thursday's parliamentary elections, despite a slight renewal of interest following the unexpected government crisis of the last few weeks.[30]

Commentary on other countries allowed for some reflection on the national perspective on Europe. In Germany, several articles expressed concern that Germany was not taking Europe seriously enough. The Prime Minister of Bavaria, Edmund Stoiber, criticised the European influence on Bavaria and the importance of the elections: 'Even if the people don't believe it, the nomination of Romani Prodi as President of the European Commission is at least as important as that of the Federal Chancellor.'[31] A similar argument is made in an article entitled 'Learning from the British and French. Germans are less determined in following their interests.'[32] It is reported (without concrete ref-

---

[29]Spanish report.
[30]French report.
[31]FAZ, June 7, 1999.
[32]FAZ, June 10, 1999.

erence) that in Brussels, German and Italian civil servants are seen as the most 'European,' whereas their French and British colleagues are more closely linked to their respective national capitals. A high-level German EU official is quoted as arguing that a fear of accusations of nationalism cause many Germans in Brussels to exercise an exaggerated restraint.[33] The second article here implies a questioning of the more 'European' perspective of German political actors.

Although the coverage of campaigns in other countries was a common aspect of the reporting, there have been some reservations as to the value of such articles. The authors of the Irish report pointed out that they felt that there is a certain amount of tokenism underlying this sudden and short-lived increase in European coverage. *The Irish Times*[34] for example, reprinted two reports on the progress of the European elections in Spain and Portugal—the paper offered no particular rationale for singling out these two countries, nor was there anything in the articles that appeared particularly newsworthy.[35]

CONCLUSION

Given this data, European Parliamentary elections continue to be a national event with, by and large, national party candidates and a focus on national issues, or in some cases an event where satisfaction with national political leaders can be expressed. Understandably, this is reflected in media coverage. The media's role, to some extent, is to report on the campaigns, candidates, and issues. The lack of debate on specific EU policy issues, decided at the EU level but impacting on the lives of citizens, is reflected in the data analysis, outlining different national approaches. There were, however, many attempts to approach the elections from a European perspective. In the press, this included publishing guides to the elections, outlining the stance of particular parties on EU issues, and covering campaign developments in other countries. The depth of analysis as regards the European debate in other countries of course varies, and whether this type of coverage is merely an example of tokenism is open to debate. At least the appearance of comparative coverage across the EU indicates a developing perspective that moves beyond national boundaries. The French and Swedish press coverage appears to be the most comprehensive in terms of range of topics and other member states being discussed.

Alongside the trends and developments mentioned so far, there has been an increase in the amount of shared and syndicated articles between European

---

[33]German report.

[34]*Irish Times*, Friday, June 11, 1999.

[35]Irish report.

outlets. For those with access, the Internet versions of media outlets offer a much deeper sphere of analysis with links to previous stories, political parties, and Non-Governmental Organisations (NGOs) involved in debate and policy process. The introduction of the Euro has certainly enhanced this process with the sharing of stories online between titles such as *Le Monde, The Guardian, El País,* and *Aftonbladet.* The online coverage of elections also allowed greater access to information about the campaigns in other countries, as illustrated by *Le Monde.* Overall, there is an incremental development of space in European media outlets for debate and exchange regarding common issues and policies. Hence, the presentation of a 'European news agenda' is more developed in some countries than in others and, due to the focus on different issues, cannot be considered as homogeneous. The extent to which the media enhances political identification or the development of European citizenship also varies across countries and sometimes across outlets within national spheres, based on both information provision and discussion.

Several obstacles are apparent that inhibit the media's role in this process. In discussions with journalists, it has been remarked that political news in general requires some controversy or 'personalisation.' This has certainly been the case as regards many of the candidates who received media attention. On the other hand, there was criticism of 'unknown' and inferior candidates.

Most debates remain focused on national issues or European issues relevant to the national interest. Inasmuch as support for, or engagement with, the European Union has, by political leaders, traditionally been couched in terms of 'national interest' or 'cost and benefit' measurement, this continued link of the 'European' with the 'national' is hardly surprising.

5

The War in Kosovo: Media Debates About a 'European Crisis'

INTRODUCTION

The dominant story during both monitoring periods was the Kosovo crisis. The purpose of this research was not to examine in any great detail the nature of news reportage of the war, at least not in the sense of outlining the propaganda battles.[1] While these events had a major impact on news agendas throughout Europe, skewing any measurement of European coverage in the media, the way in which the war was covered in each country reveals several things about the nature of media discourse about Europe and integration. The kind of coverage we refer to does not really involve the journalists 'on the ground' but rather the more considered discussion of a 'bigger picture' that commentators and writers at home may have had more opportunity to explore. This chapter refers initially to results of the coding of news items, followed by a general discussion on the media debates based on national reports and interviews.

COVERAGE OF KOSOVO IN THE MEDIA

The following is a brief overview the coverage of Kosovo and related debates in the media in the eight countries monitored. For many countries, a major

---

[1]See: *The Kosovo News and Propaganda War.* Peter Goff Ed. International Press Institute, September, 1999.

element of coverage related to the plight of the Kosovan refugees and frequently became a more 'national' story outlining what was being done in each country to help these people. This also relates to the coverage of 'others' and was the only story during both periods dealing with refugees. In this sense, in the special context of war, the coverage of refugees could not really be seen as typical of the coverage and debates on refugees and asylum seekers in general. The comparison of countries in Table 5.1 shows the percentage of the entire coverage coded for this project that was devoted to the following three topics: war in Kosovo; Common Foreign and Security Policy; and refugees. The wide remit of European news implied that this was the biggest story, but it is apparent that there were clearly differing news agendas in relation to these issues.

Table 5.1 shows the percentage of all the data that relates to Kosovo. During both periods, the European news in the British and Dutch media was heavily dominated by the Kosovo crisis, constituting 65% and over 50%, respectively, of the news items coded for the research. In both instances, they were followed closely by Spain, with Ireland having the least percentage of Kosovo coverage in relation to other European news. The actual totals in terms of quantity of news items relating to Kosovo are highest in Germany, followed by Spain, the UK, and the Netherlands (this is clearer in Table 5.3 relating to press coverage).

There were two aspects of media coverage that are of interest to this project. The first was the focus on the plight of the refugees, which was also highly significant in the UK, Spain, and the Netherlands, with considerably less attention in France and Sweden.

The second element concerns the way in which this war in Europe provoked discussions on 'European security identity' (as opposed to the role of NATO), and the development of a Common Foreign and Security Policy (CFSP) can be viewed in a quantitative sense in Table 5.1.

TABLE 5.1
Percentage of Total 'European News' That Dealt With Kosovo,
CFSP, Refugees, During Both Periods

	Kosovo May	CFSP May	Refugees May	Kosovo June	CFSP June	Refugees June
France	27%	6%	7.5%	20%	10%	1.3%
Germany	24%	2%	5%	19%	4%	5%
Ireland	21%	4.5%	8%	15%	1.2%	7%
Italy	32%	29%	7.5%	16%	8.1%	9%
Netherlands	52%	.5%	21%	48%	3%	20%
Spain	45%	3%	15%	33%	3%	15%
Sweden	28%	8.5%	6.5%	17%	3%	1%
United Kingdom	65%	0%	21%	45%	2%	12%

Discussions on CFSP were an important part of Italian news coverage at this time, although it should be borne in mind that the total quantity of coverage in the Italian media monitored is less than in the other countries. Conversely, when looking at the German data, it must be considered as relative to the fact that the German monitoring was extremely large. Although Kosovo constituted less than 20% of European news, the figures for period one and two are 447 and 458 news items respectively, referring to the war. Likewise, the number of items referring to CFSP are 24 and 101, respectively.

Discussions on CFSP also feature in the French, Swedish, and Irish media in the first period but not to any significant extent in the Dutch, while being completely absent in the UK media. During the second period of the monitoring exercise, the focus of coverage was more on the peace talks and the securing of peace in the Balkans. References to expansion of the EU were very minor (and not included in the chart) during both periods, with Sweden giving the most coverage to this issue.

Television Coverage

Television coverage illustrates how important Kosovo was on the news agenda and also the way in which the story was framed for television audiences. Again, it has to be borne in mind that different programme formats allow for more frequent but shorter reference to topics in some countries, whereas the less frequent reference per news item in others is compensated by the fact that items are often longer.

Table 5.2 illustrates the dominance of this event on television news in Spain, Germany, France, and the UK, and also shows that the issue of the refugees was given far less coverage on German, French, and Swedish television news during the second period. CFSP was not discussed on British or

TABLE 5.2
Television News and Number of References to Kosovo,
CFSP and Refugees During Both Periods

	Kosovo May	CFSP May	Refugees May	Kosovo June	CFSP June	Refugees June
France	26	3	10	38	8	3
Germany	33	0	3	28	0	0
Ireland	22	4	9	17	2	9
Italy	16	11	4	9	2	6
Netherlands	14	0	9	16	2	9
Spain	52	6	20	67	1	30
Sweden	10	1	6	5	5	0
United Kingdom	16	0	13	36	0	13
ARTE	14	8	3	18	1	14

TABLE 5.3
Press Coverage of Kosovo, CFSP and Refugees: Number of Articles

	Kosovo May	CFSP May	Refugees May	Kosovo June	CFSP June	Refugees June
Germany	414	24	78	430	101	109
Spain	294	19	97	271	26	132
Netherlands	92	1	33	130	6	51
Ireland	89	19	35	120	9	24
United Kingdom	191	0	55	93	5	21
France	64	13	17	66	43	3
Sweden	34	12	4	36	66	3
Italy	14	16	3	14	9	7

German television news (despite being two of the largest and most influential countries in Europe) at any time during the monitoring. Although there may be historical reasons in both cases for a lack of discussion, the fact that this issue is not linked to the Kosovo crisis on prime time television news is questionable. The emphasis on the refugee crisis is most apparent on Spanish and UK news but least visible on German television.

Press Coverage of Kosovo

If German television news was lacking in depth of issues covered, the coverage of Kosovo by German press (see Table 5.3) presents a different picture in terms of quantitative and qualitative coverage. The Kosovo crisis dominated the coverage of European news most markedly in Germany, Spain, and the UK during the May monitoring period.

As Kosovo coverage was largely in the form of reports, it may be more informative to look at the type of rhetoric[2] coded for coverage of Kosovo by isolating editorials, commentaries, and opinion sections of news. In the first period German, British, and Italian coverage has been coded as predominantly neutral. The Dutch media was perceived to be far more national in its approach, whereas the Swedish took a more 'European' perspective. Overall, there was more of a mix of rhetoric in the French, Spanish, and Swedish media.

The second monitoring period (during the election campaigns and the Kosovo peace talks) reflected more or less the same pattern, with an increase in 'European' rhetoric in Ireland and Italy, and an increase in 'national' in Spain. In fact, the figures for commentary and opinion coverage are very similar to that of the overall coverage, including straightforward reports. Only in the French media is there such a variety of perspectives; This is even more

---

[2]Based on the judgment of coders as to whether the perspective of the news item was 'national,' 'European,' or neutral (as distinct from positive/negative judgments).

obvious when the opinion, commentary, and editorial sections are analysed in isolation from other sections of the newspaper.

A EUROPEAN WAR AND DEBATES REGARDING A COMMON FOREIGN AND SECURITY POLICY

As already illustrated, an important aspect (in varying degrees) of the coverage of the events in Kosovo and the NATO strikes on Serbia involved discussions of the CFSP within the EU, or in a wider sense, what is also referred to as 'European Security Identity,' including the development of the Western European Union (WEU). The extent to which the war in Europe promoted debate on this aspect of political integration varied from country to country and was influenced by issues of national interest. According to the Italian report on the monitoring of the media during the conflict, 'the concepts of 'Europe,' 'European integration,' and 'European identity' emerged in war news dealing with Europe's role in the crisis, with reference to the discussion of a 'European security identity' and foreign policies.'[3]

In the Irish media, 'The conflict coincided with a public debate about Ireland's entry into NATO's Partnership for Peace. Opponents of PfP membership asserted that it would undermine a traditional tenet of Irish foreign policy—neutrality. In such a domestic political context, where neutrality in European wars has been taken for granted, perhaps it is no surprise that Irish media coverage should reflect such a stance.'[4]

Similarly, the debate in Sweden revolved around questions of neutrality. 'There were many news reports in the Swedish media dealing with European identity and the need for defence co-operation to guarantee peace and security in Europe. Nevertheless, most of the media content emphasised the unique tradition in Sweden of non–alliance and a long history of peace. These national arguments were often used to underline the difference between Sweden and many other European countries, with other experiences from the last world wars.'[5]

For these other countries, the coverage was quite different and tended to focus more on the role being played by national armies and governments in a European context.

'Concerning the role of Italy within the European Union, the issue of the Italian peace proposal was covered extensively by both newspapers and television news bulletins; not only by reports, but also in opinions and comments from experts. Comment and analysis focused on the role of Italian politicians

---

[3] Italian report.
[4] Irish report.
[5] Swedish report.

within the European Union, and the extent to which they were considered important partners in the development of a peace strategy for the resolution of the crisis in Kosovo.'[6] Hence, the CFSP was an important element in Italian coverage (see Table 5.1) in terms of Italian involvement in peace settlements and the 'future construction' of eastern Europe.

The Italian media also reflected the role played by various European left-wing governments, their attitude towards war intervention, and the criticisms of the right-wing parties, an issue that has been stressed by commentators and editorials. A large number of editorials, opinions and comments relating to the war and to the role of Europe focused on the lack of a common foreign and security policy. In this sense, the so-called 'European identity'—never quoted in the outlets analysed—was identified by its lack of presence, thus in a negative way.[7] In the second period, some Italian media commentary identified an idea of 'European identity' in relation to the postwar role of European countries.

The media are, however, criticised as to the extent of this coverage. According to one political source, the media 'certainly covered the dramatic aspects and moments of the war, but they are not covering the great debate regarding the European role which is emerging from the war experience.'[8]

In Britain, the *Sun*'s coverage of Europe focused on Kosovo, documenting the role of British and specifically Scottish soldiers (as this was the Scottish newspaper edition) involved with NATO. The three broadsheets in the study devoted extensive space and resources to covering the war and its impact. For example, *The Herald,* the largest selling broadsheet in Scotland, devoted at least two pages every day to events surrounding the Kosovo crisis. Although the focus of coverage was on the role of Britain in the crisis, it was noted that 'the reporting did not attempt to link explicitly the wider political and economic debates about European integration with events in the Balkans. The same failure to connect these events was true of both *The Times* and *The Guardian,* and this would also prove to be the case in the second monitoring phase. The Balkans conflict was neither discussed nor reported in the wider context of developments in the European Union, not least the implications of that conflict for common foreign and defence frameworks.'[9]

A particular aspect of the Spanish media during this time, which was more pronounced than in other countries, was coverage of the Russian angle on the crisis:

---

[6]Italian report.
[7]Italian report.
[8]Italian regional politician.
[9]UK report.

The Spanish media paid particular attention to the politics of three European countries Russia, Italy (terrorism), and Germany. The media have been very attentive to Russia's role as intermediary in the Yugoslavian conflict. The Moscow visits of the Spanish President Aznar were therefore a major issue in the media. Aznar had an interview with Chernomirdin (the Russian mediator with Serbia) and an appointment with Yeltsin who, several minutes before the meeting, announced to Aznar that he was not able to receive him. The discourse in May was largely characterised by the following aspects: human interest stories (the media portrayal refugees); the coverage of the different dimensions of the humanitarian catastrophe, and the diverse diplomatic attempts to stop the conflict; and the contribution of Spanish and other international military forces in the war.[10]

On French television:

Special programmes on Kosovo and its implications for Europe played a role in shaping perceptions and increasing awareness in the period under review, possibly on a more lasting basis. Similarly, a series of 30- to 90-second television news reports on the prime time newscasts showed cooperation between, and possible divergences among, European leaders in relation to Kosovo and examples of cooperation between European soldiers. There was concern that Europe was playing second fiddle to the US within NATO, and that Kosovo illustrated the urgency of a common European defence and security policy. This line was quickly taken up by media commentators in the form of radio phone-ins, and correspondence columns in the press, or edited mini random street interviews shown on some TV news bulletins. Kosovo affected man-in-the-street thinking about a need for a common European defence and military policy in a way that media reporting of defence policy consultations in the past had failed to do.[11]

Examples included two pieces in *Le Monde,* (dated 6–7 June: p. 13) which presented the importance of news-editorial coverage of the conflict. It was illustrated in an editorial how the conflict had both tested the EU's political determination and maturity, and revealed its weakness as a coherent military force, playing second fiddle to the US.[12]

A less optimistic attitude towards the effects of the media coverage in Ireland is provided by one political correspondent who claimed that:

The Kosovo crisis did not make any dramatic impact on coverage of European issues or attitudes to Europe. It is one thing to call for European troops to be sent into Kosovo but the question is whose troops? On the whole, media coverage of the 'Partnership for Peace' is neutral-to-positive. However, the real problem there is not media coverage but the lack of leadership on this issue.[13]

---

[10]Spanish report.
[11]French report.
[12]French report.
[13]Political correspondent, Ireland.

Although the German perspective on a European war was understandably different from many European states, there were still internal debates regarding military intervention.

> A specific German aspect of the Kosovo coverage was the heavy critique within the Green Party against the war and against the government whose Foreign Minister Joschka Fischer is a member of the Green Party. Many opponents of the war left the Green Party, causing severe problems for the coalition. The government had to steer between this critical position and the American position, as e.g. with regard to the question of sending ground forces to Kosovo. Here a certain concept of 'Europe' emerged during the war, one defined by a partial opposition to the United States.[14]

Although examining only a limited time period, the coverage of Kosovo highlights the differences that exist between national debates on the issue of common security policy in Europe, ranging from quite developed in France to barely visible in the UK. These differences are a reflection of historical differences and traditions. It is also apparent that, in general, national security identity and policy has not yet given way to any 'European' equivalent. That is not really surprising. Even where there was debate on European security policy, it tended to be from a national perspective; Italy, for example, focused on 'Italian' solutions to European problems.

THE KOSOVO CRISIS AS A COMMON 'EUROPEAN' PROBLEM

In connection with the issue just discussed, a sense of common European responsibility or strategic response to the events in the Balkans was reflected in different ways in the national media. Here we can make reference to debates and to the rhetoric used when referring to these issues.

While examining the nature of discourse on European issues in the Irish media, it was noted that:

> In areas such as the Kosovo conflict the inclusive European rhetoric disappears. Thus one can note that countries such as Germany, the UK, France and Italy are suddenly primarily referred to as NATO members rather than as EU states. In effect no distinction is made between Ireland's relations with them and its relationship with say China or the US. In the straight reportage virtually no qualitative distinction is made between references to NATO's European members and to Serbia itself, which has been portrayed as the arch-villain of the piece in for example the UK media. Indeed scrupulous, (perhaps over-scrupulous) neutrality is maintained. One could speculate at length as to why this might be the case—it is obvious for example that, on the whole, western media organisa-

---

[14]German report.

tions, stung by accusations that they were used as propaganda tools during the Gulf War, took a less overtly partisan approach to the Kosovo conflict. The Irish media was no different.[15]

This view is somewhat echoed in interviews with Irish journalists and politicians, although there was some suggestion that the Irish media were rather one-sided in their approach and not questioning NATO actions particularly in relation to civilian casualties.[16] Similar criticisms were voiced in relation to the Dutch media and the Spanish media.[17]

Coverage of Kosovo in the German media is described as including an interesting multilevel conception of Europe. Most of the articles, including news about the latest events and the refugees, simply refer to a NATO perspective, sometimes paraphrased as 'the West' or 'Western countries,' reminiscent of the former Cold War period. However, when it comes to strategic aspects and the basic issue of continuation of the war, many articles differentiate between 'Europe' (i.e., the European NATO members) and the United States. Another 'Europe,' that of the European Union, is referred to in articles that deal with the necessity of a common foreign and security policy. With respect to this, articles on the Italian prime minister's initiatives to promote the negotiations with Serbia take an implicit tone of 'us, the EU member states.' The more general and essay-like articles on future visions of Europe refer to a much wider concept, which is rather an idea than a concrete political or geographical space.

This was even more apparent during the second week, with a sharpened differentiation between 'Europe' (particularly Germany) and its role on the one hand and the United States on the other. This became even more the case after the end of the war, when the perspective of coverage changed from the NATO to the European level and to the future of the European Union: 'The war made Europe more self-conscious. A common foreign and safety policy is overdue.'[18] A further aspect was closely linked to the German debate on their contribution to the EU's budget. The prime minister of Bavaria, Edmund Stoiber, stated that with regard to aid for the Balkan countries, Germany has to reach a fairer distribution than is the case with EU finances: 'Germany declares its solidarity, but there has to be fairness.'[19]

It was noted in the second monitoring period in Italy that:

> The varied use of European rhetoric according to the situation was also brought out by reporting on the G8—wherein EU members are referred to in the same tone as the non-EU G8 members—i.e. from a neutral perspective. The same is

---

[15] Irish l report.

[16] Irish European editor, and Irish MEP.

[17] By a Dutch MP, and a Spanish government official, respectively.

[18] German report.

[19] German report, in reference to *Das Bild,* June 11 and June 10, 1999.

true of references to EU members when reporting on Kosovo. Although, over-all it was observed that the tone of Kosovo coverage had altered somewhat—most notably references to Serbia had abandoned their generally neutral stance in favour of a more negative outlook, particularly after the first collapse of NATO/Serbia peace talks—those EU members which also belonged to NATO were still regarded from a balanced/neutral perspective within such coverage.[20]

The reference to the Italian peace proposal in the context of a European se-curity identity also reveals an interesting variation on the use of rhetoric:

> From this point of view, it is possible to find a subtle dialectic which ranges from an 'us/them' rhetoric (we are able to propose a peace plan, while other European partners are not) to a more sharp 'European' rhetoric (we—Euro-peans—are able to reach a peace which NATO and the USA are not able to achieve).[21]

For Dutch media coverage, it is noted that an us/them rhetoric appears in relation to NATO actions[22] and, as mentioned earlier, much of the coverage was from a national perspective.

There is a sense that media coverage, whether reflecting elite opinion or political statements, allows for differing definitions of what is 'European' and at what point it is appropriate to include the nation-state in this grouping.

THE REFUGEE CRISIS, OTHER CULTURES, AND THE EXPANSION OF THE EU

The plight of the Kosovo refugees was the most important story that reflected any kind of discussion of other peoples or cultures in Europe. As mentioned earlier, in some cases the refuges were the focus of coverage of the conflict. As one journalist pointed out: 'During the Kosovo crisis, there was an awareness of Europe pulling together but it was covered more in a humanitarian context and not as a European issue.[23] It also opened up the issue of future security in the East and the expansion of the EU. In Italy the subject of Kosovan refugees has been framed within a broader issue that could be described as an 'identity' one. Mediterranean countries (an EU region) are considered in the Italian media as a sort of 'European gate' for Eastern countries, thus giving rise to a series of considerations about the links between Europe and neigh-bouring Eastern countries, and the role played by Italy in accepting people from these countries.[24]

---

[20] Irish report.
[21] Italian report.
[22] Dutch report.
[23] Irish deputy news editor.
[24] Italian report.

In several countries the refugee crisis was a major aspect of the war coverage, and in many instances this was dealt with in an emotive manner. For example, the Italian channel TG5 covered this issue in the form of a melodramatic serial story, one instalment a day, by focusing on the emotive and 'passionate' elements of the reports. In a similar vein:

> the Kosovo war and the plight of the refugees were perceived, by the Spanish media, as a humanitarian catastrophe, and a very complex issue involving many actors. This accounts for the negativity reflected in the tone of news in the May and June periods.[25]

From a different perspective, the Spanish coverage of Kosovo gave rise to few discussions of EU expansion in eastern Europe, undoubtedly due to geographical factors. 'During this time important aspects of European integration such as the expansion of the Union to Eastern countries, and European culture were hardly mentioned. Such concepts as 'European integration' or 'European citizenship' seldom appear in media discourse.'[26] In this respect, a Spanish MEP claims that the Spanish media are still unaware of Spanish international duties and obligations in the military and security domain.[27]

In reference to the (then) forthcoming European Parliament elections, the *Süddeutsche Zeitung* (May 20), in an article entitled 'Albanians to Europeans: A political chance for the European Parliament,' drew some of these debates together:

> The article referring to the forthcoming elections asks: 'What shall we think of a Parliament, which tries so hard not to attract attention and yet wants to be elected?' As a suggestion as to how the parliament could attract attention and increase its profile the author asks why no parliamentary party proposes to admit Albania and Macedonia to be members of the European Union at once. The argument would be that this is the only way to avoid an ever-increasing gap between the EU and the Balkan states. In addition this would be a model to guarantee peace in the Balkans by integrating the respective countries into the European peace order as early as possible.[28]

CONCLUSION

The Kosovo conflict presented a challenge to the notion of '50 years of peace in Europe,' and it has raised questions about peace and stability, expansion of the EU towards the east, and the future role of NATO in Europe. All of these issues were important background debates in the media during the crisis, but

---

[25]Spanish report.
[26]Spanish report.
[27]Spanish MEP, socialist group.
[28]German report.

as just demonstrated, the nature and depth of discussion varied between countries, and it was influenced by past traditions and alliances and by current concerns and interests. The Kosovo crisis constituted a complex European (and
international) event. In both the area of common foreign and security strategies, and the question of expanding the EU and our notions of 'Europe' and
'Europeans,' the discussions around the Kosovo conflict provided some insights into the different debates that exist in the national spheres.

6

News Coverage
of Economic Issues

INTRODUCTION

European integration has been largely an economic project, thus news about economic and business issues constitutes an important part of this study. During both monitoring exercises, coverage of economic integration mainly involved news about mergers and Euro oscillations. As the report from Spain emphasises, with reference to previous research,[1] economic reality has a high impact on European media discourse. References to economic integration, to the Euro, and to the European budget amount to around 8% of the news analysed in the Spanish media (without taking into account the articles focusing on the economy of the different European countries). This sort of news appears mostly in the business, finance, and economy sections of newspapers. The overall importance of economic issues in this study is significantly lower than that noted in previous research. This is due to the wider remit of the project in terms of a wider view of Europe, and also because of the inclusion of a wider variety of types of news including sport and culture. Earlier chapters already outlined the quantitative coverage of topics including economic integration and EMU.

The single currency presents a development in integration that goes beyond EU level policy making but that represents a political and economic reality. During the periods monitored, the fluctuation of the Euro in the international currency market has been an important aspect of European news.

---

[1]*La Unión Europea en los medios de comunicación* [*The European Union in the Media*], Informes anuales de Fundesco, Madrid 1994, 1995, 1996, 1997.

TONE OF COVERAGE OF EMU

Table 6.1 outlines the overall coverage of EMU by country and indicates both the tone of the coverage (i.e., positive, negative, or balanced) and the rhetoric (neutral, national, or European). This table includes all media outlets, and figures for each type of tone or rhetoric are presented as percentages. The German data show a major proportion of this coverage as balanced and neutral and the Swedish coverage largely 'European' and balanced. The Spanish and Dutch coverage is quite varied, but in each case about two thirds of the coverage is balanced and two thirds has also been considered to be presented from a European perspective.

The tone of the coverage in Spain, Italy, and the Netherlands presented a more mixed view. Coverage in the UK media is far less likely to be European and had a high percentage of negative coverage, but there are also a good deal of news items coded as either balanced or positive.

In the UK, where potential membership is still a contentious issue and (as illustrated earlier) EMU was central to debates about the European Parliamentary election, there are more obvious examples of a differing rhetoric. *The Sun* is viewed by politicians as an important barometer of British public opinion, and its support of the government of the day is seen as vital by those in power. Despite its switch in allegiance prior to the 1997 General Election to Tony Blair's New Labour Party (and in Scotland from the Scottish National Party to New Labour), it has remained strongly opposed to closer political and economic integration with Europe and often critical of Blair's 'pro-Euro credentials.' In particular, the paper has positioned itself as the crusading defender of the British pound, vigorously opposed to EMU. During the period monitored, the paper carried very little coverage of political debates relating

TABLE 6.1

News Coverage of EMU, Tone and Rhetoric by Percentage of Coverage

	Tone of Coverage			Rhetoric of Coverage		
	Positive	Negative	Balanced	National	European	Neutral
France	15	7	78	4	30	66
Germany	5	0	95	0	1	99
Ireland	20	0	80	0	33	67
Italy	0	33	67	0	33	67
Netherlands	14	20	66	20	66	14
Spain	15	28	57	28	64	8
Sweden	5	10	85	3	70	27
United Kingdom	21	48	31	21	2	67

to Europe. However, what it did carry clearly marked its position over Britain's economic relationship with wider European integration. The following summarises the rhetoric during the two monitoring periods, which despite covering only 2 weeks is quite typical of *The Sun*'s campaign against the single currency (a campaign that has been running for 3 or 4 years).

DEFENDER OF THE POUND

An inside cover page on Monday (17 May) was devoted to the 'Pound in Peril.' The paper announced that *The Sun* was 'Winning war against Euro nuts.' It claimed with some pride that despite pro-European publicity generated by the government, a recently published report indicated that *The Sun*'s anti-European campaign against joining the Single European Currency was 'the biggest obstacle to Britain joining the Euro.' An accompanying piece entitled 'Why work more for less?' told readers how people in Britain, although working more days to pay their tax bills than those in the US, would nevertheless be worse off in Euroland: 'Euroland folk toil for 171 days [In Britain it is 147 days] before keeping their cash, equal to an extra SIX WEEKS at work.' Of course, there was no mention that higher taxes may also mean better services in health, education, and transport. Rather, the message was simply that readers would be worse off if Britain joined the Euro. This point was reinforced by an opinion piece in the same edition by William Hague, leader of the Conservative Party, who set out his party's Eurosceptic line to be pursued in the forthcoming Euro elections. Once again, it was the negative financial impact European economic integration would have on Britain that was emphasised under the heading: 'Why we should never let Europe get control of the British economy,' which finishes with Hague echoing the *Sun*'s position that 'The pound is safe only with us.' This theme was reiterated later in the week when in its editorial column, *The Sun Says,* the paper warned the Labour Party that, 'We're Watching': 'The Sun will be watching every politician, analysing every move, while the Pound is in peril.'[2]

In contrast to this, the coverage of EMU in the other countries, particularly 'Euroland,' is not only noncontentious but also appears to have impacted on the general rhetoric about Europe. Although a German political party consensus on Europe and European integration has ensured cooperation across the political spectrum, the single currency has, in the past, faced criticism. Most recently there was concern expressed regarding the qualification criteria for membership prior to the launch of EMU in 1999. However, in principle the whole political elite supported the EMU. Earlier in the 1990s, this consensus was threatened by a more sceptical climate of public opinion. Despite overall

---

[2]From the UK report.

support for the process of integration, the imminent loss of the Deutschmark provoked concern and also brought home the depth of integration. The general impression is that had a referendum on the issue taken place, it would not have been passed by the people, but once the decision had been made and the common currency introduced in 1999, the discussion dissipated.[3]

Since the Euro was introduced, 'Europe' has become an everyday subject in Germany, something to be administered by the government. With the German presidency of the EU, German media did not cover 'Europe' as something that should be questioned or supported in general. Instead, there was the picture that 'Europe' is something that just has to be done. Concerning the European Union and its institutions, there were only a few articles in *WAZ* and *BILD*, whereas *SZ* and *FAZ* quite often dealt with the Commission, the Presidency, several EU Directives, and the Euro. In the *FAZ* business section, the common currency is a top subject—without giving any hint of a positive or negative tone. One gets the impression that the Euro is just there, that this is nothing to be criticised any more. Although many experts are quoted who are worried about its decreasing value compared to the US dollar, the coverage is completely neutral with regard to positive or negative tone from the side of the journalists.[4]

In Italy, the only issue that can be considered as truly 'European' is that of the Euro oscillations—and, in more general terms, the economic issues dealing with EU single currency.[5] Economic issues during this time also focused on the Telecom–Italia Olivetti merger bid. Such coverage is more extensive in *Il sole 24 Ore* than in the other outlets.

The Irish report identifies the emergence of a 'European' rhetoric in relation to issues relevant for Ireland such as coverage of the Euro in the financial news and of the CAP in the farming sections. Although stories may be considered to be of national interest, the framing of these issues in the context of European legislation and policies implicitly identified Ireland as operating within the larger context of the European Union. Where a story lends itself to a them/us structure (where 'us' refers to the EU), Ireland is explicitly identified in such a fashion (e.g., the US–EU beef imports dispute).

This 'European' perspective lacks consistency in Irish media coverage of other European countries, depending on the context. The main example given in the report refers to coverage of EMU. In this context, the UK (outside 'Euroland') is positioned as 'the other,' although with regard to stories relating to the Common Fisheries policy, the UK became 'European' (during the latter meeting of the Council of Fisheries Ministers, the UK supported Irish claims

---

[3]German report.
[4]German report.
[5]Italian report.

for increased quotas). The point about varying use of European rhetoric according to the situation was also brought out by reporting on the G8, wherein EU members are referred to in the same tone as the non-EU G8 members (i.e., from a neutral perspective). A similar inconsistency was noted in the coverage of Kosovo:

> The key point here is that within the Irish media it would appear that there is not so much a European rhetoric emerging as an EU rhetoric. Indeed it should be noted that there is a marked tendency right across the Irish media to use the word 'European' to mean 'EU.' In some articles it is virtually impossible to tell whether the author is referring to 'Europe' in the sense of the geographical landmass or 'Europe' in the sense of the institutions of the European Union.[6]

Hence, the rhetoric also reflects the fact that integration has developed in varying degrees across a range of economic and political policy areas. The breadth of discussions can be examined using the data from the media monitoring, showing where discussions of EMU are linked to other countries in Europe. In the case of the UK, the debate is very internalised, with occasional references to Germany and France. For the German and French media, the UK is the most frequently discussed country, followed by the 'Euroland' countries. The emphasis on the UK is much less pronounced in Ireland, with more of a focus on 'Euroland.' In these three countries and in the Dutch media, there is also a good deal of EMU debate linked with central and east European countries. For Italy, Spain, and Sweden, EMU is most frequently connected with Germany, then the UK, followed by other EU members.

THE IMPACT OF EMU
ON REPORTING EUROPE

Based on research into news agency activities in the French report and interview material from other countries, this section briefly outlines the impact of the launch of the Euro on journalism practice in Europe. In the months preceding the June elections, the launching of the Euro hastened the redeployment of news–editorial resources. From discussions with news journalists[7] in *Le Monde, Le Figaro,* AFP, and Reuters, it emerged that the launch of the 'Euro' had led to a major rethink in the allocation of staff and the logistics of coverage (significantly more than the 1999 election campaigns). Preparations for the Euro launch had led to the formation of teams within various news media whose brief was to cover 'Euroland' developments.

---

[6]Irish report.

[7]From French report: discussions with Reuters journalists based in Paris (Reuters Editor France: François Duriaud) and Reuters sources in London.

Within Reuters (H.Q.: London), two journalists produced a book on the Euro (EMU explained), while Reuters-Paris was reorganised in October 1998. Traditional distinctions between the English-language international service and French-language services were gradually eroding, and there was growing emphasis on integrated reporting teams, made up of international and French reporters, some of whom write in both English and French. News–editorial resources were organised into five teams. The team covering politics also covered economic policies, energy, foreign affairs, and general news. Although sharing resources from across the organisation, the European teams source Euro and related stories, many of which have to do with international finance and banking and the reorganisation of major European companies. According to financial journalists, the coverage of European mergers and cross-border take-overs is an important aspect of news about economic integration—for example, the Olivetti hostile bid for Telecom-Italia in Italy and the BNP, Paris-Bas, Société Générale battle in France. Offices covering these stories were asked to think outside 'the national frame' and consider the story to be at least as important for 'the other country.' Journalists were constantly pooling resources and holding telephone conferences to check who was covering which angle, and pooling ideas.[8]

The extent to which the launch of EMU has affected day-to-day reporting in the media outlets varies. Most Swedish journalists felt that there has been a change in coverage and an accentuation of the importance of the EU. 'Before the introduction of the Euro few Swedish politicians and people in finance thought that the EMU project would actually come to life. We report on a continuous basis on the Euro, how it changes the EU as a whole and the debates in the other member states.'[9] One Swedish politician commented that media coverage is too centred on Sweden rather than Europe and questioned state influence. Alongside other transnational issues, Dutch journalists also felt that EMU has and will continue to impact on the approach to European news.

Irish journalists largely felt that the introduction of the EMU had not impacted on their approach to covering European news although the impact for Irish companies was an important aspect of business news. This was expected to change when EMU became a reality, and one political correspondent pointed out that EMU served to underline the fact that 'decisions regarding interest rates are being made in Frankfurt at the headquarters of the European Central Bank'[10] and not in Dublin.

For many, the introduction of the single currency is considered as contributing to the development of Europeanness: 'The Euro is certainly an important factor in European integration as it is going to be felt in everyone's

---

[8]French report.
[9]Swedish journalist.
[10]Irish political correspondent.

wallet—this should give a boost to the European idea, which has not really gone beyond the embryonic stage' (Dutch press journalist: interview 1999).

CONCLUSION

Business and economic news is a fundamental part of European media coverage. The areas that have been politicised or that inspire deeper debate, include EMU, which in the past was a matter for debate in Germany and is currently such in the UK and Sweden. EU funding and budgetary issues were previously a contentious issue in Britain and currently are a problem in Germany. The on-going problems of corruption in expenditure of EU funds at both the national and European levels are widely discussed. Discussions of EMU within 'Euroland' were more focused on currency fluctuations and the consequences for business, whereas in the UK the battle for the pound continues. The debate in Britain remains a highly domestic one, unlike in other countries where the coverage is more 'Europeanised.' Frequent reference to UK debates on EMU in the national media of other EU members, reflects a concern about the debates there.

The extent to which the introduction of a single currency has affected the activities of the media in covering Europe is more apparent from the perspective of the news agencies already operating from a European perspective. Many journalists and editors working for national media outlets, particularly Dutch and Swedish, indicated that EMU has played a role in the development of news coverage of Europe.

Coverage of EMU is generally balanced and neutral, with a 'European' perspective being noted in all countries except Germany and the UK. Ireland and Germany display little or no negative aspects in the tone of reporting on EMU, whereas the UK coverage is distinctive from other countries in regard to being more national and more negative; this is most prominent in the case of specific outlets.

7

News About Other Countries and People in Europe

INTRODUCTION

This chapter gives a brief overview of news about other people and countries in Europe, first recapping the data analysis results from the previous sections. Coverage of other countries in the context of EU politics has already been explored in the chapters dealing with the European elections and also with reference to EMU debates. Here it was shown that in relation to coverage of the European Parliamentary elections, the UK, followed by France and Germany, are the countries most frequently discussed.

Coverage of EMU in relation to other people in Europe (aside from the more technical economic coverage) varies from an internal political debate in the UK to wider discussions on the implications for eastern and central Europe and the expansion of the EU, as observed in Germany and Ireland. Despite the more isolationist or national perspective of the UK regarding European political issues, the UK is, for most other countries in this project, of central importance to European debates. Although the Irish media pays most attention to the UK, in the context of EMU, the UK remains the 'other' in European news, with more focus on the 'Euroland' countries.

References to immigration, refugees, and 'others' in the 2 weeks of monitoring for this project were largely confined to coverage of refugees in the Kosovo crisis. As mentioned earlier, the issue was treated as a humanitarian crisis and a large percentage of coverage focused on what was being done by 'our country' to help these people. In this sense the coverage was not typical of debates regarding these issues (in many countries, those earlier humanitarian discussions have recently given way to less sympathetic discussions when faced with the reality of long-term solutions for refugees and asylum seekers).

COVERAGE OF EU MEMBER STATES

The figures used here (see Tables 7.1 and 7.2) refer to the number of news items that contained a reference to any of the relevant countries, and many of these countries may have appeared in the same article. In relation to the EP election news and EMU, the UK emerges as the most frequently referenced EU member state in most countries. When looking at all coverage and references to member states, the pattern changes slightly. Whereas the UK is most frequently referred to in German and particularly Irish media, Germany is more frequently referred to overall in France, the Netherlands, and Sweden.

Although the Swedish and French media show a greater variety and frequency of reference to member states in the context of the European elections, overall coverage shows a rise in the attention given by the German, Irish, and Dutch media. Again, the amount of media attention devoted to other member states in the UK and Italian media monitored is very low and does not increase during the second (election) period (an exception in Italy are the references to Belgium).

In general, for both periods of the study, the UK, France, and Germany feature most prominently in the news. This is the case with all countries monitored except the UK, where the Kosovo crisis dominated European news. (In this case Serbia, Russia, and Scotland were the top three countries.) Second in line after the main three, other EU member states feature, but this is somewhat dependent on events (the Netherlands cabinet crisis and the Belgian dioxin scandal pushed these two to the fore).

Spanish coverage of European information is described as having a heavily political focus regarding the coverage of other countries, which was particularly focused on Russia, Germany, the United Kingdom, Italy, and France. As mentioned earlier, Russia featured in Spanish media mainly because of the role played by Russia as a mediator in the Kosovo conflict. Media coverage of Germany was more varied dealing with, among other things, politics, economic issues, and the Blair–Schroeder manifesto. In relation to the UK, the coverage was less political, with the economy as a major feature and including a good deal of information regarding society, health, and television programming. Likewise, the coverage of France covered a wide spectrum of politics, the economy, terrorism, racism, and, in the realm of culture, archaeology and history.

TABLE 7.1

Reference to EU Member States in News Items From Both Periods

Monitoring Period May

	France	Germany	Ireland	Italy	Nether	Spain	Sweden	UK
France		329	81	5	26	25	5	6
Germany	84		63	23	62	41	20	14
Ireland	8	26		0	7	3	0	2
Italy	66	257	33		37	33	6	17
Netherlands	13	109	11	0		5	3	0
Spain	28	116	38	1	19		5	0
Sweden	8	67	14	0	14	0		0
UK	55	366	180	6	39	26	24	
Belgium	14	59	9	1	27	2	4	3
Denmark	4	45	9	0	1	0	9	0
Portugal	13	19	5	1	1	1	4	0
Finland	9	62	17	4	26	1	33	2
Austria	2	136	6	1	1	2	3	0
Luxembourg	5	26	5	0	0	2	3	0
Greece	8	49	5	1	6	1	9	2

Monitoring Period June

	France	Germany	Ireland	Italy	Nether	Spain	Sweden	UK
France		406	82	6	58	24	11	9
Germany	96		94	9	101	34	35	7
Ireland	13	36		0	4	5	2	3
Italy	45	232	56		34	14	9	2
Netherlands	24	153	51	4		9	11	0
Spain	36	136	26	0	19		4	1
Sweden	12	77	17	0	9	0		0
UK	102	465	233	14	66	25	16	
Belgium	53	148	46	37	54	80	13	6
Denmark	14	79	12	3	10	3	13	0
Portugal	20	28	9	0	9	6	7	0
Finland	18	63	24	0	45	1	13	1
Austria	12	166	22	9	7	2	5	0
Luxembourg	5	23	6	0	8	0	3	0
Greece	12	50	12	0	10	1	12	1

During this period, Italy is portrayed in Spanish media as the home of the Mafia and terrorism, with some space dedicated to other issues such as society, economy, and justice. The other countries were featured in the context of political issues and crises, including the Dutch cabinet crisis, the problems in Northern Ireland, and the countries involved in Kosovo. According to the Irish report for the study:

The overview of Irish European news coverage concludes that there is little to suggest that Irish newspapers regard themselves as 'having a mission' to educate the Irish about other peoples and cultures in Europe. The only possible exception to this is *The Irish Times,* which publishes weekly feature articles from correspondents living in European capital cities under the 'Letter from' heading. For the most part, the references to other European people and cultures are fleeting with the occasional newspaper article focussing on the political culture of an individual nation, but only at times of extreme crisis such as the collapse of Wim Kok's Dutch government during the first monitoring period. However even this story did not carry the 'newsworthiness' required for television coverage.

Obviously, the Kosovo crisis introduced another range of countries that are next in line in terms of prominence. A further group includes central and eastern European countries, the coverage being most significant in Germany and Ireland. The coverage of 'other Europeans' in the Irish media is heavily dominated by the presence of the UK, with 384 references in the election week, and a further 65 references to Scotland (mainly in the context of sport). France, Germany, and Italy are also dominant, with the Kosovo crisis influencing the overall range of countries. The range of other countries and cultures covered in the German media is extremely wide, as illustrated in the following section.

NEWS ABOUT EUROPEANS OUTSIDE THE EU

This section builds a picture of which national media have most news about other people in Europe, and also determines which 'other' countries have more or less significance in the national news, whether cultural or political. Table 7.2 combines the total coverage of other European countries and people for both monitoring weeks (the trends in each week are quite similar). The countries included in this section are those that were entered by coders in each country. No predesigned list was given to the national partners, so if any European countries do not feature, it is because they did not receive any news coverage during the two monitoring weeks. These figures do not include references to sport, which was extensively coded in both Germany and Ireland (although not in other countries). There were more references to all countries, in the context of sport, due to the qualification process for the Euro 2000 football championships with, for example, the England game against Poland.

The first group includes European countries that are not EU members and not particularly anxious to join. The coverage of these countries was limited, aside from news about Switzerland in the German press.

The second group consists of the 13 applicant countries. In all cases the German media give the most wide-ranging coverage, but there is also a great deal of reference in the Irish media, perhaps due to discussions on expansion of the EU and the implications for Ireland. The German media are naturally most aware of the countries immediately to its east such as the Czech Republic, Poland, and Hungary. The German media also not surprisingly, given the German Turkish population, include a good deal of news about Turkey. Sweden pays some attention to Latvia, Estonia, and Lithuania in EU expansion debates, whereas all countries appear in the German media.

The amount of news about the Balkan states is largely due to the Kosovo crisis. Again, sport articles were left out of this analysis for comparative purposes, although during this time there were even more references to Mace-

TABLE 7.2
Europeans (Non-EU) in the News Not Including Sport

	France	Germany	Ireland	Netherlands	Spain	Sweden	UK
Norway	6	70	15	14	0	6	0
Switzerland	11	278	8	10	2	0	0
Iceland	1	9	7	0	0	2	0
EU applicant states in the news							
Czech Republic	3	103	10	0	1	2	1
Poland	4	124	19	3	30	6	0
Hungary	3	78	15	5	2	2	2
Slovakia	0	36	2	0	4	2	0
Slovenia	4	34	10	19	1	0	1
Lithuania	0	8	0	0	0	2	0
Estonia	0	4	2	0	2	0	0
Latvia	0	1	2	0	0	2	0
Bulgaria	0	34	8	5	0	1	0
Romania	3	47	7	2	0	0	0
Cyprus	1	8	10	3	0	3	2
Turkey	2	145	19	10	0	0	2
Malta	0	5	3	0	0	0	0
Balkan states in the news							
FRY	18	317	148	14	20	60	14
Serbia	5	181	67	20	13	0	68
Albania	12	235	71	54	5	0	8
Bosnia	1	97	20	6	4	0	1
Macedonia	12	145	57	55	2	0	2
Croatia	1	43	14	4	1	0	0
Kosovo	8	13	27	5	9	0	8
Montenegro	0	22	8	2	0	1	0
CIS countries in the news							
Russia	13	229	74	72	27	9	10
Ukraine	1	55	6	0	0	0	0
Belarus	0	10	0	0	1	0	0
Moldova	0	2	0	0	0	0	0
Kazakhstan	0	1	0	0	0	0	0
Armenia	0	1	0	0	0	0	0

donia, Croatia, and Yugoslavia in Ireland due to Euro 2000 football fixtures. Many of the references that remain still relate not only to sport but also to the political debate and crisis over whether to cancel these fixtures due to the war.

The Dutch focus on Macedonia and Albania mirrors the focus on the refugee crisis during this time as illustrated in chapter 5. The Swedish coverage of the Kosovo war did not particularly focus on refugees, which is again apparent from the lack of references to any states aside from Yugoslavia.

The final group of European countries that appeared in the news during this time are the former Soviet states now known as the Commonwealth of Independent States (CIS). Obviously, Russia is the most commonly featured CIS member in the media, particularly in the context of the Kosovo war, although there is a marked difference between the German and the French and British media as regards reference to Russia. Most of the other states only appear in the German media.

Overall, the coverage of other countries and cultures in Europe in the context of news stories reveals the prominence of the big powers in the EU: the UK, Germany, and France. This is naturally due to the fact that the eight countries of the study are EU members, and EU member states are also very prominent, although this varies between countries. Coverage of others in the news depends on events like the war in Kosovo and subsequent coverage of the Balkan states. These countries and the East European and CIS countries do not frequently appear in the EU member states' news media, as they are not as relevant to political or economic events, hence they appear during crisis situations. Some exceptions are, of course, Russia and the EU applicant countries. The attention paid to these states is dependent on geographical factors—for example, the German and Swedish coverage—and also perhaps to debates on the implications of enlargement, as witnessed in the Irish media.

Aside from sports coverage, particularly the qualification games for Euro 2000, which incorporates a wide view of 'Europe,' there is very little news about non-EU Europeans in the national media outlets with reference to other cultural, musical, or art events. The major exception is the German press, which aside from having the widest coverage of 'Europeans' also features many articles on art and culture in other countries. The following outlines the nature of media coverage of background information relevant to news events and also cultural news in general, with reference to national reports and interview material. This section also addresses the issue of whether the media, particularly news media, have a role to play in the promotion of cultural understanding.

BACKGROUND INFORMATION IN NEWS EVENTS

In this section the focus is on the news media and not on other types of factual or fiction programming. Generally speaking, as has been observed in other research, news coverage of foreign cultures outside the nation-state tends to occur in times of war or crisis, as too often media coverage of minorities within a country also focuses on issues of conflict. In these instances, there is often a lack of background information that would help clarify events.[1] In this sense, we are looking at culture in terms of a way of life, alongside historical, political, and economic events that may lead to certain actions such as immigration, war, famine, or internal hostility. A major issue, therefore, concerns the extent to which the media should fulfil an educational role by providing more background information in contextualising stories.

Many of the media professionals interviewed for this study felt that such provision of background information was a central tenet of news journalism. However, the opinions of politicians were rather mixed on this issue:

> In my opinion it is an absolute canon of good journalism that a story should be placed in a context. In our increasingly complex and disparate societies, background is essential to understanding. Understanding must be the basis of informed judgement. The media, in its everyday work, has an informative rather than an educational role—we live in a world which is becoming increasingly professionalised and it would, I believe, be unfair to impose upon journalists, the weighty and onerous task of acting as mentors to their fellow citizens.[2]

This illustrates the balance between informative journalism and the media taking on an educational role. There were further expressions of caution against imposing obligations on journalism from another European politician: 'Politicians should not give the media obligations. I think that the media in Sweden is just as good or bad (as any other) at educating its citizens.'[3]

Similarly, an Italian politician claimed that 'it shouldn't be expected that media perform a particular educational role. That is a task for institutions.'[4]

CULTURAL INFORMATION

The cultural news, in the media outlets monitored, involves a mixture of news about other people and cultures in Europe and also reference to other people in the context of sport, music, art, and literature and was largely dependent on events. In the press this type of news appears in the culture, art, entertainment, or foreign sections, or more generally in feature rather than news sections of the paper. It was recommended that sports news only be coded if it were of a more rhetorical type and not straightforward information about

---

[1] See for example: Beattie, Miller, Miller, and Philo: 'The media and Africa: Images of disaster and rebellion' in Philo, 1999.

[2] Irish MEP.

[3] Swedish MEP.

[4] Italian MEP.

results, but the amounts of coverage in this area varies widely. News about cultural events and lifestyles of others is questioned somewhat in the Irish report. It could be argued that articles promoting continental regions or cities as holiday destinations are promoting cultural understanding. It may be more realistic, however, to describe such articles as simply commodifying the areas they describe, containing, as they do, little in the way of in-depth description of the people and cultures who live there.[5]

UK media coverage of Europe is less wide-ranging and often more heated than in other countries, but the UK report points to 'another' Europe, which receives 'broadly positive' treatment in the media. Examples included arts sections dealing with the Cannes film festival and the growing importance of Scottish film within a broader European film culture.[6] *The Sunday Times* (23 May) carried a similar piece, 'Ruling the Waves,' in which it talked about British rather than Scottish cinema, whereas *The Times* arts section (17 May) discussed Spain's top director Pedro Almodovar's new film being screened at Cannes.

In the *Herald*'s travel section (22 May) there was a two-page feature on the 'hidden beauty and character of Catalonia's capital,' Barcelona. Reference to the political position of the city within Spain was made: Gaudi, but never gaudy. 'With an identity as separate as Scotland's is from that of England, Catalonia has an ongoing debate and struggle over independence from Spain.' Europe as an up-market holiday destination was similarly sold in positive terms in travel sections in both *The Times* and the *Guardian.*

In the sports section (21 May) of *The Herald,* a form of European integration was vigorously advocated. However, this centred on the overdue nature of a major European football final being staged by the governing body of European football (UEFA) in Glasgow. The importance of European football success was discussed in all the papers as they set the scene for the following week's European Champion's League Final involving England's Manchester United and Germany's Bayern Munich.

The UK report concluded that:

> Europe was continually talked about in newspapers, however these differing versions of Europe are rarely connected, so the political and economic Europe remains separate from the Europe to which people may travel on holiday, or the Europe which is viewed by football fans as staging competitions of major importance.[7]

The issue of cultural identity is not central to Italian news media debates on Europe and neither is the coverage of other peoples and cultures in Europe.

---

[5] Irish report.

[6] 'The Mix,' a weekly section of *The Herald.*

[7] UK report.

TABLE 7.3
News About Europeans by Themes

	EU General	EU policies	Wider Europe	Kosovo War	Art/Culture
France	UK, Germany, Italy, Spain, Sweden, Ireland	EU and Czech Republic, Balkans, Russia, Turkey	Balkans, Turkey	UK, Italy, Germany, Balkans, Russia, Turkey, C+E Europe	Very little
Germany	All, mainly UK, France, Italy, Austria	All EU, 'applicant' countries, Russia, most other Europeans	Balkans, applicant countries, Central Europe, Norway	UK, France, Italy, Finland, most other Europeans	EU and Czech, Russia, Poland, Turkey and Switzerland
Ireland	All, mainly UK, France, Italy, Spain, Germany, Sweden	UK, Italy, France, Germany, 'applicant' countries, Russia	Balkans, Russia, Eastern Europe	UK, France, Germany, Italy, Finland, Greece, Sweden, Balkans, Russia	UK, France, Italy, Spain, Sweden, Greece, Russia, Turkey and Norway
Italy	UK, France, Germany, Belgium	UK, France, Germany, Belgium	Turkey	UK, France, Germany	Very Little
Netherlands	All, mainly France, Germany, UK, Belgium	France, Germany, UK, Belgium, Pol cul of all 'applicants,' Russia	Balkans, Russia, Turkey	UK, France, Germany, Finland, Balkans, Russia, C+E Europe	France, Italy, Ireland, Belgium
Spain	All, mainly Germany, France, UK, Belgium	France, Germany, UK and other EU	Yugoslavia, Russia, Poland	UK, France, Germany, Italy, Yugoslavia, Russia	Little on EU and Russia
Sweden	All, mainly UK, Germany, France, Denmark, Finland	UK, France, Germany, Political culture EU, Russia, 'applicants'	Applicant countries, Russia	France, Germany, UK, Italy, Greece, Spain, Balkans, Russia, 'applicants'	Belgium, Czech Republic, Yugoslavia, Russia
United Kingdom	France, Germany, Ireland, Italy, Spain	Political culture most m/s	Russia	France, Germany, Yugoslavia, Serbia, Russia, Kosovo	Very little

The Italian news media does not seem to place much importance on cultural events in Europe or on the peoples and the cultures of the continent. However, a different trend emerges in relation to non-fiction television programmes, as will be discussed in chapter 10.

The Cannes film festival was again the main cultural event, with a certain amount of discussion on the cultures of the peoples and countries portrayed in the different films presented during the festival, and with articles and reports focusing on their cultural traditions. Similarly, but to a lesser degree, some reviews about exhibitions focused on the historical and cultural role of some countries in establishing a broader European cultural identity. In the second week, the main news event concerned Italian qualification for the European Football Championships.

CONCLUSION

Table 7.3 summarises the coverage of other Europeans and other cultures for each country in the monitoring exercise related to particular themes. The German media outlets, particularly the press, deal with the widest range of European countries and cultures in the context of the widest range of issues.

In relation to the EU, the Italian and UK news media are most limited in reference to coverage of the other member states. In the context of specific EU policy discussions, the German, Irish, French, Dutch, and Swedish media are already including references to applicant countries as part of the coverage, implying a wider view of the development of Europe.

As regards the coverage of cultural information in the sense of art, literature, music, etc., the Mediterranean countries present less information about these subjects in relation to other countries.

According to the national reports, other people feature in the news when linked to specific events whether political or cultural and there is little evidence that news media have a role to play in educating the public in a more general sense about the lives of 'others' in Europe.

8

Reporting Europe: Trends and Developments

INTRODUCTION

An analysis of media coverage of European news should also take account of changes and trends in the way that European issues are reported. Based partly on the perceptions of both journalists and politicians interviewed in the eight countries of the study and supplemented with reference to other studies on journalism in Europe, this chapter examines some of these issues.

JOURNALISM IN EUROPE

The work of journalists everywhere is influenced by the state, by business, by national traditions, and by technological change in terms of production, information sourcing, and distribution. Concentration of ownership, integration of media industries, and the influence of corporate public relations on content affect all media practitioners. It is important to remember these pressures on the profession when looking at the specific aspect of European coverage. Journalism in general is perceived to be suffering from trivialisation and a deterioration of quality due to both commercialisation and cross-ownership.

It appears that the debate on the role of the media, particularly the press, in the democratic process has itself a 'European' nature. As regards public trust:

> French journalists do not enjoy a high standing in public opinion.[1] Radio news
> tends to have a higher reputation than TV news, while both media maintain a

[1]This impression is based on annual opinion polls commissioned (since 1987) by the weekly *Telerama,* and the daily *La Croix* (conducted by the Louis Harris institute; cited in French national report).

higher reputation than that of print media. In the early 1990s a combination of instances of 'mis-reporting', of over-reporting (saturation coverage) of events linked to Romania—the 'false' or purported massacre in Timasoara—the Gulf crisis and war (1990-1) and various domestic scandals, have served to weaken public confidence in the media.[2] According to the data for 1998, 49% of French people believe that news reported in a newspaper is more or less exact; 50% believe TV news reporting is more or less exact, and 57% believe radio-news reporting is more or less accurate. The survey does not analyse coverage of European affairs. In this case one suspects, such issues hardly suffer from 'over-reporting'—certainly not the regular activities of the European Parliament, the European Court of Justice or even the European Commission aside from the internal crises.[3]

From Eurobarometer data gathered in the spring of 1999, it is apparent that television (55%) and daily newspapers (32%) are the preferred methods of receiving information about the European Union.[4] Those surveyed also responded to questions on their levels of trust in different types of media. In general, television and radio are deemed more reliable than the press. People express higher levels of trust in the press in the Netherlands (73%), Finland (65%), and Belgium (64%), and least in the UK (24%).[5]

A further important factor in the standing of the media is the commercialisation of the media, and market forces are frequently referred to as having an impact on journalism:

> The increased competition among all media in Sweden has led to a backlash for political journalism in general. In a society where the public interest in political affairs is dropping, with decreasing confidence in political actors, it is not surprising that the media tend to play down political reporting and focus more on articles and programmes that are competitive in an effort to maximise the audience, and the profit of the media organisation. Even if Swedish newspapers and public service media still pay considerable attention to political affairs, especially during election campaigns, they have to adjust to a new media market situation where stronger commercial interests in the long run have become more important than traditional values about the role of media in democracy.[6]

Similarly, in Britain the competition for a shrinking audience has also led to controversies over newspaper content. The 'dumbing down' of newspapers— sensationalism and superficiality—seems at odds with the changing composition of the UK newspaper audience. Papers such as the midmarket *Daily Mail* have benefited from significant changes in both the numbers of people staying

---

[2]*La Croix,* 19.1.1999; *Le Monde* 20.1.1999 (cited in French report).

[3]French report.

[4]Eurobarometer 51, July 1999 (field work March–April 1999).

[5]Ibid. A more recent survey (Eurobarometer 55, October 2001) indicated similar trends, although with only 15% of UK respondents expressing a trust in their press.

[6]Swedish report.

on into further and higher education, and the increase in the population of working, newspaper-buying, women (*The Economist*, 31/1/98: 30).[7]

PERCEPTIONS OF EUROPE

In the course of interviews with both media professionals and politicians, some questions were asked with a view to assessing general attitudes to Europe and European integration. A view of 'Europe' as a philosophical concept was frequently described by Italian and Spanish interviewees by referring to 'countries that received the Greek heritage, were Romanised and also influenced by the Christian faith and have a political and even cultural common denominator' (Spanish Socialist MEP: interview, 1999).

Other nationalities, such as Irish and Dutch, linked Europe far more directly with the EU, which is perhaps due to a mixture of geographical and historical factors. In the Netherlands, 'Europe is a very complex concept. The EU is often confused with Europe, whereas Europeans intuitively see things in a broader perspective. There's this notion that Europe is really the current 15 member states only' (Dutch press journalist: interview, 1999).

In many cases the terms 'Europe' and 'EU' become interchangeable in debates, in media coverage, in political statements, and in public discussion. The research was intended to look at European political and cultural news in the widest sense possible; this necessitated a specific examination of coverage of EU issues. The following gives an indication of how these terms are used and also, more specifically, how media professionals and politicians view concepts such as 'European identity' and 'European integration.' The sample is not exhaustive and perceptions are personal, but one can assume that this summary gives an overview of attitudes that influence the work of the interviewees. Some journalists are quick to admit that the term 'Europe' can be used in a loose sense:

> The concept of what 'Europe' is depends largely on the context in which it appears. If it is an EU-related story, 'Europe' usually refers to the member states. However, in the case of issues such as Kosovo, the concept of 'Europe' is extended to encompass a broader cultural and geographical area. Likewise, in coverage of the Commission, the European Parliament and other EU topics, 'Europeans' refers to members of the EU. When we run stories on Bosnia, Kosovo, Romania, etc., the category of 'Europeans' widens to include Eastern Europeans and a more general definition of what it means to be European. (Irish broadcast news editor, interview, 1999)

Attitudes to 'Europeans' and the perception of who is or is not European vary, as can be seen in these comments of journalists and politicians:

---

[7]UK national report.

> I would hope that most journalists regard Europe as the continent which stretches from the Atlantic to the Urals and Europeans as the people who were born on it, while recognising there are also lots of people born on the continent who would belong to an ethnic origin, which would not be classified as European. (Irish European editor, interview, 1999)

> I find it very difficult to determine what Europe is and what it is not, who the Europeans are and who they aren't. Turkey and Cyprus want to become members of the EU, but do these countries really belong in Europe? Romania also wants to become a member of the EU, but what does this country's culture have in common with Europe? (Dutch politician [Socialist Party], interview, 1999)

Such distinctions between European culture and the cultures of Turkey, Cyprus, and Romania are surprising coming from a socialist politician. Such a remark might be more typical of the 'right,' for example, with the suggestion that Russia, but not the other republics that formerly belonged to the USSR, shares cultural or political similarities with the rest of Europe, reflecting a narrow definition of Europe: 'European integration is firstly, an economic concept, secondly a political one and lastly, a cultural idea. The political and cultural Europe includes Russia but not republics such as the Ukraine, Georgia and the transcaucas' (Spanish MEP [Partido Popular], interview, 1999).

European Integration and European Identity

In relation to the question of the media playing some role in the process of European integration and identification with Europe, it is useful to see how some opinion formers and media practitioners view concepts such as integration and identity in a European context. Although these responses tend to be a mixture of both personal and professional perspectives, they help to build an impression of the framework of European debates in the media. As far as European integration is concerned, perceptions varied widely. For many, it was clearly just a political and economic process, not cultural, stemming from the growing transnational policy processes of the EU:

> European integration means growing interconnectedness and growing interdependence of the nation states within the European Union. There are some cultural competencies attached to the treaties and it is possible to say that there is a sort of cumulative cultural effect. The concept of cultural integration is really an afterthought and refers to improving linguistic compatibility, tourism, travel, communications and cross-cultural exchange. However, this is not attributable to European integration but is part of a much larger, global trend toward cultural homogeneity. (Irish foreign editor, interview, 1999)

The idea that identification with Europe does not exist in a broad sense for most European citizens is also shared by politicians who attributed this type of identity only to particular elite groups:

> European identity only exists in the minds of those who are working in one way
> or another on European matters, such as policy makers, politicians, corporate
> leaders, etc. It has no place in the heads of the people yet, although things are
> changing now, with Europe becoming ever more important for everyone. For
> people to feel more involved, a more democratic substructure is necessary for
> the success of Europe. (Dutch politician [Democrats 66], interview, 1999)

Others, particularly southern European interviewees, were more likely to express a belief in the existence of a European identity:

> I strongly agree with the existence of a 'European identity' in several fields—
> political, philosophical, cultural and even commercial. Nevertheless the devel-
> opment of the European identity is still the most important political task at the
> turn of the century. In my view a full integration could very much contribute to
> improve the international relationships and the scientific and technological
> development of the entire world, as never happened in the past. (Spanish MEP
> [Socialist], interview, 1999)

Those who did not feel such a close identification with Europe were more likely to be from northern Europe:

> I don't think there's a European identity. The Swedes are just as much like peo-
> ple from New Zealand as people from Germany. I don't think such an identity
> is important. (Swedish MEP, interview, 1999)

> European identity is fiction. Europe as it is now is a patchwork of different
> countries. If we achieve the goal of the United States of Europe, then a certain
> kind of European identity will eventually come into being. (Dutch broadcaster,
> interview, 1999)

OBSTACLES IN REPORTING EUROPEAN NEWS

Journalists who cover European issues are the first to admit that there is room for improvement. European Union news, particularly, is still largely refracted through the national public sphere and this occurs for several reasons. According to journalists, one issue is the lack of information or difficulty in accessing information:

> Trying to get information from EU institutions can be difficult; they're not very
> transparent and people who work there don't always speak in terms that the
> rest of the world can understand. Trying to get straight answers from MEPs
> can also be difficult but that applies to politicians in general. (Irish European
> editor, interview, 1999)

A similar view is given by a Swedish journalist who claims that the EU is a very closed organisation for journalists, and the citizens in Sweden are not very interested in the EU, so there is not that much reporting on it.

The problem is exacerbated by the intergovernmental nature of the Council and the secret negotiations between member states. After meetings of the Council of Ministers, each national minister tends to meet his or her national press representatives, and the secrecy of the meetings allows them to give a national slant on the outcome, which obscures the bargaining and compromises entered into by the ministers. This is, of course, important for their position in the national political space; the lack of a 'single sphere'[8] for EU news allows for this 'nationalisation' of issues.

Alongside this, the complexity of the issues involved requires an understanding of the constitutional make-up of the European Union and the balance of powers between the institutions, coupled with knowledge of the policymaking process. Journalists first have to comprehend what is happening in the EU and then successfully mediate that to the general public: 'The major obstacles to reporting on European and EU politics include the complicated decision making process within the EU, which also is very slow. This makes it difficult to report in an effective and comprehensible way to the readers' (Swedish journalist, interview, 1999).

The complexity is a problem for the journalists' own understanding of what has happened and why. Furthermore, the issues relating to policy making or events then require clear and concise mediation to the public, ideally with a view of both pros and cons of decisions and the probable significant outcomes or effects. 'Concepts and procedures are complex and it is hard to explain them, but that is precisely our work' (Spanish press journalist, interview, 1999).

The fact that EU policies impact on ever-increasing areas of national politics implies also that it is not just Brussels-based EU correspondents that need to acquire an understanding of the system:

> What is happening in journalistic coverage of European integration is a breakdown of boundaries between foreign and domestic. This creates issues of comprehension and different levels of knowledge between foreign and domestic affairs departments. For example, there may be some confusion as to the degree to which sovereignty has been pooled and the issue is no longer determined in Ireland (e.g. the foreign correspondents know more than the people on the news-desks). We must therefore ensure that knowledge is pooled and integrated more and we hold conferences with a view to doing this. (Irish foreign editor, interview, 1999)

Thus there are also problems in categorising news, whether it should appear in the foreign, national, or economic sections. A further problem is that when Europe becomes a national issue (i.e., enters the national public sphere), editorial staff do not understand the issues involved, and no clear distinction is

---

[8]Andreas Ortega, *El País,* during a discussion of European correspondents at the conference: 'Media literacy as a topic of civic and political education in Europe,' 28 Nov–1 Dec 1998, Granada. (See also Schlesinger & Kevin, 2000.)

made in reporting issues between the impact of national parliaments on politics and that of the EU on politics.

This, of course, allows politicians to set the agenda and present successful policies as national triumphs over 'Europe,' or unpopular ones as 'European' failures. An example of a failure of the political elite to control the agenda on Europe is apparent in the UK. Writing about the press reaction to the Vienna summit and tax harmonisation, Tony Blair stated:

> The two weeks in which the tax harmonisation row raged were bizarre. There were screaming headlines, about the Germans setting our taxes, VAT on children's clothes and our veto on tax being abolished, all from newspapers hostile to the EU. As ever, the papers more neutral on Europe simply caved in to the same agenda.[9]

The implication is that the agenda is being controlled not by the government or the opposition, but by the media. Or more specifically by Rupert Murdoch through *The Sun*. But why would the 'more neutral' papers follow this discourse?

A further problem is identified as a 'lack of personalisation' wherein it is claimed that European politics are dull in the sense that they do not supply editors with personalities, arguments, or headlines. This was apparent in our findings from the last week of the European Parliamentary election campaigns. The problem is partly due to the lack of European-level political parties or politicians that campaign for election to the EP with clear indications of who their allies are in the European Parliament and what manifesto they might share. The recent coverage of the European Commission fraud scandal and the threat held over the Commissioners by the European Parliament was certainly newsworthy. Journalists interviewed also referred to the issue of finding stories that not only catch the public interest but also appear interesting to editors at the outlet. Reporting on Europe is described as a

> bit of a turn-off to the editor and although these issues are very interesting, they are also quite abstract and it is difficult to find a story or hook which would interest our readers. Scandals and resignations make headlines—that is the nature of news—but the everyday running of the various political and economic structures is not really of interest to large numbers of people. (Foreign editor, Ireland, interview, 1999)

The resulting coverage tends to focus more on drama, scandals, and personalisation of issues. As with most actors in the news industry, the battle for readership in an increasingly competitive market has a major impact on the 'newsworthiness' of stories:

> Europe remains a rather dull subject matter since it is very institutional. The recognisability of Europe is not great either. Issues are not 'sexy' enough;

---

[9] 'The papers miss the real story,' Tony Blair, *The Times*, December 14, 1998.

dossiers dealt with are too complex and unattractive to be tackled in the press. You can write about it once, but you cannot afford to talk about the technical details, since you always have to wonder whether people are going to read you. (Dutch European press journalist, interview, 1999)

THE INFLUENCE OF NATIONAL INTERESTS

The continuing impact of national agendas and national interest debates on coverage of EU news, as in the case of the European Parliamentary election campaigns, highlights the way in which the integration process is viewed in the media as intergovernmental rather than 'European.' One journalist stresses that 'the EU is a permanent negotiation between 15 different countries with national interests, and it is important for all journalists to keep this in mind' (Swedish EU correspondent, interview, 1999).

From the interviews carried out with journalists we can say, in general, that with reference to reporting European news, 'everything is influenced by national interests.'[10] This impacts on the importance of Europe in the news agenda. The national focus on EU news, in particular, seems to fall under three categories: particular policy issues of importance to the country; the question of funding; and the actions of national representatives and commissioners who, in theory, should not act in the national interest. 'Unless it is a big story like the sacking of the Commission, all European news needs to have some Irish interest in order to make news' (Irish political correspondent, interview, 1999).

The focus on particular policy issues varies between member states. Agriculture and fishing policy are generally cited as being of greatest importance and these could be considered two of the primary areas of EU policy-making:

> The sort of European news more influenced by national events and interests are those linked directly to Spanish citizens and interests, for example, fishing and other agricultural topics. (Spanish press journalist, interview, 1999)

> Agriculture and structural funds have been very prominent because of their direct impact on Ireland. Foreign policy, on the other hand, is less salient for us than it is for some of the larger states. Naturally, the most effective reportage is that which can link local or national issues into a knowledge of the whole but sometimes it is easier said than done. (Irish foreign editor, interview, 1999)

For other countries, different issues are considered important in this sense. In Sweden, for instance, discussions on the expansion of the EU, the environment, and social policy are influenced by national interests. In the Netherlands:

> One continues to look at European matters from a national perspective, for instance regarding European subsidies. The first question asked is how much of

---

[10]Swedish journalist.

it will find its way to the Netherlands. Dutch sentiments are also at stake when European monies go to mostly Mediterranean countries. (Dutch journalist, interview, 1999)

The coverage of the European Parliament campaigns also revealed how national interests have changed: budgetary issues are now more important in Germany than in the UK (as was the case during the Thatcher years), with the UK focus now switched to the single currency.

National coverage tends to focus on activities of the home commissioners or national representatives at the European Parliament rather than other European actors. One journalist claimed that when 'writing a story about the European Parliament I'm going to focus more on what Irish MEPs are doing than their counterparts in France or Germany.'[11] Likewise, in the Netherlands, 'Coverage is also very much related to the Dutch commissioner only and to subjects that have to do with his responsibilities.'[12] Part of the reason for this involves the need to 'personalise' the news and give the stories a 'face.' Stories that are personality driven attract a lot of media attention.

EUROPE IN THE NEWS AGENDA

The discussions that were held with media practitioners proved useful for assessing whether, in terms of the national news agenda, 'Europe and the European Union is a subject of secondary importance.'[13]

One indication of the extent to which European issues have become more salient in national news outlets is the levels of increase of coverage and increased resources for European and EU news. Although this project does not compare the amount of coverage over time, we can refer to the comments and explanations given by media practitioners such as foreign and business editors and European correspondents who work in this area. Their comments are also a useful indicator as to why coverage may have increased. 'Coverage of Europe has increased due to a lot of issues that need to be dealt with beyond national boundaries, such as asylum seekers, the Euro, environmental issues' (Swedish political editor, interview, 1999).

In general, there is an impression that currently there are more news stories about Europe and more areas of the news agenda that require a European angle. The extent to which policy issues are increasingly decided at the EU level is given as a major reason for development in this area of coverage:

In recent years, nearly all aspects of business and public affairs are in some way influenced by Europe—every sphere or department of government has an EU

---

[11]Irish European editor.
[12]Dutch press journalist.
[13]Dutch television journalist.

branch—so there is a lot more media attention being given to European issues. (Irish political correspondent, interview, 1999)

Media coverage of European issues has increased along with the integration process and with the relevant specific areas, which are closer to us. Since last year, *El Mundo* has a European section and publishes every Sunday an interview with European political or cultural personalities, not only from the European Union Member States. (Spanish press journalist, interview, 1999)

The analysis in chapter 3 illustrated the way in which news about Europe is spread through a variety of sections of media outlets. This has a major impact on the work of journalists:

Throughout the whole newspaper, in all sections, coverage of Europe has increased. Although we have two permanent correspondents in Brussels, the Hague-based journalists always have to take into account the European dimension of a given issue, i.e. agricultural reforms, they have to go to Brussels too and this has its impact on the newspaper content. The traditional Dutch-centred approach is being demolished by this practice. (Dutch press, Brussels correspondent)

Although it is apparent that specific policy issues affecting the national interest have increased coverage, there are also larger, more 'European' events that have changed the nature of European issues in the news agenda, such as the fall of the Berlin wall and news about the single currency.

Several journalists also pointed out that levels of coverage are subject to change and dependent on the relevance for national debate. One such example is the point of preparation for entry into membership of the European Union, a time when important national actors and the public in general tend to be more focused on the issues. (This aspect of media engagement with EU news is dealt with later in connection with television programming about Europe.)

Coverage of European issues was huge at the start when Ireland joined, then it tailed off, and now it is increasing again. We have two reporters in Brussels who don't just cover EU-related issues but travel all over Europe covering diverse stories. (Irish broadcast journalist, interview, 1999)

RESOURCES

In reference to there being a specific budget within the news outlet for European coverage, or whether there had been an increase in resources deployed in this area, most respondents answered in the negative. 'Europe' and the 'EU' are generally considered news stories on the basis of 'newsworthiness,' rather than being issues that are considered a necessary part of the daily news agenda:

When Sweden became a member of the EU in 1994, one person on the politics section was set aside to report on the EU only. The economic section of the paper has also increased its reporting on EU. Furthermore personnel from the foreign-, politics- and economical sections have been sent on internal education in Brussels a few times during the last couple of years. (Political editor, Sweden, interview, 1999)

In general there appears to have been no major change in the amount of resources dedicated to European or EU reporting, although it is apparent that all sections of outlets and all journalists increasingly require knowledge of European issues in order to report on a variety of subjects. Likewise, coverage has increased where it is relevant to the news agenda. The spread of news indicated one aspect of a developing 'Europeanisation' of the national sphere; the way in which stories are sourced and the extent to which knowledge is shared at the European level may illustrate a further aspect.

In terms of financial and economic news, Europe is frequently seen as an 'economic bloc' in a global context. 'There have been no particular developments in terms of resources. We are concerned primarily with business and politics, and so Europe has no more significance than, for example, the United States' (Irish newspaper editor).

According to the Fundesco (1997) report, there are growing trends in media coverage of Europe including an increase in resources going into this area, and in general the tone of coverage has improved. The research suggests indications of the beginning of EU-centred reporting (tinged with local culture and politics) but notes an absence of ideological content. Again, reference is made to the absence of a pan-European media and to language barriers. Other developments mentioned include an element of cultural homogeneity among younger Europeans, assisted by education and university exchange.

EUROPEAN NEWS SOURCES

The following looks at the sources of European news and is partly based on the data from the project. Overall, there is a surprisingly large number of 'unidentified' news sources for television news, but this situation is slightly clarified in the election period, particularly on the public service channels. During the second monitoring period, both types of outlets make greater use of news agency material, perhaps due to the election campaigns. The general newsroom output increases in the second period, implying an overall increase of outlet-generated European news reports and also a good deal more input from people coded under the 'pundit/guest writer/expert' category. The 'other correspondent' category (generally a foreign correspondent) was larger during the first period where the news was slightly more focused on the Kosovo crisis.

When discussing these issues with practitioners, we get a clearer picture of day-to-day practice. For example, many broadcasters share news items via ENEX (European News Exchange):

> We send pictures—and sometimes script—to Sky News in London and vice versa. We also take stories from all of the members of ENEX, for example when the earthquake happened in Greece, we got our pictures from *Antenna 1* which is the Greek national station. Obviously the scripts are in foreign languages, so we have to rewrite them in English. (Irish broadcast editor)

The European Broadcasting Union (EBU) also involves a network of 50 to 60 stations exchanging news programmes. For the Dutch public broadcaster *NOS,* sources consulted include telexes, foreign newspapers, Associated Press, and Reuters; images come from AOP, Reuters, and other EU material.[14] As regards the sharing of stories and news articles, this varies between news outlets—many outlets appear to have a policy of exchange with other European newspapers and channels. The extent to which news is shared between newspaper outlets indicates a shared news agenda and a developing transnational sphere. In the absence of large-scale pan-European media, shared stories and access to news about other countries is both a practical and a financial consideration, while providing a wider perspective on European issues. This development is not apparent in our analysis of news sources, as the items coded under 'syndicated news' or news from 'another outlet' are minimal; however, a good deal of news emanates from news agencies. It is possible that in many cases such 'news sharing' between outlets is not clearly identified. For the EU news, it is not entirely clear where the majority of news items and articles are sourced, although a large number are obviously written or reported by the correspondents in Brussels. In both cases, there are many items originating from news agencies.

The exchange of articles between newspapers is becoming slightly more widespread. In Spain, *El Mundo* exchanges articles with other European newspapers such as *Il Corriere de la Sera* and *The Guardian.*[15] The Swedish *Aftonbladet* shares cultural articles with *The Guardian* and *Le Monde Diplomatique* on a monthly basis.[16] 'The Sunday Tribune in Ireland shares articles with the *Herald* in Scotland (Scottish or British stories which might be of interest here) and we send them general features but we don't share in the European context' (Irish journalist, interview, 1999).

---

[14] Foreign news, Dutch public broadcaster.
[15] Spanish press journalist, international editor.
[16] Swedish political editor.

This seems to be a less common practice for the Swedish press (aside from *Aftonbladet*) and where sharing does occur, it appears to be problematic. '*Dagens Industri* sometimes shares articles with papers in Poland, Russia and the Baltic States, but this does not work that well. Also the paper shares news lists with a Danish paper, but this is not working very well' (Swedish EU correspondent, interview, 1999).

Similarly, there was not much indication of exchange in the Dutch press, although a different approach occurs in broadcasting. In the Netherlands, *RTL4* buys some images from Reuters, DTN, WTN, or from their commercial colleagues in Flanders, VTM.[17] 'We are always looking for attractive ways of covering the news. We almost always write our pieces ourselves; we hardly collaborate with other news organisations. From time to time we adapt stuff from *The Guardian* or *El País*" (European specialist, Dutch press, interview, 1999).

Exchange of news within common language areas is obviously more convenient as the following example illustrates:

> We have one person out in Brussels and if something big happens, we tend to look to other sources of information, for example the English Independent and the usual sources such as Reuters. The same applies for the Irish Independent. For example, if the Telegraph runs an article lambasting Europe we will use it providing that it is a good piece, in spite of the fact that, on the whole, the Independent has a pro-Europe stance. More important than whether a piece is pro- or anti-Europe is the fact that it is well-written and well-developed. (Irish news editor, press, interview, 1999)

OVERCOMING OBSTACLES

Journalists themselves have frequently proposed solutions to the obstacles in reporting European news. There is continued emphasis on the need for education of journalists regarding European issues, not just Brussels correspondents but also those focused on the national space. The European Journalism Centre (EJC) in Maastricht has a mandate: 'to further the European dimension in media outlets—to enhance the quality of journalistic coverage of European current affairs; to analyse and describe the developing European media landscape; and to provide strategic support for the European media industry.'[18]

They organise a wide range of courses for journalists from national and regional papers, educating them on policy issues and policy-making procedures. The journalists no longer come from just EU member states but also from applicant states and central and southeastern Europe. Many journalists claim

---

[17]Political editor, Dutch commercial television.
[18]http://www.ejc.nl/aboutejc.html

that a good deal of understanding is also picked up after a few years on the Brussels news beat.

Many of the quality papers are building networks, syndicating stories, and sharing information. There has been a cooperation (since December 6, 1998) among seven European newspapers sharing stories on the single currency via their Web sites. The section entitled 'European Perspective' links the reader to stories in *El País, Le Monde, Süddeutsch Zeitung, The Guardian, Le Soir,* and *Aftonbladet* (with a link to an Internet translation programme). Such cooperation is, of course, a more elite development and requires online access.

From an institutional perspective, it has been suggested that a change in the nature of press relations at the EU is recommended wherein the European Council and Council of ministers press conferences would involve all ministers (or prime ministers) and journalists together and not be divided by country. In this way, of course, there would be less opportunity for individuals to place a particular spin on the outcome of negotiations.

Russ-Mohl (1992) suggested possible instruments of self-regulation, including cross-national exchange of ideas and information regarding quality standards, media observatories, building and linking infrastructures, and an inventory that registers and describes existing networks and infrastructures particularly those that crosscut traditional national boundaries. This is echoed by a declaration of Mediterranean journalists who hope to:

- Encourage the European institutions to assist in developing training for journalists of the local and regional media.
- Adopt action programmes and fund policies of promoting contacts and professional exchanges among journalists, media and press associations, in order to further the creation and implementation of a network of journalists of the Mediterranean countries.
- Assist in providing the media with the means to improve coverage of European issues by, for instance, financially supporting access to new technologies, setting up tailor-made news-files for local and regional journalists, and giving practical tools to the Mediterranean journalists for the creation of a Mediterranean network.[19]

The Association of European Journalists also proposes changes, including the encouragement of less complexity in policy making, which may be impossible to achieve. They also encourage the use of investigative journalism to show where the actual power lies and suggest reform wherein EU politicians can be held to account for decisions, and that there be names rather than party lists for elections.[20]

---

[19]'Connecting Europe with its Citizens,' Declaration of the Mediterranean Journalists, meeting in Matera, Italy, December 4–5, 1998.

[20]Athanse Papandropoulous, commenting at Granada conference, 1998 (cf. footnote 8).

CONCLUSION

The impetus for interviews and discussions with journalists concerned the need to balance the research findings outlined in the previous chapters with a perspective on the realities for practitioners in reporting European news. As such, we find that on top of the normal pressures on journalists as outlined in chapter 2, whether commercial, editorial or political, there is an added dimension of developing an interest in European issues. This is one of the reasons for the constant need for a 'national hook' in stories. In terms of professionalism and continued education, there is a general movement towards acquiring more knowledge about the processes of European governance. There is also a gradual development in sharing and syndicating stories.

There is, of course, a difference between the impetus shown by these journalists for developing a public sphere, or spheres, for political debate and discussion, and the idea of the media playing a part in the promotion of a European identity. Indeed, some would claim that 'uniting Europe is not a task for the media who have no obligation to make propaganda for Europe.'[21] But certainly the provision of clear unbiased information and analysis will go a long way towards developing an arena of public debate.

---

[21]Discussion of European correspondents at Granada conference, 1998 (see footnote 8).

9

Overview of Programmes Dealing With Europe

INTRODUCTION

The first phase of this aspect of the research involved taking a look at how much television programming on the main national channels deals with European issues (see Table 9.1). Channels were monitored during a 6-week period from mid-May to the end of June to get a flavour of the overall quantity of programmes and to identify relevant types for deeper analysis in the second phase of the project.

The principle of selecting two channels, one public service and one private, on the criterion of having the largest audience share proved problematic. In the Italian case, there was nothing of relevance on the commercial channels, implying the necessity to focus only on the RAI programming including all three channels. In the British case, the second public service broadcaster featured more programmes than the first, whereas in the Netherlands all three public service channels needed to be considered. In Poland both public service channels appear to provide a good deal of relevant programming; in Germany the two channels selected fit the initial audience-reach criterion. Hence in most cases, the criterion for the most suitable channels related more to where people can seek out this information, rather than to the audience reach of the channels.

Much of the time period of analysis was dominated by the Euro 2000 football tournament, an event that in some ways was the most important 'European' aspect of programming during this time. Despite this, the range of programmes was quite broad, as we looked at the entire schedule for 'Europe-related' television. Consequently, there are representations of Europe that included

TABLE 9.1
Total Number of Programmes Identified as Having a European
Theme or Element, From Mid-May to the End of June

	Channels (Number of Programmes in Brackets)
France (63)	France 2 (21), France 3 (9) TF1 (7), and ARTE (5), Le 5me (21)
United Kingdom (117)	BBC2 (74 including the Learning Zone) and Channel 4 (43 including sport)
Germany (34)	ARD (25) and RTL (9)
Italy (60)	RAI 1, 2, and 3 (60)
Poland (51)	TVP1 (30), TVN (21)
The Netherlands (84)	NED 1, TV2 and (78) and SBS6 (5) RTL5 (1)

education, language and culture, sports and travel programmes, specific policy issues, cultural and historical documentaries, and night-time entertainment programmes.

United Kingdom

In the British case, BBC1 and ITV broadcast mainly holiday programmes in relation to Europe. The channels selected were BBC2, the second public service channel, and Channel 4, a commercial but regulated channel with some public interest obligations. According to the British expert, BBC2 fulfils more of the public interest role, as BBC1 is somewhat compelled to be more competitive and populist in order to compete for audience shares. Channel 4 is also under pressure to secure advertising and this has apparently led to an increase in 'pop-trash' programmes aimed at the late teens and early twenties age group. Leaving aside the large number of educational programmes on BBC2, the two channels had a relatively equal amount of 'Europe-related' programmes. In this case, both channels are performing rather a similar role in the provision of information about Europe, although BBC2 focuses more on education and Channel 4 has more entertainment programmes. On the one hand, there were political/cultural programmes such as Correspondent Europe (a once-off series) cited as giving a wide view of European issues. On the other hand, a major area of programming portrays Europe as an 'exotic playground' (i.e., *Eurotrash*), and somewhat linked to this theme was a range of programmes dealing with tourism and holidays.

The Netherlands

The Dutch public service channels featured most of the programmes relevant to Europe, whereas on the commercial channels SBS6 and RTL5, programmes were largely related to holidays and tourism similar to the UK representations of Europe as a playground. The division of tasks between the three Dutch public service channels was reflected in the types of programmes, whether documentary, educational, or news analysis.

Italy

Over the 6-week review period, no relevant programmes were identified on the Italian commercial channels. Mediaset channels, perhaps reflecting the Euro-scepticism of Berlusconi, tend to focus on Italian issues. According to the national partner, the only commercial channel that could be considered to have a European flavour was MTV Italy; Commercial programming is characterised by programmes such as *Who wants to be a millionaire?* On RAI the most relevant programmes were in magazine format, dealing with historical and cultural issues representing a construction of European cultural identity through culture, history, and an invention of tradition. This European identity is more focused on the Mediterranean area of southern and southeastern Europe and North Africa. However, the overall attention paid to European issues, particularly political and economic, is very limited.

France

The launch of the French presidency of the Council of the EU at the beginning of June (2000) appears to have had little impact on programming about Europe in France. Most of the relevant programming in the 6-week period appeared on the public channels, France 2 and France 3, and also on the more educational La Cinquième. One of the more notable points about these programmes is the attempt by both public service and commercial broadcasters to use 'key figures' to sell Europe. This was described by the French experts as an attempt to revive the tone of debate about European issues and promote a more positive, enthusiastic discussion. The issue concerns 'pitching Europe' to the 20s–30s age group and 'promoting a Euro-consumer enthusiasm.'

The French commercial channel TF1 has an editorial policy of providing general family programmes, exclusive original programmes, and events and live broadcasting. The extent of its focus on European issues is minimal, the exceptions being the miniprogramme *L'Euro en poche* and the national programmes that frequently deal with Europe, *Les rendez-vous de l'entreprise* and *A vrai dire*. ARTE also broadcast the series *EUtopia* during this time entitled *Putain d'Europe* and *Mein Gott Europa* in French and German, respectively.

Germany

In the German case, the public service and private channels did satisfy the criterion of having a large audience share. Alternative channels ARTE and 3sat, due to international cooperation in public broadcasting, almost by definition present more European content, but they have significantly smaller, more niche audiences. The regional channels of the ARD broadcasters in general feature a good deal of information and educational programming and offer special programmes for foreigners living in Germany. From the two channels chosen, more than three times as many programmes appeared on the public service channel ARD. Within the ARD, the decentralised structure affects programming. The schedules are frequently filled with productions from different ARD broadcasters, even with the same programme title. An example is the culture magazine presented on Sunday evening sometimes called *Titel, Thesen, Temperamente,*[1] or *Kulturweltspiegel,*[2] and sometimes *Kulturreport.*[3]

RTL programmes, due to the licensing system, are frequently produced by independent broadcasters with their own separate licences, using the terrestrial band-width in North Rhine–Westphalia used by RTL during a specified time per week for information programmes (DTCP and Center TV). Based on these rather limited licences, they have an agreement with RTL that their programming will also be included in the RTL terrestrial and satellite transmission for all of Germany. On RTL, programmes with content related to Europe are scheduled late in the evening, whereas on ARD the scheduling includes prime time, late night, and afternoon, most of which were broadcast at weekends. Relevant German programmes consisted of mainly regular magazines dealing with political, economic, or cultural issues. Political and economic topics that deal with Europe tend usually to focus on one country and do not have a comparative aspect. Other 'Europes' are those involving sport, travel and tourism, and places and people.

Poland

The two Polish channels monitored for the study were the public service channel TVP1 (both public service channels had a good deal of programming), and the commercial channel TVN, which has a growing audience share. European and EU issues are, at this time, highly relevant in Poland due to preparations for, and debates over, accession to the European Union. Hence, the issue of legal adjustment in order to incorporate the *aquis communitaire,* and the impact of accession on small businesses and agriculture are frequently dealt with on television. Both channels dealt with these issues, with the public channel providing more of the afternoon programming and the commercial channel covering these issues on late-night programmes. A second picture of Europe, more particularly on commercial channels, revealed a darker side of Europe

---

[1]Produced by HR.

[2]Produced by WDR.

[3]Produced alternatively by BR, MDR, NDR, and SFB.

focusing on scandals, crimes, sex, and prostitution. Very little was observed that dealt with Europe in terms of culture, art, or music.

In all of the countries in the study, the public service channels produce most of the relevant programmes, but only in Italy is there a serious lack of interest expressed by the commercial channels. A major contrast between two countries in which a large amount of 'Europe'-relevant programmes were noted was provided by Poland and the United Kingdom. The focus on language, culture, and travel in the United Kingdom reflects a completely different idea of Europe than that of the policy-oriented approach of the Polish broadcasters.

WHERE CAN WE FIND EUROPE?

The content of these programmes is described here in the context of scheduling. In this way we have mapped the different kinds of 'Europe' that are represented or discussed throughout the day in each of the countries. Television schedules on one level indicate the target audience for a type of programme, whether during children's viewing hours, prime time, or late-night viewing. In another sense, the schedules reflect the importance given to different aspects of European cultural or political issues within the national sphere.

Table 9.2 indicates the number of programmes in each country placed into categories based on viewing times. We categorised scheduling times in the following way:

- Early morning: 5 A.M. to 9 A.M.
- Morning: before 12 P.M.
- Lunchtime: 12 P.M. to 2 P.M.

TABLE 9.2
Scheduling of Programmes With a European Theme or Element
During Six-week Overview Period

	France	Germany	Italy	Netherlands	Poland	United Kingdom	Total
Early morning	10	0	0	15	1	11	37
Morning	2	4	11	1	1	23	42
Lunchtime	4	3	5	7	12	11	42
Afternoon	0	10	7	12	12	2	43
Early evening	3	2	0	13	8	12	38
Prime-time	8	9	0	25	1	24	67
Late night	13	4	5	18	11	13	64
Very late night	7	5	14	1	3	45	75

- Afternoon: 2 P.M. to 5 P.M.
- Early evening: 5 P.M. to 7 P.M.
- Evening prime time: 7 P.M. to 10.30 P.M.
- Late night: 10.30 P.M. to 12.30 A.M.
- Very late night 12.30 A.M. to 5 A.M.

Prime-Time Television

Prime-time television seldom deals with European issues, but in the UK and the Netherlands there were more examples of Europe as a prime-time topic. In the case of the UK, most of these programmes were documentaries dealing with aspects of European history, or cultural or travel programmes. On the Dutch channels during this time, there were several programmes dealing with aspects of the Euro 2000 championships including the Yugoslavian soccer team, Euro 2000 safety issues, and black market tickets. Other programmes dealt with crime problems in Europe such as the export of women and diamond trafficking in Belgium, the relationship between Holland and Belgium, and a series of biographical portraits of scientists and philosophers. Programmes that appeared during prime-time slots in Germany were generally magazine formats dealing with economic, consumer, or crime issues. In France, the topics were mainly political and cultural including a programme on the rise of right-wing politics in Austria. Prime-time programmes in Poland or Italy did not deal with Europe. One example of a successful prime-time programme is the talk show *Union Libre,* another interesting French approach to European programming. The programme consists of seven or eight guest journalists from European countries who talk about various aspects of life in their own countries.

Hidden Europe

The tendency of the countries to broadcast Europe-related programmes during the early-morning and late-night programming was most apparent in the United Kingdom. Most of this programming falls into the BBC2's 'Learning Zone,' which contains a range of educational programmes, often including European issues, aimed at school, university, and adult education. The Open University also broadcasts on BBC2, in the very late night to very early morning slots. Many of these programmes were focused on language instruction and cultural aspects of other European countries. Similarly, in France relevant programming is generally scheduled early in the morning or late at night (in relation to quota requirements for other European productions, the scheduling patterns are similar). The early-morning programming included the current affairs and press review programme *Télématin.* In the Netherlands, early-morning television involved features on Europe on breakfast television. The only programmes in Italy that dealt directly with European and EU political issues were the Rai Uno broadcasts of *Euronews* at 6 A.M. The later programming on Italian television was a literature series presenting important books by European (and world) authors. *Un Mondo a Colori*, broadcast in the morning, features multicultural Italy and Europe.

Lunch-Time Europe

Lunch-time programming appears to be quite important in Poland, the UK, and Italy. In Poland a good deal of the lunch-time programmes were EU focused, particularly with relation to agriculture, including market issues, agritourism, regional policy, and EU farming comparisons. The main EU-specific programme at this time is *12.20 to the Union*. Other programmes looked at accountancy standards in the EU, science, Kosovo, and Expo 2000. In the UK the programmes are mainly sports related. There was, however, during this period a magazine series presented by the head of the European Commission representation in the UK entitled *Powerhouse*. Italian programmes, for example *Mediterraneo*, dealt with cultural and geographical aspects of Europe. In France the miniprogramme (formats are discussed later) *A vrai dire*, broadcast at lunch-time, presents short features on various consumer issues, often with reference to Europe. Although this was broadcast every day, the programmes are only 2 minutes long, so the total programming at this time is quite short.

Daytime and Early Evening Programmes

Polish programming continues throughout the day, often focusing specifically on EU-relevant issues, including the EU labour market on *Euroexpress*. Aspects of policy such as agriculture, rural development, environment, and waste management are discussed. The adoption and implementation of EU legislation is discussed with relation to trade, food, the impact on small and medium enterprises (SMEs), and topics included EU audio-visual policy and the 'Television without Frontiers' directive. There are also more general features and discussions on aspects of European integration such as 'visions of the future EU,' 'relations between Poland and the EU,' and the impact of membership on various aspects of the economy including tourism. The Polish focus on the EU is understandably much stronger than in the other countries in the study due both to the preparations and incorporation of a vast amount of EU legislation within a short time, and to internal debates on the pros and cons of membership. French daytime and early-evening programming included the miniprogramme *L'Euro en poche*, a 2-minute slot briefly explaining various aspects of the workings and legislation of the EU. Le Cinquième also aired an early-evening cultural programme, *Correspondance pour l'Europe*.

Dutch television featured a variety of documentaries dealing with cultural issues in European countries, including Turkey, Greece, and Italy, and the experiences of immigrants living in the Netherlands. Other programmes featured travel and language. In the UK during this period, there was a one-off series, *Correspondent Europe,* that looked at various political issues throughout Europe including Belgium's far right, environmental pollution of the Danube, Dutch euthanasia, Islam in Germany, and older people in Russia, Holland, and Austria. Similarly, German programmes, particularly *Europamagazin,* looked at various current affairs and cultural issues throughout Europe, including the oil spill in Brittany, prisons in Italy, Romanian orphanages, and football hooliganism.

After-Dark Europe

Late-night and very late-night programming about Europe varies widely throughout the countries. Possibly the most unusual selection of programmes appears on the British channels. Programme titles such as *EUtopia, Eurotrash, Euroballs* (the *Eurotrash* Euro 2000 special), *Eurotica,* and *Exploitica* perhaps conjure up some images of what after-dark Europe in the UK represents. *EUtopia* (BBC2, four editions broadcast on Tuesday through Friday of one week) is a programme series filmed in the 15 EU member states dealing with various aspects of living and moving throughout the EU. Two of the programmes were broadcast in the UK and one in the Netherlands during the second phase of the project and are dealt with in more detail later with regard to programme themes.

The other programmes are all broadcast by Channel 4. *Eurotrash* (broadcast on various evenings) has been described by the UK partners in the project as 'off-beat,' 'pornographic,' or 'humorous' and is basically a magazine programme looking at various aspects of sexual deviance and other 'wacky happenings' with reports from around Europe. *Euroballs* was the special edition broadcast during the football championships featuring, among other things, an Italian nun who manages a football team. *Eurotica* and *Exploitica* (Fridays) both appear to present film directors from Europe who made erotic, horror, or 'horrotica' genre movies.

Late-night Europe is not so frivolous in other countries, although some very late-night programming on the Polish commercial channel TVN dealt with sex shows in Europe and also with Polish girls becoming involved in the sex industry in EU countries. In contrast to the British programmes, which were more humorous, in Poland these issues were seen as problematic and as representing a sleazy side of Europe. Other late-night programming in Poland, particularly from 10.30 to 12.00 P.M., continued to look at aspects of EU policy and other problematic issues such as prostitution, smuggling, and immigration.

Similarly, late-night programming in France dealt with problem areas such as the handling of public money in relation to the Eurotunnel on the programme *Argent Public.* In the Netherlands, an educational programme, *Correspondent in Avondland,* covered various aspects of EU democracy.

LEVELS OF COVERAGE

We categorised programmes under three levels of relevance to Europe, which included programmes that are specifically about Europe or the European Union, national programming that regularly deals with Europe, and general programming that has a European flavour. This helped to identify in which countries there is dedicated programming dealing with the EU or Europe. (See Table 9.3 for an overview of programme levels and broadcast times.)

Italy

The regular programmes on Italian television dealing specifically with Europe are geographical or cultural magazine formats such as *Giorni d'Europa* (*European Days*), *I viaggi di giorni d'Europa* (*The Journeys of European Days*), and news programmes such as *T3 Europa,* a television news bulletin dealing with European news. No regular, once-off, or special programmes dealing specifically with the EU appeared during the monitoring period. However, prior to the monitoring period, there was a series entitled *Maastricht Italia,* a programme where the economist Alan Friedman outlined in a straightforward way the dynamics of European economics. No one-off or special programmes dealing specifically with Europe were broadcast during the monitoring period (aside from those dealing with Euro 2000). Programmes focused on national issues that deal regularly with European topics were not identified. On the third level of programming, there were a number of magazines dealing with culture, travel, and literature.

The Netherlands

In the Netherlands there was a wide range of programmes that could be considered to deal specifically with the European Union or Europe including *Correspondent in Avondland.* All of these were on the public service channels and broadcast from afternoon to late night. The second level of more national programmes also had a wide range that frequently dealt with Europe, mainly in the format of current affairs and news analysis. The more general cultural programming focused on travel, culture, and language, and this was the main level of coverage that appeared on the commercial channels.

TABLE 9.3

Programmes on Three Levels of Relevance to the EU and Europe;
I = Specific, II = Relevant, or III = General

Time	France	Germany	Italy	Netherlands	Poland	UK
Early morning 39	EU I Public 10		Euronews RAI Public	**Europe II** Public 14 Private 1	**Europe II** Public 1	General Public 8 Private 3
Morning 38	**General** Private 2	**Europe II** Public 2 **General** Public 1 Private 1	**Europe I** Public 3 **General** Public 8	**General** Public 1	**General** Public 1	**Europe II** Public 2 **General** Public 15 Private 6
Lunchtime 38	**Europe II** Private 4	**Europe II** Public 1 **General** Public 2	**Europe II** Public 5	**Europe II** Public 1 **General** Public 2 Private 4	EU I Public 7 **Europe II** Public 1 **General** Public 5	**Europe II** Private 1 **General** Public 8 Private 2
Afternoon– Early evening 88	EU 1 Private 3	**Europe I** Public 3 Private 1 **General** Public 6 Private 2	**Europe I** Public 6 **General** Public 1	**Europe I** Public 5 **Europe II** Public 7 **General** Public 6 Private 6	**Europe I** Public 7 **Europe II** Public 3 Private 4 **General** Public 3 Private 3	**Europe I** Public 5 **Europe II** Public 1 **General** Public 7 Private 1
Primetime 67	EU I Public 5 **Europe II** Public 3	**Europe II** Public 4 **General** Public 4 Private 1		**Europe I** Public 2 **Europe II** Public 19 Private 1 **General** Public 3	**General** Public 1	**Europe II** Public 1 **General** Public 12 Private 11
Late night 60	**Europe I** Public 5 EU II Public 6 **Europe II** Public 2	**Europe II** Public 1 Private 2 **General** Public 1	General Public 5	EU I Public 4 **Europe II** Public 11 **General** Public 3	**Europe II** Private 11	EU I Public 4 **General** Public 1 Private 8
Very late night 61	EU II Private 1 **General** Private 6	**Europe II** Private 1 **General** Private 3 Public 1	General Public 14	**General** Public 1	**General** Private 3	General Public 33 Private 12

The United Kingdom

Very few UK programmes were identified that relate specifically to the European Union or Europe. Those broadcast were mainly on the public service channel including *Correspondent Europe,* a current affairs and cultural series, which looked at issues in Europe (on BBC2 early evenings). For example, on May 20th the programme focused on environmental issues and looked at the cyanide pollution of the river Danube in Romania. *Correspondent* is a regular current affairs programme, but the seven-part European series was commissioned during the time period of the study to 'investigate the human stories shaping Europe.'[4] The other series during this time was *EUtopia,* a European cooperative production focusing on living in the European Union (BBC2 late night). There was not a great deal of national programming that was considered strongly relevant to Europe or the EU, but the more general cultural programmes (level three) included a wide range of sport, language, history, and magazine and entertainment programmes.

Poland

Both Polish channels broadcast programmes that were specific to Europe or more precisely to the European Union, some of which had quite a high audience share (between 20% and 40%). The private channel TVN had more 'national' programmes covering European issues than the public service channel, particularly late-night programmes. The more general cultural type of programming dealt with travel and tourism.

France

Programmes that deal specifically with Europe or the EU are considered a rarity on the French television channels. One programme that possibly sums up the approach of French broadcasters is *France Europe Express,* as all programming is essentially more focused on the national perspective wherein France remains the central theme. An example of this was a programme in May about the launch of the French presidency of the Council of the EU. The TF1 programme *L'Euro en poche,* mentioned earlier, frequently deals with EU issues.

Germany

Neither of the channels had a regular programme or series dealing with the EU, and during the 6-week period, there were no one-off programmes specifically dealing with EU issues. A 'Europe specific' programme is *Europamagazin,*

---

[4]http://www.bbc.co.uk/alert/spotlight/sci_0518_corre.shtml

which deals with general current affairs throughout Europe. Some of the national current affairs regulars that touch on European issues are *Weltspiegel,* *Spiegel TV,* and *Stern TV.* On the business/consumer front, ARD broadcast a consumer/economic magazine programme *Plus–Minus.* General programming included sport, culture, and art reviews.

Overall, we can see that there is a concentration, in each country, of EU- or Europe-related programmes during afternoon and early evening schedules, particularly as regards programmes dedicated specifically to EU issues. Specific programming dealing with the European Union or Europe in general was most often noted on the Dutch and Polish channels. Programmes that were considered relevant—that is, more nationally focused programmes that regularly deal with Europe (in this case they were only counted when they actually had European themes)—are least common in Italy and the United Kingdom. In both of these countries, the more general cultural references to Europe were most frequent; in fact, in Italy this was the only area of coverage. However, the approaches used, the themes dealt with, and the representations of Europe vary from country to country.

PROGRAMME FORMATS

In general, in France, Germany, and Italy, magazine-type programming is used in programmes dealing with Europe. In this context we consider *magazine* as a programme mixing studio discussion and short reports, often with different topics being covered in each programme. In contrast, Dutch and British programmes tend more towards documentaries, with more of an in-depth focus on one particular subject. In Poland the range of formats is wider, with documentaries and magazines supported with a good deal of discussion, debate, and news analysis programmes. This reflects the focus on current EU policy issues and the national debates on the pros and cons of membership.

As already noted, there are quite a few educational programmes with a European flavour on BBC2 that constitute a different type of format. The new format types that are most noticeable are those of the French channels, particularly the miniprogramme comprised of 'information packets' sometimes dealing with EU affairs or EU-relevant consumer issues. These programmes are usually presented by well-known or popular journalists and are intended to impart practical information regarding specific issues. According to the French researchers for this project, the subjects (particularly on *L'Euro en poche*) are presented in a cheerful and optimistic light, simplifying as much information as possible aimed at an audience who would normally be least informed on, and least interested in, these issues.

A further interesting format is that of the aforementioned programme *Union Libre,* which is broadcast in a prime-time evening slot on Saturdays on France 2, the talk show that deals with European lifestyle issues with a wide range of European regular and guest participants.

TELEVISION PROGRAMMES ABOUT EUROPE AND REFERENCE TO OTHER EUROPEANS: TOPICS AND THEMES

As mentioned earlier, Italian television programmes, when they deal with Europe, seldom appear to cover political and economic issues and the representations are mainly cultural. Migration and issues such as the rights of immigrants, particularly those moving into Italy, is the most frequently covered topic. Although the main focus was on Italy, migration, cultural and historical issues, and travel in Germany, Yugoslavia, and other parts of Europe were also portrayed.

There was a great variety in Dutch programming during the 6-week period. Political and current affairs, the Euro 2000 football championships, and the Srebrenica hearings in the Netherlands were major topics. There was an interesting mixture of programmes including profiles of philosophers, filmmakers, sociologists, and researchers from various countries. Cultural issues such as film, art, and architecture are mostly covered for Italy, Greece, Germany, and the UK.

In Poland the most important issues covered were agriculture and Poland's integration into the EU. Specific countries, generally the major EU members, were dealt with in relation to various topics, from the sex industry in Sweden to a flower and garden exhibition in the UK. No reference was made to Poland's other neighbours, including the other applicant states. The French programming in this period focused more on economic, political, and current affairs issues. Europe and the EU in general were the main topics. No programmes were recorded where one specific country was covered, although some comparative aspects are used in reference to particular topics like education and taxation.

A large amount of the general programming in Britain is educational, with language instruction in the most important EU languages. French, Italian, Spanish, and German, and cultural issues, art, film, and sports are the main topics. The series *EUtopia* deals with a broad range of topics concerning Europe and Europeans. Quite a lot of German programming deals with live events such as sport, royal birthdays, and Clinton receiving the Karlpreis in Aachen. A wide range of other Europeans are dealt with including eastern European countries such as Romania, the Czech Republic, and Russia.

CONCLUSION

Italian commercial channels do not provide much programming that deals with Europe in either the political or cultural sense, aside from aspects of multicultural life. Berlusconi's Euroscepticism is suggested as a reason for this lack of programming on the Mediaset channels, which focus on Italian issues. The programmes on RAI are more likely to be cultural than political, with the Euronews broadcasts providing the only coverage of political and economic issues. Italian programmes about Europe are generally of a magazine type and are most frequently broadcast in the early-morning or late-night viewing slots. Europe as a theme is therefore not particularly important in the Italian national sphere, and the cultural and historical links presented are more focused on the Mediterranean. This echoes the lack of Italian media engagement with Europe revealed in the analysis of news.

In the UK the most relevant programming is to be found on BBC2 and Channel 4, presenting several pictures of Europe: a political Europe; Europe as business; Europe as exotic playground; Europe as a holiday destination; and European sports events. Both magazine and documentary formats are used, with the latter being more frequent during prime-time viewing. On the edges of the television schedule, we find a great deal of educational programming including language instruction and cultural information about other Europeans. Late-night viewing provides a range of entertainment programmes that present exotic or sleazy pictures of Europe. British television, particularly BBC2 and Channel 4, therefore offer a wide range of programming about Europe for those who wish to seek it out, but the central policy and legislative aspects of the European Union are seldom featured.

In the Netherlands, due to the nature of division of tasks between the three NOS channels, it is important to consider programmes from them all. With a recent restructuring of channels, the first is intended for an older, more traditional audience and will most likely feature European programming. The second channel is likely to focus on documentaries, whereas the third channel concentrates on culture. The majority of Dutch programmes are broadcast between evening and late night. As with the British programmes, prime-time television tends to be more historical and cultural and in documentary format.

Due to the moves towards accession to the European Union, European issues are highly relevant in Poland. The second public service channel recently dedicated a whole day of programming to Europe, including informational programming and films. The main politico-economic issues dealt with on Polish television relate to the *aquis communitaire*. Whereas the public channel covers European issues during the day and early evening, the private channel TVN takes over in the evening and late night. It still deals with EU policy issues but also provides a range of entertaining programmes more similar to the British, although the focus on sleazy aspects of Europe is more in a context of concern than amusement.

There are no television programmes on the German channels monitored that deal specifically with the EU, in comparison to the Dutch channels where a great deal of European-specific programming was observed. However, *Europamagazin* presents problematic political issues from all over Europe.

Two trends are emerging in France in the portrayal of Europe. The first involves the need to 'pitch' Europe in a more positive, enthusiastic way with well-known or popular journalists. Another development is the emergence of miniprogrammes—short (2-minute) pieces that deal briefly with particular issues.

The majority of programmes focusing specifically on Europe or the European Union are broadcast in the afternoon and early evening. This is also the time of day where 'Europe' is most likely to feature in programme titles. The exceptions to this are the late-night UK programmes where the prefix *Eu* is played with in a variety of ways, in most cases having little to do with the EU. In all the countries, public service channels broadcast most of the programmes that were identified as relevant to Europe.

10

Analysis of European Television Programme Content

INTRODUCTION

The programmes selected during the 2-week period of analysis were those considered most relevant to our research criteria and in many cases constituted the entire range available on the selected channels during this time (see Appendix II). Despite this being a more selective range of programming, the scheduling times more or less mirrored the findings from the first phase in relation to when programmes were broadcast in each country. There are some apparent differences between the countries as regards the scheduling of informational or entertainment programmes that have a European perspective. The French and German channels in the study are more likely to deal with European political or economic issues during prime-time broadcasting than the other countries, although these are conveyed through national current affairs programmes rather than specific European programmes. This possibly reflects a different perspective on what 'Europe' means in two central states of the European cooperation project. Alternatively, for Dutch and British channels in the study, this is the appropriate time to feature documentaries of a historical or cultural nature. A reasonable spread of programmes throughout the day can be observed in the scheduling of the Polish, French, and Dutch television. Daytime television is particularly significant in Poland. Unfortunately, many of the more interesting cultural programmes, particularly in Italy and the UK, are lost at the edges of the broadcaster's schedules.

VISIONS OF EUROPE: REPRESENTATIONS
OF A COMMON IDENTITY?

The themes that were common to all countries give a further impression of the 'Europeanisation' of the content of national broadcasting. The media's role in the development of national identities is generally considered as being complementary to the national education system and to both educational and oral history traditions. Elements of the media that contribute to identification with a collective space at the national level include the use of a common language, not really applicable in a mass media sense to identification with Europe.

The media also play a role in documenting the past in historical documentaries, an area that is examined later in the chapter. General fictional programming such as films and soap operas, through the use of cultural references, also serve to reinforce regional and national communities. 'European soap operas' do not exist, but at one point it was claimed that the European Commission had considered investing in soap operas in exchange for Euro-friendly plot lines. A European official quoted in an article in *The Times* stated, 'Sitcoms are the best way to get the message across because they are set against the background of a particular national reality. We just have to broaden into a European one.'[1] Whether such investment ever took place is not clear, but one range of programming from a slightly different genre, the 'fly on the wall' documentary, did receive some EU funding. Some of these programmes are analysed later in the chapter.

The European Union

Programmes that deal specifically with the European Union, and programmes that regularly cover European Union issues, were selected for analysis in the second phase of the project. The extent of such programming may indicate the way in which the media fulfil some role in enhancing European citizenship with the provision of information, the explanation of EU politics, and the provision of a forum for debating these issues. Some of the programmes fall into a category that could be described as 'civil education' programmes particularly for young people, such as the Dutch *Europe, History of the Future* and the Polish *Euroexpress* with news from Europe for young people. The programmes are broadcast during the day and probably intended for use in the classroom. These two are quite similar and often deal with quite complex aspects of the workings of the European Union. One edition of *Europe, History of the Future* looked at cigarette advertising in Europe and included both an explanation of

---

[1] 'EU bankrolls sitcoms to sell its message' by Peter Conradi, *The Sunday Times*, June 1, 1997, p. 23.

how legislation works in the EU and what role the European Parliament plays. It also outlined the other organisations (including lobbyists) that can influence decision making. The BBC2 *Landmarks of Europe,* also aimed at schoolchildren, took a different approach: It did not directly deal with the European Union but moved through a range of EU countries. The presenters outlined economic, geographical, cultural, and historical aspects of different areas including the Rhineland, the 'economic corridor of Europe,' and the programme was presented in a more up-beat way than the other two.

Only one Italian programme fitted into this category, *Europa Come . . . ,* which looked at the workings of the European Council presented by an Italian representative in Brussels. No nationally focused current affairs or news analysis programmes were identified that deal with Europe.

More specifically, European or EU-focused programmes, as noted earlier, are broadcast on the Polish and Dutch channels, indicating a more developed European current affairs genre in these countries. One interesting example is *Correspondent in Avondland,* which, although educational, also comprises elements of investigative journalism. The presenters set out to answer questions about various aspects of European Union democracy including the lack of 'openness and transparency' of the EU and the European Parliament. The differences in European law are also examined with reference to the legalisation of soft drugs, combining interviews with officials and visits to coffee shops in Amsterdam.

In Poland a range of such programmes have been analysed including *12.20 to the Union* and *Facts, people, money.* These programmes and others present and discuss the incorporation of European laws into Polish law and their implications for the country. One area of prime importance is agriculture, with comparative features from Sweden and Germany (including regions of the former GDR). The Swedish example outlined how CAP works in practice, and Europe was presented as a positive, ordered, rich region of the world.

Polish television looks at a wide range of facts and figures concerning recent economic development in the European Union, unemployment, trends in the labour market, the petrol protests, and the Euro rate against the dollar. An analysis of the implications of all of these developments for the Polish economy is provided throughout the programmes.

Another programme, the first in a series entitled *Europeans,* was devoted to discussing what it means to be 'Europeans.' Among the elements mentioned were openness, tolerance, optimism, positive thinking, and generally a good level of education. Participants in the programme also stressed the importance of preserving Polish tradition and cultural identity in an era of globalisation. The programme was not particularly innovative in form, being of the 'talking heads' genre, but had some vox pop contributions from a variety of citizens.

The provision of a forum for debate about European issues is, by and large, carried out in the sphere of national current affairs and news analysis programmes. Some examples from the UK included *Newsnight* and the coverage of the annual Trade Unions Conference. The morning of the second day of this conference was focused on Europe and included a speech by social affairs commissioner Anna Diamontopolou. Discussions included social cohesion, competitiveness, and membership of the Euro, and reflected an area of civil society (labour rights) that is increasingly 'Europeanised.'

On German television, current affairs and economic programmes such as *Plusminus, Spiegel TV,* and *Stern TV* frequently deal with European Union issues such as the Euro and economic integration. In relation to the attempted stock exchange take-over by the Swedish stock exchange, the participants in one programme concluded that European integration is an on-going process that proceeds at a fast rate often unacceptable to many important political and business actors.

In France such programmes include *Envoyé Special, Argent Public,* and *Les rendez-vous de l'entreprise* dealing with various political and economic issues, including a feature on Haider's Freedom Party in Austria and the question of the EU's ability to deal with right-wing extremism. There are also a couple of 'on the surface' European programmes such as *Correspondance pour l'Europe,* looking at comparative issues between France and other countries as regards education and child care, and *France Europe Express,* which, for example, focused on the plans to reduce the French presidential term. Although the perspective is always French, there does appear to be an attempt to learn about how other Europeans do things in a range of areas including education, taxation, company law (less complicated in Britain than in France), and labour flexibility (in Germany).

Representations of the European Union, in an institutional sense, varied quite widely between countries, with the least in Italy and the most comprehensive programming in Poland, the prospective member of the club.

Common Problems, and Common Solutions?

Many common issues of concern are dealt with in the television programmes including crime, smuggling of tobacco, illegal immigration, the petrol crisis, and prostitution. These were, in many instances, issues that go beyond both the geographical and institutional reach of the European Union. Looking at the way these issues are presented allows us to judge whether such 'common problems' are viewed from a European perspective with the possibility of working together to find solutions.

The protests around Europe relating to taxes on fuel prices constituted a major common theme that appeared during the 2 weeks of analysis. As an example of a pan-European issue, it allowed for some discussion of the different forms of industrial action and the various government responses to this action that occurred in different countries. The BBC2 news analysis programme *Newsnight* initially approached the story from a British perspective, with, for example, contributions from British holidaymakers stranded in France. A later edition revealed some empathy with the actions of the French hauliers, as the chief executive of the UK road haulage association claimed that the French had achieved more in 48 hours than the British had in 2 years. The Polish *Kropka nad I* (Dot on the i) looked more closely at how the protest issue unfolded in different countries. It concluded that although Europe has common problems, it does not necessarily find common solutions as each country takes its own approach. Although the presentation of the problem in Germany was from a more internal perspective with some comparisons with France, the conclusion reached was that Europe consists of a group of countries with similar problems but different political cultures.

In the aftermath of the Kosovo crisis and the NATO war with Serbia, several programmes looked at on-going projects in Kosovo including a visit by Dutch singer Marco Borsato, a representative of the Netherlands in the War Child NGO. This organisation helps children to express their feelings and emotions with music, art, and theatre. A German documentary followed a woman (a former terrorist in the 1970s) as she reflected on her life and current work with people in Kosovo coping with war trauma. The French *Envoyé Spécial* looked at French and British industrialists rebuilding the infrastructure in Kosovo. All three programmes reflected 'European cooperation' on the issue of rebuilding the Balkans. French programmes during this time tended to look at financial issues including the funding of UNESCO, the costs of the Eurotunnel (between France and the UK), and Internet credit card security. The latter issue involved a comparison between European and US security systems, claiming Europe to be more secure for online transactions.

A major theme in most of the countries deals broadly with the issue of immigration, illegal immigration, racism, and xenophobia, and included the sanctions against Austria over Haider's Freedom Party role in government. Regarding immigration in general and the experiences of immigrants in European (particularly EU) countries, the Italian programme *Un Mondo a Colori* focuses specifically on this theme. The programme has been described as an attempt to

> take immigration out of the crime news, out of the darkness of ignorance, out of a kind of 'non-existence' inflicted upon it by the media. We would like to show the Italian public the other side of the story. Immigration is a social and cultural process happening all over Europe as well as in Italy. Immigration is not simply an emergency since many people coming from other cultures and other continents have been living in Italy for decades. Italy has for the first time an important number of second-generation immigrants, born in Italy and having very distant relationship with their (home) country and culture. These people are changing Italian society and Italian culture.[2]

---

[2]Jean Leonard Touadi, RAI, speaking at the WDR Conference: Cultural diversity against Racism, Köln, 1998.

This approach is similar to that of several Dutch programmes that try to portray multicultural issues in a less problematic way.[3] The German current affairs programme, *Europamagazin,* dealt with a range of such issues, highlighting problems of racism throughout Europe. Themes include the poor treatment of African soccer players in Europe and a comparison with the smuggling of women for prostitution. The Belgian right-wing political party Vlaams Blok was a subject of one programme, with a report on a Belgian project aimed at providing a better understanding of African (particularly Moroccan) culture in an attempt to fight against xenophobia. Another report looked at the rise of Nazism in Denmark, where one academic has been placed on a 'hit list' published by an extreme right-wing organisation.

Illegal immigration is more frequently viewed as a 'European problem' with, for example, a report on Chinese immigrants coming to Europe through Belgrade and Montenegro or through Slovenia to Italy, but no particular solution is offered in the context of these programmes. Other problems from around Europe featured on German television included the situation in Romanian orphanages and the low pay for Russian public sector workers.

Although common problems were identified by virtue of being dealt with in the programming of each of the countries, there was, overall, little attempt to bring people together to work out solutions. For example, the rise of right-wing extremism in various countries is outlined, but common underlying problems contributing to this are not really discussed. The issue of immigration is interesting, as within the nation-state there is an attempt to address issues of multiculturalism. Illegal immigration, on the other hand, tends to be discussed as a wider problem with reference to other parts of Europe, but again without proposing solutions and portrayed as an issue of fear or concern. These issues are dealt with in a more 'personal' way with reference to the experiences of individuals in some of the programmes described in the following section.

Living and Working in Europe

An important theme in the programming of all the countries concerns the movement of people in Europe and, in a sense, provides a more practical view of the actuality of life in a multicultural Europe or a Europe of 'free movement.' Both illegal immigration and the experiences of immigrants in other countries are addressed in these programmes. The representations of experiences of living in a different country in Europe, or being an immigrant to Europe from another part of the world, are extremely interesting and varied.

---

[3]Many of the German regional broadcasters, which were not part of the remit for this project, also feature such multicultural programming, an example being *Funkhauseuropa* on WDR radio.

One German programme portrays a Turkish writer and a Turkish film director living in Germany. Their collaborative work addresses a fundamental issue, which they describe as the problem in Germany of 'angst' in relation to foreigners. The director tries to decide if his work is Turkish or German but considers that, as he has lived his whole life in Germany, he is German. The programme is described as having some interesting complex interpretations of the problem of xenophobia from the perspectives of natives with foreign passports.

A Dutch programme broadcast on Polish television concerned a young Moroccan woman who told her own story and that of her mother and grandmother and their experiences of marriage. This allows audiences to contrast Moroccan and Dutch culture, and Dutch Moroccan culture where traditions have merged. She quotes her father: 'Women leave the home twice in their lives, once to get married and later when they are dead.' The central issue is the confrontation between the traditional Moroccan model of family with the reality of life in a European country.

Another regular programme that contrasts different cultures is the Dutch *Parallel*. The cities of Amsterdam and Istanbul are always featured, with similar people being interviewed about their lives. In Amsterdam a Dutch amateur singer presents his life, his old neighbourhood, his friends, and his bar. A real 'Amsterdammmer,' he sings the old, typically Dutch Schlager songs from past times. In Istanbul an older lady is followed who tries to make a living by playing the accordion in and outside of restaurants. Her impression of Europe is that 'you need a Greek as your lover and an Armenian cook but Europeans are cold.'

Two Polish programmes are interesting from the perspective of the relatively recent experience of free movement for Polish people in Europe and beyond. In one talk show, six people of various ages and educational and socioeconomic backgrounds tell their stories about experiences of living in different countries, including Greece, France, and the Netherlands. Europe is described as a highly competitive area, where it is difficult to find a good job and probably more difficult (as an immigrant from Poland) to be socially accepted, but this is possible if you work hard, learn a lot, and are optimistic.

Geezers is the title of a report where a female reporter meets people from Poland who are 'moonlighting' workers in France or just 'geezers' living there. Along the way she meets drug addicts, alcoholics, unemployed poor people, and beggars; some of them do not allow the cameras to show their faces. They left Poland looking for a better life in Paris but cannot speak the language, have no work, and finally, live on the margins of society on the street or in ruined houses. They all declare they will go home but have no money to do so. The report is generally balanced and concentrates on serious social problems. The impression of Europe is negative, as despite the fact that some have a good attitude towards the French and France, it is clear that not all the people have been able to establish a normal life there.

A similar theme is addressed in the Dutch edition of *EUtopia* concerning young French people living in squats in London recounting their experiences in France and in Britain. Although they have trouble finding stability as the police move them and they have to search for a new squat, they also express some positive impressions of Britain. 'Here you don't have to show your ID all the time, it's cool here.' They comment on employment benefit and free accommodation in the squats. According to the programme, there are about 65,000 British people living in France and about a quarter of a million French living in Britain.

The experiences of one such British person in France is outlined in another edition of *EUtopia*, broadcast on BBC2. This programme deals with a young Englishman who goes to work on a French vineyard owned by a German businessman. This programme shows ordinary Europeans interacting, living and working together, and frequently commenting on each other. For example, the father of the Englishman bemoans the fact that Europe is not more 'Thatcherite' and claims that the Germans are too socialist. The German vineyard owner feels the British have no respect for manual labourers; he is also frustrated at having to deal with the centralised government system in France. The Frenchwoman who oversees the vineyard does not hide her contempt for the rich English youth sent to France for the summer to get his hands a little dirty before moving on to bigger and better things. Although there is an element of stereotyping, particularly as regards the character of the English youth's father, these are real people participating in this 'fly on the wall' documentary, and the dialogue flows easily, often referring to central issues of integration in Europe.

Moving higher on the scale of 'living abroad' is the experience of the Baker family in another edition of *EUtopia*. The family owns an estate in a Greek village, which their ancestors bought from a Turk in 1832. This initial fact is one thorn in the side of some of the villagers—that is, the property was originally stolen by invaders. The programme provides an interesting snapshot of the interaction between one British family and a local Greek community. We learn that Propoki is in a depressed ex-mining region of Greece, earmarked by the EU for development funding. The current Mr Baker has obtained an EU grant to renovate and convert the house into a bed-and-breakfast. There is a certain amount of local resentment towards the Bakers for receiving funding, which is considered by some to be of no benefit to the wider community. Only the two loyal and humorous housekeepers offer a different opinion. Baker acknowledged local resentment but made limited efforts to overcome this. He speaks excellent Greek in his interactions with builders and suppliers, but he trusts no one.

Although more consumer based, the UK programme *A Place in the Sun*, dealing with living abroad, is about people buying their second and third homes in Spain, Italy, and France. The contrast with the homeless Polish people in

Paris underlines the variety of experiences in the 'open Europe.' Similar to standard holiday shows, the programme goes one stage further in assisting a couple in buying a holiday home. The opening animated credits interestingly depict a flight from Britain to 'Europe' with a large signpost visible over the continent pointing to Europe. There is a strong emphasis on the relative cheapness of property and the start of a property boom so that they should receive a good return on their property if sold. The Costa Blanca is presented as both a popular British holiday destination and a place to buy property. In one village the impression given is of a 'separate' British community, with a cinema showing films in English, and the three estate agents involved were English. As mentioned earlier, this programme (unintentionally) reflects the tendency of British (and German) holiday-home owners to colonise parts of Spain and create a 'home away from home,' thus not really interacting with the local culture.

All of these programmes were broadcast either in the afternoon or late at night, implying that some of the more interesting approaches to looking at Europe are still considered as peripheral viewing and not of general interest. This occurs despite the fact that, for example, the *Parallel* and the *EUtopia* series were particularly innovative, incorporating real personalities and elements of humour. In reference to this, the producer of the *EUtopia* series claimed that even though the BBC had commissioned this series, the channel decided to schedule the programmes late at night, before they had viewed them, in fact, before they were even made. The assumption made was that they would be boring (Luke, 2001, p. 147).

Telling European Stories

Several programmes, mainly documentaries, have emerged that deal with the past, frequently a conflictual past, often from personal viewpoints. These appear on Polish, British, and Dutch television. Many relate to a particularly troubled period of European history such as World War II or the Cold War. One British documentary followed a former prisoner of war on his journey back to Auschwitz, 50 years after he was imprisoned there for 14 months with several hundred other British soldiers. He returns and reminisces about the past, reliving some of the distress of both his experiences in Poland and his return home. The programme presented a balanced account of his experiences. A Polish documentary outlines the research activities of the Gauck Institute regarding the practices of the STASI, the secret police in the former GDR, and its special interest in the situation in Poland, particularly after the establishment of Solidarity. Due to the political changes in central and eastern Europe, Europeans can leave certain dark episodes in their history behind them, and Europeans (in this case German and Polish) can cooperate in establishing historical facts.

One Polish documentary proposes a strong probability that the UK was responsible for the death of the Polish prime minister and army chief, Sikorski, during World War II. In 1942 and 1943, the UK was seeking support from Stalin on the eastern front during the war. Historians, a former Polish agent of MI5, and other experts formulate the thesis that the UK had a great interest in Sikorski's death. Recently J. Nowak-Jeziorański (former chief of Radio Free Europe) publicly appealed to the UK authorities to release, after 50 years, the files on this issue. The programme presents another example of cooperative research.

A Dutch documentary shows the period of Stalinist rule in Russia and how the country became isolated and feared during this regime. Comparisons are made with Spain (under the reign of Franco) and the rise of Hitler's Nazi Germany. The views and opinions of a variety of nations including Russia, America, and the United Kingdom regarding the relationships between Russia and Germany, and Russia and the West, are presented in the documentary. *Secret Agent,* a BBC2 documentary, looks at the work of Churchill's Special Operations executive in 1940. Four European agents from Britain, France, and Norway recount their experiences working behind enemy lines. References to Germany and Italy were necessarily in some cases negative but the primary focus was on the inspirational recollections of four European agents.

Two other documentaries looked at different aspects of European history. One of a five-part series in the UK on BBC2 (made in cooperation with the Irish broadcaster RTE), *The Irish Empire,* explored the history of Ireland including the reasons for and consequences of emigration. The programme is described as balanced and objective. It describes how Irish emigration to Europe prior to the 18th century diminished as American demand for labour supplanted the Irish connection with Europe. There is some discussion of the strong relationship between Ireland and Europe in the late 16th and early 17th centuries, largely through the Catholic Church. Political exiles also moved to fight with French and Spanish armies against England. The narrator commented on the new form of relationship with Europe: 'Ireland's membership of the EU has been a huge influence on its emergence as a modern society.'[4]

The Dutch documentary, *Prisoners of Buñuel,* looks at a period in the history of Spain as portrayed in the Buñuel film *Tierra sin Pan.* The film portrays the poverty in a particular region of Spain, and in Spain in general, in 1932, and was originally banned by Franco. This documentary shows the extreme poverty, diseases, and lack of food and facilities, and criticises the Catholic Church, which according to the film did little to redistribute its wealth. The documentary asks whether the Buñuel film was a blessing or a curse for this part of Spain. People from the region view the film for the first time and express what it means to them and for Las Hurdas, the local town. According

---

[4]The Irish Empire, BBC/RTE, BBC2.

to some, several scenes in the film were staged and untrue. This documentary gives voice to the various opinions there are in Las Hurdas about Buñuel and his film.

Such documentaries serve as a review of history, an attempt to redress an issue with new evidence or insight, and there is some indication of the 'Europeanisation' of these histories with cooperation in production, in research, or in the representation of historical cooperation and links between Europeans.

A Shared Cultural Heritage

Another aspect of shared history in Europe includes art, heritage, music and architecture. Although generally located in, or identified with, a particular place or person, such heritage is frequently described as European. For example, a Dutch programme describes Roman art and architecture as founded on Etruscan and Greek art and declares it as the basis of further European architecture. Another German programme looks at the worrying issue of floods in Venice, in particular, and in other parts of Europe.

There are also portraits of artists, film directors, philosophers, scientists, opera singers, and writers throughout Europe, reflecting more recent 'shared' artistic and intellectual culture. Film festivals and art exhibitions are dealt with in an interesting way in *Kulturweltspiegel,* giving perspectives on controversial and strange events throughout Europe. Such reports included a portrait of the Spanish writer Javier Manas and his new novel, the suspected fake paintings at a Salvador Dalí exhibition in Germany, and the opening of a controversial exhibition by two brothers in London. A further example is the Italian late-night literature series featuring short profiles of writers such as Hesse, Mann, and Camus. The life and work of art critic and cultural commentator Robert Hughes are outlined in one BBC2 documentary describing his visits to Italy and Spain, during which he praised Barcelona for its 'beauty, eccentricity, history, cooking and utopianism.'[5] Religions and other cultures feature most prominently on Dutch television with a series *Religions of the World,* in this case dealing with the Russian Orthodox Church, that looks at issues such as religious heritage and religious freedom.

Europe in the 21st Century

Whereas our 'shared past' is reflected in the previous programmes, there is also a sense in which we have a 'shared future' in Europe. Science and technology, particularly with reference to transport, the 'information superhighway,' and genetics, are important television topics and are often viewed from a 'European' perspective. Comparisons are frequently made between the ap-

---

[5]The shock of the Hughes, BBC2.

proaches in Europe and the American or Japanese developments and debates in these areas. The BBC2 documentary, *Concorde: The Plane That Fell to Earth,* highlights the Anglo–French cooperation in developing the mass market for air travel in competition with the USA, and the programme featured both British and French participants.

Similarly, a Polish documentary, *Focus Magazine: Swifter Than Wind,* on the development of high-speed trains, contrasts the experiences in European countries, particularly France, Germany, and the UK with Japan. Reference is made to the difficulties in the area of technological development and research. The development of fast rail lines between Paris, Brussels, and London, plans for future lines to Berlin and Frankfurt, and the role for high-speed travel in integrating Europe are also discussed.

Genetic science and cloning, a new area of worry and uncertainty, was dealt with from a European perspective in several countries, largely with comparisons between the US and Europe. One *Newsnight* edition examined multinational control of genetic technology and referred to an effort by the European People's party to put an end to this area of research. A documentary broadcast on Polish television claimed that Europe has a different approach to the problems of cloning than the US, in that Europe is more likely to have a public debate on ethics than the US, hence implying a superior intellectual culture in Europe. Conversely, a Dutch report on the 'Siamese twins' debate in Britain highlighted the different cultural approaches in these two countries to the issue. A Dutch expert in medical ethics claims the ruling on the separation of the twins was very 'English,' as in the Netherlands the opinion of the parents would be taken into consideration and would be respected.

Our Strange Neighbours

Some programmes that bring us stories from other parts of Europe fall into the infotainment or entertainment genre, and many of these were stories from Britain. *Wizjer TVN* (*Viewfinder TVN*) on the Polish public channel is one example. The stories during the monitoring period were all from Britain and worthy of a British tabloid newspaper. They included a piece on a 16-year-old boy who accused his ex-parents (now he lives with another family) of feeding him chips every day, causing him to be overweight. Another concerned an English aristocrat in his large estate with a safari garden (open to tourists) and focuses on his love of art, women, and strange clothes. *Nie do wiary strefa 11* (*Unbelievable zone 11*), also on TVN, investigates different paranormal happenings and phenomena in Poland and around the world. One programme dealt with the mysterious power at a graveyard in Edinburgh. One section of the German *Europamagazin* dealt with a 'name and shame' campaign in Britain in relation to prostitutes' clients, which was considered a bizarre approach by the German commentators, comparing it to medieval pillorying.

The British programme *Eurotrash* (Channel 4) in turn takes a look at 'strange activities' in the rest of Europe. The programme is obviously European in its focus, featuring stories and people from France, Germany, Majorca, Athens, and Norway, and one edition of *Eurotrash* was introduced as 'your regular Friday flesh-fest. It's crude, it's rude, and not for the prude.' The programme regularly features breast enhancement and other nonsense and has a French celebrity TV presenter, Antoine de Cannes. On the show, a German celebrity TV presenter, a French singer, a Greek TV presenter/politician, and a Norwegian TV personality were interviewed. The guests regularly speak English, but where their voices are dubbed, the text is changed in order to make them look even more ridiculous. The programme presents an 'us versus them' attitude to the 'strange people' from other parts of Europe, with stereotyping and offensive comments about German tourists in Majorca and references to 'cheeky Greekies.' In a vaguely humorous way, it portrays the rest of Europe as a world of tacky, amusing pornographic lifestyles.

Other light-hearted programmes with a European flavour include the Dutch version of *Games Without Frontiers* (*Spel zonder Grenzen*), wherein a variety of Europeans compete in various games. Between games, a short impression is given about the cities the competing teams are from. The French *Union Libre* combines a mixture of gentle stereotyping with regular guests, usually young European journalists, discussing 'soft news' from their country and touching on topics such as European culture, European identity, or sport.

The Polish *Z plecakiem i walizką* (*With rucksack and suitcase*) on the public channel is a more serious treatment of 'European neighbours,' looking at Dutch people who like to travel in the Orient. The programme suggests that Dutch people are well travelled and also have a great ability to accept and assimilate different cultures and incorporate them into their own, and that this traditional tolerance is a perfect example of the benefits of being open to others.

Pictures of Europe

A final major area of programming concerns travel and portraits of other European countries and cities, and in general reflects positively on the cultures and places featured. Such programming generally promotes tourism, in cooperation with airlines, hotels, and tourism agencies.

Many of the programmes that provide pictures of Europe could be considered more general interest or educational. This includes the aforementioned *Landmarks of Europe,* one of two programmes featuring the Rhineland. Aimed at schoolchildren, it incorporated information on industry, pollution, history, travel, culture, and wine production. The presenters of *Landmarks of Europe* travelled from Spain to Sweden during the series and the programme was more informative than standard travel shows, with cultural and historical references. Another programme, aired on Italian television, showed the historical, cultural, and geographical aspects of the Rhine area, connecting the country with the cultural and political origins of a united Europe. Further examples were the French *Fenêtres sur . . .* and the Channel 4 *Waterways,* both featuring aspects of Ireland. In both cases, local people featured strongly and the programmes were quite informative.

The Channel 4 programme *Wild Europe* (providing a different view of 'wildness' from that of *Eurotrash*) looked at a wildlife region in central Spain with reference to agriculture and industrial development. The Dutch *Rail Away* takes a look at countries from the perspective of a train journey, in this case through Norway.

ACTORS AND PARTICIPANTS: HOW EUROPEAN ARE NATIONAL PUBLIC SPHERES?

In the programmes selected for analysis, we looked at the range of both actors and participants appearing on television in relation to Europe, and also the actors (countries or people) who were subjects of discussion in the programmes. This allowed for an impression of where and when other voices or opinions are included in debates about Europe. In the first phase of the project, regarding programmes about others in Europe, we outlined, in particular, the most frequently covered countries in a range of programmes and their relevance to particular topics. Here we try to give an overview of the approach in each country to including other Europeans in the discussion and portrayal of political and cultural issues.

Current Affairs

The study confirmed the assumption that for the French media, France and one other European country remain the broad angle of comparative treatment in dealing with European issues. Although this does not necessarily imply an 'us versus them' approach, it indicates that bilateral relations are more important than a Europe-wide perspective. All European programmes have a French host, even when the programme discusses a European issue such as the German car industry. French rather than other European nationals are the primary persons interviewed. The French 'prism' is favoured, for instance, in a programme on Finnish nursery schools, in comparison with French nursery schools. The only two actors interviewed are French (an economics professor and the French minister for social affairs).

On German television, *Presseclub* and *Plusminus* are the more EU-relevant programmes. *Presseclub* tends to focus on one issue in a studio discussion, which regularly includes foreign journalists. Covering a range of topics in short but substantial reports, *Plusminus* includes commentary from a wide range of people from other European countries in relation to economic issues including tobacco smuggling, featuring a German EU commissioner and institutional and business actors. These programmes appear to try to reflect European issues from a relatively European perspective. For more general European programming, the situation is similar, as is the case with *Europamagazin,* which has short but relatively informative reports about European issues. When these programmes focused on problematic issues such as the plight of refugees, right-wing extremism, or the smuggling of people across borders, they tried to include the opinion of all sides involved, including Chinese, Italian, and Yugoslavian citizens and officials. *Europamagazin* does seem to focus on European problem issues and generally attempts to present the issues from a wide perspective. *Spiegel TV* and *Stern TV,* national-interest magazine programmes, also presented European topics with contributions from various European actors and experts relevant to the issues including German, Russian, and Italian people.

As is the case with France, there is a very limited range of 'European voices' or participants in Italian programmes. The only programming in Italy during this time that directly dealt with political issues were the RAI broadcasts of *Euronews.* One RAI programme, *Europa Come . . . ,* presented by the Italian ambassador in Belgium, attempted to explain some of the workings of the EU. In Dutch programming such as *Europe, History of the Future* and *Correspondent in Avondland,* the actors were mainly Dutch with some French EU representatives. National presenters and commentators largely dominate the programmes with a more national focus, even when they deal with European issues.

As regards specific EU programmes on Polish television, the actors are mostly Polish, although comparative reference is made to the activities in other European countries such as France and Germany. What is notable is the lack of discussion or involvement of the other applicant countries in relation to EU policies or adoption of EU legislation. The programme *Europeans* was very much from a Polish perspective including opinions from academics, business people, and citizens, with one contribution from a German businessman. The educational series *Euroexpress,* aimed at young people, was more varied in the range of actors with several French European Parliamentary members and a Luxembourg government representative appearing. Two regular national-interest programmes dealt with agricultural issues, one a farming meeting with only Polish actors, the second looking at Swedish farming methods with mainly Swedish participation.

None of the British programming during these 2 weeks dealt directly with EU policy issues aside from some analysis on *Newsnight.* The BBC2 news analysis programme generally focuses on two or three issues per edition. One of the more important topics covered during this time was the petrol protests, featuring French and British contributions. The debate on this issue (involving haulage association representatives) moved from initial anger with the French protesters to almost admiration for their tactics. Coverage of the TUC (Trade Union Congress) conference included the debate on Europe where the Greek EU Commissioner responsible for social affairs and employment was invited to speak. Perhaps both of these examples reflect some solidarity between British unions and their counterparts on the continent.

Documentaries

Documentaries, by their nature, require participation from a range of people involved in the issues and, in the case of European issues or elements of history, such participation was generally reflected in the programmes. Two relevant documentaries in the analysis were from Dutch television, one dealing with the Kosovo War Child organisation and the other with the Cold War, both having a range of European participants. European programmes in Poland included two that were produced by foreign channels, one a Dutch production and the other made by ARTE. The ARTE programme looked at the issue of cloning and included French, British and American contributions. The Dutch documentary, *In the House of my Father,* concerned the life of a Moroccan woman living in the Netherlands. Two programmes focused on the experiences of Polish people living abroad so although the perspective in terms of locations was quite European, the actors and discussants were all Polish. Other programmes of relevance were historical documentaries such as *Regime's Shield and Sword—STASI,* which also featured German participants.

The relevant documentaries featured during this time on British television dealt with various aspects of European history and included relevant participation from other Europeans including Polish, French, Irish, and Norwegian experts, actors, and commentators.

Culture and Living

Exceptions to the French tendency to have a particularly French perspective as regards participants are travel programmes such as *Fenêtres sur . . .* featuring local people and French people living in the country of focus, and of course *Union Libre,* which has a variety of European participants.

Cultural programming in Germany focused on art, travel, and film in Spain, France, and Britain including the Cannes film festival, with a range of European participants. One interesting combination of cultural and political issues appeared on *Titel, Thesen, temperments,* where the work of two Austrian cartoonists, critical of Haider, gave an interesting perspective on the internal Austrian debate regarding his party's participation in government.

The majority of Italian programmes are cultural, with *Un Mondo A Colori* portraying the lives of different cultures in Italy. Other programmes generally feature a presenter, usually Italian, or a voice-over, and deal with issues of geographical, cultural, and historical links in Europe. In this sense the 'European' actors are really the countries under discussion. Exceptions are the literature series *42 Parallelo–Leggere Il 900,* again with one presenter, but focusing on the lives and works of famous authors.

The series *EUtopia* can be considered highly relevant to the EU as it reflects the actuality of the 'free movement of people' between EU states. The two programmes in the research period focused on British people living or working abroad and their interactions with others including Greek villagers, and a German businessman and his French vineyard employees. Cultural programming featured travel, which generally includes local people in the programmes, wildlife, and film, a particular exception being *A House in the Sun,* which had only English participants buying or selling homes in Spain.

The Dutch *EUtopia* episode coded for the research featured French and North African French actors who live in squats in London. More general European programmes often deal with specific countries and hence the people reflect the issues, as in the case of the Buñuel film, with mainly Spanish people commenting on the film. Cultural programming, biographies, or features are again dependent on the topic in question and the country or person featured. The programme *Parallel,* for example, is quite an interesting series contrasting life in Amsterdam and Istanbul with, naturally, Turkish and Dutch people appearing in the programmes.

Entertainment

Wizjer TVN (View-finder TVN) is a programme featuring unusual stories, some of which are from other European countries. The four stories coded for the project were all British and similar to tabloid news. They ranged from the boy who wanted to sue his parents for making him obese to the English eccentric with a private safari on his estate. Similarly, the *Unbelievable Zone,* which looks at paranormal phenomenon, had a British story regarding ghosts in Scotland with Scottish, English, French, and Canadians. The programme *Eurotrash* has a regular French celebrity TV presenter, Antoine de Cannes. On the show coded for the research, a German celebrity TV presenter was interviewed, also a French singer, a Greek TV presenter/politician, and a Norwegian TV personality.

CONCLUSION

At the national level, although a variety of Europe-related programming can be found, there is not yet a strong propensity to include other Europeans in the discussion of European issues. An exception is in the area of reporting on a specific issue in another country, where German television appears to feature the most representative range of participants. European debates, particularly economic and political, are therefore largely centred in the national sphere. In the case of Poland, other European 'actors' appear in these discussions but usually only by reference and as countries rather than individuals. Cultural and travel programming tends naturally to deal with people and cultures from other countries, and entertainment programming such as *Eurotrash* or *Union Libre* feature other Europeans sometimes more for their 'exotic' or entertainment value.

11

Europe in the Media: Summary and Conclusions

INTRODUCTION

Looking at the media with reference to the process of European integration implies examining why the media may play a role and what this role should or could be. For the purposes of researching media coverage, we began with the simple premise that economic and social integration between people in Europe is a reality, and that it impacts on people's lives. It affects the nature of production and distribution of goods and services, increases the variety of goods, and has led to changes in the regulation of working life. Assuming that the media should play a role in informing people of issues that affect their daily lives and in orientating people and helping them understand central aspects of integration was the basic area of interest for the project. In this sense, we could assess the extent to which the media contributes to a more informed citizenship and to a wider, rational debate on the pros and cons of policy developments. As such, media activities contribute to the national public sphere of debate and exchange concerning European policies, while also bringing about the Europeanisation of national public spheres through identifying and reporting on common trends, obstacles, and opportunities in other countries.

For many actors, the expectations of the media's role may be stronger when accompanied by a belief that European integration or cooperation is an important development and should be enhanced. Different actors or interest groups may have varying reasons for wanting the European project more positively promoted in the media. For example, European Union representatives, particularly parliamentarians, may want their activities to be more visible.

However, the understanding of integration, the interpretations of agendas for cooperation, and the complications of globalisation and diverse national cultures imply that there is no universally understood 'European project.' The premise for this work does not then assume that there is a given ideal form of European integration that is being pursued and should therefore be promoted.

The tendency for national media to present a national slant on European events has been explained and discussed. This is often most visible after an intergovernmental meeting or conference wherein a quick glance at news headlines in each country reveals the same pattern of reporting on what the leaders have achieved in the national interest. For national actors, this representation of Europe is important in the context of national politics as it helps to keep certain aspects of integration in the domain of 'intergovernmental relations' wherein the prime minister, president, or minister has gone to the table and negotiated the best deal for the nation-state. Aside from the need to clarify common ideas and agendas, coverage of Europe should move beyond such national rhetoric in order to allow for cooperative investigative journalism as a way of checking the democratic elements of governance at the European level.

Looking at the media provides the most clear picture of how European affairs are presented and debated in what are obviously the most widespread modes of engagement—national press, national news, and television. The combination of the two research projects provided several comparative snapshots of media activity in order to outline characteristics, similarities, and differences in European countries, allowing, in one sense, an assessment of the media's fulfilment of a prescribed role in informing, questioning, and providing platforms for debate. In another sense, the coverage highlighted the diversity of ideas about Europe and also underlined the difficulty of prescribing any universal media approach to European affairs.

Political Identification and European Citizenship

The exploration of the concept of European identity in chapter 1 revealed the need to consider any such identity as being complex and undoubtedly more influenced by personal experience than is the case with equivalent national or ethnic identity. At the same time, attitudes to Europe are strongly influenced by elite debates reflected in media discussions of Europe that can often reveal different 'visions of Europe' in different countries. The logic of treating separate elements in the form of political or cultural identification with Europe was due to the recognition of the complexity of impressions and ideas that 'Europe' may conjure up in the national psyche or within the individual. A political European identity seemed a useful framework in which to examine certain aspects of the media's role in the functions of information provision and debate. The obvious focus for such identification is the European Union itself as a structured political and legal entity. A European political identity where it may exist or develop cannot be separated from national political engagement. This in itself is problematic as total engagement with a European perspective can imply a disengagement from the national or regional as a prerequisite, something that many of the European Commissioners themselves cannot achieve. A consideration of a European political identity as a type of add-on element to national citizenship does, however, require some compromise of loyalties and an ability to see the world in a manner that functions beyond national perspectives.

An important element of the research in this sense involved looking at the last week of the 1999 European Parliament election campaigns. Again, it should be stressed that this was a snapshot, yet it covered the output of 31 newspapers and 16 main evening news bulletins for a week, a sample that provides a comprehensive picture of the media at work in mobilising European citizenship. Such campaigns have traditionally been carried out through a national system of party structures, campaigns, and media and, to a greater and lesser extent in each country, have been conducted on the basis of national issues often of little direct relevance to the European Parliament. However, the mobilisation of support, on the part of political actors, for European integration and EU policies has in many cases always had a basis in economics and the economic welfare of the nation-state. The benefits of membership have to be translated into a national gain in the same way that national policies must relate to the individual level (as often witnessed in attempts by political parties to focus on particular niche groups of society, for example pensioners, during election campaigns). The way out of this dilemma lies in the idea of 'cosmopolitanism' as referred to in chapter 1, or the development of 'postmaterialist' values. In essence, some national acceptance of a level of societal success and prosperity in comparison to others allows politics to partly move beyond the concerns of the nation. Unfortunately, despite the fact that a country or region may have a successful position in the world economic scale, this does not imply that all sectors of society benefit. It would be difficult, therefore, to imagine media outlets as vehicles for encouraging the population to begin to consider the welfare of others in Europe when they may be faced with their own social and economic problems.

On an objective level the media, in the context of an election campaign, should fulfil some basic criteria: to provide information on policy issues and political agendas that relate directly to the activities of the European Union; to examine the democratic process at work; and to provide a space for discussion and debate. As far as the provision of information is concerned, the research revealed stark differences both in the quantity of coverage and in the extent to which it was 'Europeanised' (as opposed to Europe viewed through a national lens). A role in assisting a development of European citizenship would include some explanation of the political process in Europe, that is, the role of the Parliament in decision-making. The impact of the resignation of the

Commission on public perceptions is uncertain. In one sense, it again raised the issue of corruption at the European level. On the other hand the Parliament's role in this issue received significant media attention and may have increased the level of public awareness as to the interaction between the institutions.

The extent to which the media discussed 'European political culture' or the nature of democracy at the EU level was relatively limited, occurring mainly in the Swedish and UK media. Although this implies a somewhat critical examination of European politics, none of the coverage was particularly negative. In the Swedish context, EU democracy and accountability was compared with the Swedish system. Exceptions to this more neutral approach in the UK involved a couple of articles in both *The Sun* and *The Times,* which considered the election process to be a waste of time. As part of an overall news agenda, the election campaigns possibly did not allow space for discussions of the intricacies of the divisions of sovereignty between national governments and EU institutions. This did occur, however, in special supplements that attempted to provide information about the Parliament and policy issues, more particularly in the Spanish and German press but also in *Le Monde,* the *Irish Times,* and the *Herald.*

From the analysis of nonnews television programmes, it was apparent that, in general, discussion and presentation of EU affairs on television is quite limited. Some educational programmes try to outline the workings of the EU but are, in general, not presented in a very appealing format. Perhaps this type of 'civic educational' approach is not the responsibility of the media, as programming of this kind is not generally produced with reference to national or regional governance. However, these programmes could be seen as useful resources for schools.

With regard to more concrete aspects of citizenship in Europe, the presentation of EU policy issues in the context of the election campaigns was examined. Here the findings varied between countries and generally were rather more an issue for press coverage. Internal political rivalries or items of specific national interest within the context of European politics continue to dominate the presentation of the European elections. Here again, the issue of European politics requiring national relevance for public support, for reader interest, or for editorial interest was highlighted. Interviews with journalists confirmed the need for a 'national hook' on which to hang European stories. However, the extent to which certain national media spheres lacked a wide-ranging coverage of European issues remains a concern. One could expect the development of some type of parallel coverage dealing with the nationally specific areas of concern such as EMU in the UK, and also separately presenting a European framework of common debates and problems. This did occur in the media of several countries, namely in the French, Swedish, and Spanish press, where a variety of EU policies were addressed. Instances of the EU becoming front-page news in the period of the final week of election campaigning only really occurred in France and Germany, and to a lesser extent in Italy.

Outside of election campaign periods, the research looked at the extent to which EU politics constitutes an important part of national news agendas and television schedules. In a quantitative sense, most news appears in the German press, as is the case with European news in general, reflecting a strongly Europeanised political and cultural Germany. Alternatively, the extent to which EU membership is still a contentious issue in the UK and Sweden is reflected in the concentration of EU news in the categorisation of EU news as a special or separate issue, while also a highly political one. The lack of media attention paid to the European Union (outside of the economic press) in Italy is a recurring problem and will be discussed later.

As another indicator of the media activity in the development of European citizenship, we can say that television programmes specifically about the European Union, as observed in the second study, are most frequent on Polish television (both public service and commercial channels). Poland was the only non-EU country in the study, and the extensive coverage is undoubtedly due to preparations for membership. Although no other applicant country was observed, a similar pattern for applicant states or new members is suggested in interviews with journalists. Hence the need to adapt legislative and policy areas for membership, as well as discussing the pros and cons of membership, lead to greater attention to European politics. It would be interesting to compare media activity in this area between the various applicant countries. In the case of Poland, there was very little coverage or programming that looked at the activities of, or debates in, the other applicant countries. The Dutch channels in the study also provided some 'civic education' programmes, particularly for young people, indicating a more developed European current affairs genre, with one or two interesting formats. Outside of specific EU programmes, national current affairs programmes regularly feature European and EU affairs in all of the countries in the second study except on Italian television.

Any role that the media may play in enhancing citizenship or political identification at the European level is therefore dependent on several factors. News coverage of the EU is dependent both on news agendas and events and on the relevance of policy issues for national interests. In the case of the elections, the opportunity for a civic educational role may not be so prominent, but many media outlets did try to deal with policies and the political process. Aside from this, the elections tend to bring to the fore the central issues of debate for each country, some of which are common, and many more of which indicate the differing perceptions of Europe or European integration between states.

Some of the suspected pulls between the regional and national level, in the context of European integration, were not really borne out by the research. However, one suggested reason for the lack of attention paid to European affairs in the Italian media was the regional nature of Italy. One politician interviewed, commenting on European identity, summarised the problem: 'We're still seeking an *Italian identity*.' An overall impression of a slightly more pro-European stance in the Scottish paper in the study vis à vis the single currency, coupled with more attention to particular policy areas (i.e., common foreign policy), indicated a somewhat different political outlook. This was precipitated, perhaps, by devolution, and also an element of comparison with Ireland as an (economically) successful model of self-assertion within Europe. Most of the regional papers, although serving a particular community, were already considered, or were in some ways striving to be, a national outlet within their own landscape; hence, themes and agendas tended to replicate those of the national outlets.

Connecting With a Wider Europe

Although the European Union provides the central focus of European integration, the research was also designed to examine news about Europe in a wider sense. Much of the media focus on Europe is centred on problematic issues and European, particularly European political, themes are generally framed in terms of conflict or cooperation. Within the timeframe of the news project, the Kosovo crisis was the dominant news story and hence the central issue of European conflict. Coverage of Kosovo and where this linked with common security issues, or the 'future construction' of Eastern Europe, revealed quite wide disparities in the debates. In Sweden and Ireland, the discussions were generally influenced by the traditions of neutrality. For other countries, the coverage was quite different and tended to focus more on the role being played by national armies and governments in a European context, for example the Italian peace proposals, or Spanish–Russian discussions.

In Britain, the media tended to focus on the role of Britain in the crisis, with little reflection on cooperation at the European level. The German media dealt with the internal debates over military intervention in Kosovo, and also featured discussions on the necessity for a common security policy. A European perspective appeared in the French media, with more reflection on the implications for Europe and more illustration of cooperation between Europeans. Foreign policy and security questions have always been a central aspect of nation-state sovereignty, and hence it is not surprising that these debates varied in the different countries. In reference to the outlook on international cooperation in security issues, the British media reflected the relationship with NATO and the US, whereas the Dutch, German, and Italian media made distinctions between a European role in the crisis and an American-led NATO intervention. A year later, in the aftermath of the Kosovo crisis and the NATO war with Serbia, several television programmes observed in the second study looked at on-going projects in Kosovo involving cooperative action by European countries or transnational NGOs such as War Child. All the programmes reflected a type of 'European cooperation' on the issue of rebuilding the Balkans.

Topics of common concern in Europe were reflected in documentaries and current affairs programmes, which allowed more time for reflection than news coverage. One major 'European' issue is that of immigration, and more particularly illegal immigration. Connected to this are the problems of racism and xenophobia and the rise of right-wing extremism. On one level, an interesting range of programmes, particularly on Dutch and Italian television, dealt with real-life experiences of immigrants in different parts of Europe. In fact, this is the only area of Italian television programming that reflects any of the issues central to European integration. Immigration was generally presented in a problematic way on German current affairs programmes dealing with racism and 'people smuggling.' What was interesting about the German approach was the tendency to take a European perspective that included reports from other countries with the programmes not requiring a 'national angle' in order to be of interest to the viewer.

Further problematic issues, which arose in the context of the second study, included the petrol crisis, crime, and various transborder illegal activities. The extent to which common solutions were discussed, or any cooperative 'European' solution found, was rather limited. This propensity to ignore the necessity to work together in solving particular problems has been played out more recently with the 'European' BSE crisis. Ironically, the initial crisis in the UK in 1996 was viewed as a 'British' or more specifically an 'English' problem, and it would appear that a lack of rational debate about 'European' food production at the time led to the problem not being properly addressed until 5 years later.

Aside from issues of conflict and cooperation, television programmes dealing with Europe also revealed further themes, which connect the viewer with a wider Europe. In a sense these could be considered 'future themes' as they referred to science and new technology. Presentations of technology development in the areas of transport and communications illustrate the way in which horizons have been broadened beyond the nation-state. Not only do these developments allow a greater flow of information, ideas, and people between countries, they also are being considered in media representation as obvious 'European' themes in terms of policy and cooperation. Comparisons are frequently made with US or with Japanese technological developments. Such comparisons also occur in relation to scientific questions. Science, particularly genetic science with reference to humans and to food production, emerges as an issue of uncertainty and fear that requires a common approach in term of regulation and policy. Although 'future themes' provided a European perspective in programmes, 'past themes' also emerged as frequently having such a perspective. Historical documentaries in Britain, Poland, and the Netherlands were frequently coproduced, hence combining resources and historical data, and often attempted to look at historical issues from a European rather than a national angle. The aspect of cooperation between countries or media outlets is dealt with later as a key development in European news and European programming.

A CULTURAL EUROPE

The extent to which the media provides cultural information about Europe was a central part of the research. Cultural Europe was considered from the perspective of news or information about cultures and people outside the national borders in both news and television programmes. Some relevant programmes also dealt with foreigners or other cultures living within the national borders.

In looking at both the coverage of other people and the information about other people in cultural, sport, and art/literature news areas, we hoped to gain some insight into what role the media has or could have in the promotion of cultural understanding. This was most comprehensive in the case of the German press.

Sporting events are the most widely covered 'European phenomenon.' Travel, culture, literature, and music are also important but may constitute a 'comodification' of other cultures rather than any educational function. Spain, Italy, France, and Greece feature most prominently in articles about culture and travel. However, in the Spanish, French, and Italian media, little attention is paid to these elements of culture in other European countries. Coverage of other people in Europe is naturally also a function of geographical proximity, common languages, and historical links. For Ireland and the Irish media, the most important European neighbour is Britain. For all countries, the UK, Germany, and France are most frequently referred to in the context of EU affairs. The German media pays close attention to its eastern neighbours, whereas the Swedish media covers the other Scandinavian countries.

While the UK retains an 'isolated' approach to European issues as reflected by the media, including the low attention paid to policies and to other Europeans, the UK is for all other countries the most frequently discussed member of the EU. In the time periods of the project, there was little discussion on immigration or the movement of people in Europe, with the focus being on the Kosovo refugees. This follows a pattern revealed in other studies of the media only focusing on the 'other' in times of war and crisis, or when linked to specific events, whether political or cultural, and there is little evidence that news media play a role in educating the public in a more general sense about the lives of 'others' in Europe. Many politicians interviewed felt that the news media, in particular, should not be obligated to provide extra information on other cultures outside of particular events, although background explanatory information in times of crisis or conflict was considered important. In terms of cultural news about people and events around Europe, the German press provides information on a wide range of European countries and cultures in the context of a wide range of themes.

Television programming outside of the news had more to offer in this area in the countries monitored. This is most likely due to both the differences between print and electronic media and the differences between the news genre and more general programming. Although the printed media can provide more detail and information on European political or cultural issues, television by its nature can deal with these themes in a more attractive or emotive manner. Relevant programmes ranged from straightforward arts and cultural programmes, to travel programmes, to programmes focusing on the lives and experiences of different cultures in Europe. In particular, many programmes outlined the experiences of people who had moved or emigrated around Europe, thus providing a more practical 'real' picture of European integration. As mentioned previously, this was the only area of programming identified in Italy (e.g., *Un Mondo a Colori*) that in any way reflected the central themes of the research, although the focus was generally more on Mediterranean cultures. Dutch and Italian programmes tended mainly to reflect the lives of different cultures living in these countries.

On British television, the cultural aspect of Europe was presented in a more exotic way, that is, 'Europe as a playground' in terms of travel, food, art, and language. The German cultural programming was also much more focused on art, film, and theatre than on the lives or experiences of immigrants (aside from policy problems in the context of current affairs programming).

THE DEVELOPMENT OF A EUROPEAN PUBLIC SPHERE

To what extent can we say that some type of common European space for discussion and debate is developing through the media? The description of the European audiovisual landscape establishes clearly the limitations of a common space for audience reception of news, information, and entertainment relevant to Europe. The central way in which we tried to investigate the approach of the national media in filling this gap involved looking at news agendas and the quantity of news about Europe, which became an assessment of the extent to which national public spheres have become 'Europeanised.' This revealed both qualitative and quantitative differences between countries in the way that European political and cultural affairs are reported. The most Europeanised areas of reporting are business, economics, and of course the single currency, although the latter is far more developed within the 'Euro zone.' Economics transcends borders more easily than politics, whereas the politicisation of certain economic policies ensures that they remain within a national debate.

Another way of considering this is through the impact of 'European' news on the national news agenda, that is, how 'Europeanised' the national news agenda has become. This provided a picture of how the integration process is reflected in the news media of different countries. When asked about the task of covering Europe and making it part of the national agenda, interviewees agreed that European political issues are complex and it is often difficult for correspondents to convince editors at home that stories are important. With the general 'commercialisation' of media, news stories need 'a national angle,' a 'personality story,' or an element of scandal or panic (e.g., BSE, dioxin, fraud, commission resignation, and war). As is often the case with national affairs, European political and cultural news is seldom priority on television news unless it meets those criteria.

In the press, European news appears across different sections. The EU was frequently presented in the Dutch press as being 'world/foreign' news, whereas in the French, Italian, and Irish press it was considered under 'home news.' Sharing and syndication of news is less common than would be expected, but the same news agencies are frequently used by European media outlets and the development of Internet links between outlets in dealing with specific issues offers opportunities for a wider view of Europe.

Despite some of the drawbacks in reporting European news, there is a slowly developing space in each national sphere, more developed in some countries than in others, where information about and discussions of political and cultural affairs are increasingly available. The perceived preferences and interests of the consumer also shape cultural news. Essentially, the news media now operate in a competitive system dictated by circulation and scoops. The problems that the journalists face in getting their stories printed concern both access to sources (EU and other political actors), and in a more institutional sense, to publication when competing within the outlet with other stories. There remains a necessity to link events and policies with issues of national interest both for the readers and for the editors. It is obviously not possible for news outlets to inform the public of all political and cultural events in Europe. What constitutes the 'news value' of Europe is therefore the link with the nationality, the proximity, and the 'sensationalism' of the event. This implies that in different countries, different criteria may determine what policies or events are dealt with.

As far as EU politics is concerned, political actors strongly influence the agenda, as was apparent in the coverage of the European Parliament elections. One exception to this was the difficulty for the main political actors (i.e., the UK government) to control the agenda concerning the EMU debate in Britain, wherein business interests and even media owners have had a major influence on the debate.

In the area of television programming, the extent to which a wide range of opinions and representations are given voice on television with reference to

European political and cultural affairs is, across the board, rather limited. One aspect of a developing Europeanisation of debates would include political, civil, business, and NGO representatives from other countries in programmes, allowing a wider perspective on policies and problems. When programmes contain reports from, or focus specifically on, other countries, there was naturally a wider range of nonnational participants, as was the case with a good deal of German current affairs magazine programmes and Polish, Dutch, or British documentaries.

In many cases, however, most 'other' actors are other countries treated in a generalised way and referred to indirectly. In terms of politics, this occurs usually with reference to the national governments or the particular industrial or policy sector, for example, 'Swedish agriculture' or the 'Spanish education system.' Prime examples were the comparative aspects of programming in Poland, particularly to do with agriculture, and also on French television in programmes looking at education or transport. Although there may be a variety of Europe-related programming, there is no strong tendency to include other Europeans in the discussion of European issues.

The approach of media outlets to European affairs was addressed in both research projects and also in interviews with professionals. In conversations with journalists, the familiar obstacles in covering Europe were cited, including the complexity of policy making, the access to information on decision making, and the influence of national interests including the 'spin' on events by national representatives. Editorial staff and management generally claimed that resources had not increased particularly over the years with regard to European reporting. Some exceptions were noted in the Swedish press wherein staff and resources were increased after EU membership. As was the case with the European elections, efforts are made to increase information and provide supplements and guides during important events. EMU has been an important aspect in the development of transnational journalism, but by and large journalists, with some exceptions in Dutch and Swedish outlets, claim it has not affected the overall approach to European affairs. What is discernible is an increasingly common agenda when dealing with EMU news, particularly within the EMU countries, that is aided by Internet links and sharing of stories. The extent to which the introduction of a single currency has affected the activities of the media in covering Europe is more apparent from the perspective of the news agencies already operating from a European perspective.

Activities in the area of television production, particularly nonnews programming about Europe, revealed quite different approaches in the various countries in the study. Poland, as already observed, has a great deal of television programming that deals with Europe on both public and private channels. The activities of the Polish commercial TVN can be contrasted with the Italian case, where the commercial channels have no programming that deals with Europe in either the political or cultural sense. In the UK, very little relevant programming was identified on commercial channels. The Dutch public service NOS channels were also the main source of European programming. In contrast to the large amount of press coverage of Europe in Germany, there was much less focus on the television channels, although both private and public dealt with European issues in current affairs or cultural programming. Wider European affairs feature on German television and undoubtedly the geographical reality of Germany being at the centre of a much greater Europe influences this wider interest.

In the French case, it is considered that perhaps because of the 'difficulty' of examining European themes and topics, they are tackled in either an educational, informative manner or in light entertainment, often chat-show-type programmes. New approaches and formats on French television were observed in terms of both length of programme and style of presentation. Attempts to make the discussion more positive, to simplify information, and to make use of popular television figures were noted. One could conclude that Europe and the EU (i.e., the full extent of political, economic, and social integration), is largely taken for granted by the media in the member states, yet is much more important for potential member states like Poland.

Looking at programme formats, we see that innovative forms of addressing and presenting European topics, which might reach younger audiences, are also very rare, although the Dutch *Correspondent in Avondland* is a good example of an interesting format in terms of content, music, editing, and presentation. This programme also provided one of the few examples of a constructive investigation into the nature of democracy and the political process at the EU level. It is understandable that programme makers apparently find it difficult to develop programme formats that adequately cover the complex theme of Europe. The interesting range of documentaries observed, some broadcast during prime time, indicate a well-developed tradition in this area of programme making, at least in Britain, the Netherlands, and Poland.

A major relevant problem was the scheduling of the programmes. The majority of programmes focusing specifically on Europe or the European Union tend to be broadcast in the afternoon and early evening. This is also the time of day where 'Europe' is most likely to feature in programme titles. The exceptions to this are the late-night UK programmes where the prefix *Eu* is played with in a variety of ways, in most cases having little to do with the EU. In all the countries, public service channels broadcast most of the programmes that were identified as relevant to Europe, more particularly in the case of programmes dealing with the European Union.

The scheduling patterns in each country were also quite similar, with the overall message being that outside of relevant news, Europe is not a subject that is dealt with during prime time. Where there is prime time representation, Europe is, in the cases of the Netherlands and the United Kingdom, viewed in documentaries both historical and cultural and viewed occasionally in France and Germany with reference to political issues in national current affairs programmes. The only programme that emerged as being quite popular (with an audience of five million) is the Saturday evening prime time talk show *Union Libre* on France 2. The majority of programmes with a good deal of European content or European titles are broadcast during the afternoon or early evenings in all of the countries. Polish television in particular focuses its scheduling at this time and also at lunchtime. A strong emphasis on agricultural affairs may account for this as rural life more easily accommodates lunchtime viewing. Many other programmes, often cultural, particularly in Italy and the UK, were broadcast late at night or early in the morning, with British television offering an alternative late-night perspective on Europe in the form of *Eurotrash, Eurotica,* and *Euroballs.*

Popular television, particularly prime time, has not yet given the theme of Europe or European integration the attention that it deserves. Useful information is frequently made available, but usually on the fringes of the programme schedules. The lack of attention paid to Europe in a cultural or political sense during prime broadcast hours is perhaps easily explained. Broadcasters competing for viewers perhaps legitimately feel that substantive programmes dealing with European politics are not of interest to the general public and in such a competitive age would only imply a decrease in audience figures.

In this sense European issues perhaps constitute an area of broadcasting that can be sought out by people who have a particular interest, rather than an area that is considered necessary for popular viewing. This implies a type of 'vicious circle' in the scheduling of Europe-related programmes as a lack of coverage inhibits interest, while a lack of interest makes it difficult for broadcasters to justify a more popular viewing time. Of course, this problem applies to current affairs and political information in general.

In some cases, more serious efforts were made to present a multifaceted picture of the complex European reality and the way Europeans live together (e.g., *EUtopia*) with reference to issues of integration. On the other hand, a number of programmes used stereotyping (often ironic) of European countries and people (e.g., *Eurotrash,* Channel 4) and others, such as travel programmes, presented clichés about the lives and cultures of others. The objective of increasing understanding cannot really require that we censor all aspects of humour used in the representation of others in Europe. In one sense, the use of stereotypes is part of the communication process between different cultures allowing for a 'way in' based on prior assumptions. Indeed, in the *EUtopia* series, many of the participants tended to 'play up' or conform to their own national stereotypes. This was, however, at least one series of programmes that may have fitted into a more popular viewing time. The *EUtopia* series falls into what has in the past been a very popular genre on British television, that of the 'fly-on-the-wall' documentary wherein the focus on ordinary people going about their daily work proved highly interesting to audiences. Perhaps the broadcasters could have been more adventurous in the scheduling of this interesting series.

Differing 'Ideas of Europe'

One of the key reasons why the developments previously outlined are uneven is the lack of an homogeneous idea about what 'Europe' is, what 'European integration' involves, and, essentially in many countries, a continued 'national relationship' with Europe too frequently based on issues of cost and benefit. On the whole it must be concluded that a European element permeates across a great deal of German news, perhaps implying a stronger 'Europeanisation' of German political and cultural life, at least as it is reflected in the quality press outlets. News outlets in Spain and Ireland reflect the importance of European political and economic issues but with a strong continuing influence of domestic politics, and the Swedish media tend to put forward questions about EU democracy. Italian television programmes and Italian news largely ignore Europe, particularly the political Europe. Cultural questions are important and some attempt is made to reflect the growing multiculturalism of Italian society. In the Netherlands, this multiculturalism in Europe, as experienced in Dutch society, is strongly reflected in television programmes. In Poland the media promotes a positive, important idea of Europe while allowing room for debate and analysis. In programmes that examine the development of the economy and the infrastructure, the focus is always on the activities of the large member states and little reference is given to the preparations of the other applicant countries.

Overall, the pictures or images of Europe as presented on television are still strongly influenced by national issues and debates, and different ideas about what Europe represents have emerged in the examination of programmes. It is logical that different nationalities have different identifications with Europe due to historical or current political trends. Although these differences in some ways obstruct the development of such a sphere, some aspects of integration could be more homogenised precisely through common discussion. The diversity of representations are valid and interesting, but problems arise when a single dominant idea of Europe emerges, for example in elements of the British press where the overall 'idea' of European integration is not simply ignored but often demonised. Perceived public rejection of Europe based on limited debate allows certain media to reinforce negative attitudes with further negative coverage.

Any examination of broadcasting practice, particularly the provision of political information or the facilitation of debate, must be placed in the context of an overall changing media landscape. This attempt to examine 'national spheres' of debate and information about Europe is rooted in a particular time with the advent of digital television and uncertainties as to the future of public service television, implying that such spaces may not, in terms of audience figures and common agendas, be so easy to define. Alongside this, competitive forces of the global media market put pressure on public service aspects of broadcasting, as the genre of entertainment proves to be far more lucrative than that of information. Comparing the output of public with private broadcasters, it is apparent that the public service channels play a greater role. However, it was observed that the news programmes of the commercial channels during the last week of the EP election campaigns performed as well as those on public service channels. Similarly, the exceptional circumstances in Poland perhaps underline the importance of European issues wherein a new commercial channel, which is gradually increasing audience share, considers such programming an essential part of the schedule.

The case of news media coverage of European affairs is just one aspect of journalism that is subject to external pressures. An influencing force on what is described as a 'dumbing down' of political journalism has been the on-going development of 'image promotion' and message control in politics. Political life has in some sense been required to enter the realm of entertainment in order to engage public interest. At the national level, politicians still command an audience, or a public—one that their equivalents at the European level do not appear to have. Part of this game also includes the frequent unwillingness of national politicians to admit to the existence of a European project or acknowledge the actual amount of power that the nation-states have ceded to the European level. Against the background of these developments, which influence any 'public sphere' development, it is difficult to prescribe what the media as actors in this sphere should or should not do. A revival of interest in political issues, more frequently witnessed in the globalisation of certain issues such as the environment and the opposition to the globalisation of capitalism, may also require some basis in civic education.

The activities in the area of the print media illustrate where efforts are made to add to news coverage of events and topical issues. Internet links and additional guides during election times could be extended to, for example, intergovernmental meetings. With common issues, the tendency to report on media coverage in the news outlets of other countries is also increasing. This has been most notable in the coverage of EMU, as a common area of interest, and also in relation to problematic issues such as BSE, but could be extended into other policy areas.

In addition to the range of television programming available in these six countries, some type of European (in terms of both themes and participants) current affairs programme would be useful to present other perspectives on the problems or opportunities cooperation in Europe may bring. Such programming should not be 'pro-European' in the sense of promoting an agenda of integration but rather provide some clarity and honesty about the process.

Further cooperation between broadcasters in the production of innovative programmes should be encouraged. This and similar programming could perhaps appeal to some sort of empathetic identification with other people in Europe. Of course, the end result—that is, the programmes—will need to be promoted, and aired at a more popular viewing time. Such developments would not necessarily homogenise any view or vision of Europe, which would be a loss, but may help to enhance an understanding of our need to cooperate, and enhance the prospect of developing a proper accountable democracy at the European level.

Appendix I

Outlets Monitored for the News Study: Audience Figures, Circulation and Market Share[1] (%) Indicated Where Known

	Public Service	Commercial TV	Quality Press	Quality Press	Quality Press	Regional Press	Tabloid
France Circulation/ audience share	**France 2** News 9-10% ARTE[2] News	TF1 News 15%	**Le Figaro** 360,441	**Le Monde** 385,254	**Libération** 169,814	**Ouest France** 757,841	
Germany Population reach/ Programme share	ARD Tagesschau 9.5 m (35%)	RTL Aktuell 4.23m (20.6%)	**Frankfurter Allgemeine Zeitung** 1.3%	**Süddeutsche Zeitung** 1.8%		**Westdeutsche Allgemeine Zeitung** 4.6%	**Bild-Zeitung** 4.4m copies 17.9% reach
Ireland Circulation/ Channel share	RTE 9 o'clock 44%	TV3 News 6%	**Irish Independent** 165,657 **Sun Independent** 315,599	**Irish Times** 112,623	**Sunday Tribune** 84,566 **Sunday Business Post** 49,621	**The Cork Examiner** 60,578	**The Star** 87,443
Italy Readership/ Programme share	RAI UNO TG1 34%	Canale 5 TG5 25%	**Il Sole-24 Ore** 1,551,000	**Corriere della Sera** 3,159,000	**La Repubblica** 3,086,000		
The Netherlands Circulation/ programme share	NOS Newscast 32.1%	RTL 4 Newscast 20.8%	**NRC Handelsblad** 266,254	**De Volksrant** 347,055	**De Telegraaf** 777,010	**De Gelderlander** 179,505	
Spain Circulation/ Channel share	TVE-1 Telediario 24.9%	Antennae Noticias (23.4%)	**ABC**	**El País** 440,628	**El Mundo** 284,519	**Diarro de Navarra** 63,000	
Sweden Circulation/ Channel share	TV2 Rapport 47%	TV4 Nyheterna 48%	**Dagens Nyheter** 350,000	**Aftonbladet** 400,000	**Expressen** 340,000		
United Kingdom Circulation/ market share/ viewers	BBC 9 o' Clock News 5m viewers	ITV Evening News 5m viewers	**The Times** 737,000 (4.7%) **The Sun Times** 139,800 (1.4%)	**The Guardian** 398,000 (2.5%) **The Observer** 400,000 (.4%)		**The Herald** (Scotland) 100,938	**The Sun** 3,739,000 (23.6%)

[1] Based on figures for 1999 supplied by national partners, and/or web-sites.

[2] 'ARTE's average share of the market rose from 3% (France) and 0.5% (Germany) in the first half of 1997, to 3.5% and 0.7% respectively between July 1997 and mid-June 1998.' Source: http://www.arte.fr/ (Figures for overall channel viewing only.)

Appendix II

Full List of Television Programmes From Phase Two

France	Public Channels	Private Channel

September	France 2
	• *Union Libre* (2 editions)
	• *Mots Croisés / crosswords*
	• *Télématin. Press Review*
	  (2 editions)
	France 3
	• France Europe Express
	Le Cinquième
	• *Correspondance pour l'Europe /*
	  Correspondence for Europe
	• *Eco et compagnie–Europe /*
	  Eco and company–Europe
	• *Fenêtres sur . . . / Windows to*
		TF1
		• *L'Euro en poche / Euro in the*
		  pocket
		• *Sept à huit / Seven to eight*
		• *A vrai dire / To tell the truth*
		  (2 editions)
		• *Les rendez-vous de l'entreprise /*
		  Business agenda
		• *Célébrités*

June	France 2
	• *Envoyé Spécial / Special Reporter*
	  (2 editions)
	• *Argent public / Public funds,*
	  Envoyé spécial / special reporter
	La Cinquième
	• *Correspondance pour l'Europe /*
	  Correspondence for Europe
		• *Les rendez-vous de l'entreprise /*
		  Business agenda

Germany	Public Channels	Private Channel
September	ARD • *Europamagazin (2)* • Presseclub (2) • Weltreisen: Mein Paris • Titel, Thesen, temperments: • Plusminus (2) • Kulturweltspiegel • *Plusminus* • *Mein Neues Leben*	RTL • *Spiegel TV* • *Future Trend* • *Stern TV* • *10 Vor 11 (10 to 11)* *Kulturmagazin*

Italy	Public Channels	Private Channel

September	RAI Uno
	• *La Guerra Civille Spagnola* (2)
	RAI 2
	• *Europa Come . . . / Europe as . . .*
	• *Un Mondo A Colori / A coloured*
	  world (5)
	RAI 3
	• *Geomagazin (4)*
	• *42 Parallelo–Leggere Il 900 /*
	  42nd Parallel–Reading 900 (6)
	• *Euronews* (shown on RAI Uno,
	  12 editions)
		RETE 4
		• *Mappamondo / Globe* (3)

United Kingdom	Public Channels	Private Channel
September	BBC2	Channel 4
	• *The shock of the Hughes*	• *Waterways*
	• *Edinburgh Review*	• *Wild Europe*
	• *Secret Agent*	• *Eurotrash*
	• *Newsnight* (5 editions)	• *Concorde: The plane that fell to*
	• *Irish Empire*	*earth*
	• *TUC (Trade Union Congress)*	• *A Place in the Sun*
	conference programmes	
	• *Home Ground*	
	BBC1	
	• *Summer Holiday*	
	• *Blue Peter*	
June	BBC2	
	• *Eutopia* (2)	

Poland	Public Channels	Private Channel
September	TVP1	TVN
	• *Spotkanie rolników "Farmer's*	• *Automaniak (Automaniac)*
	meeting"	• *Nie do wiary (strefa 11) /*
	• *12.20 to the Union* (2)	*Unbelievable (zone 11)*
	• *Tarcza i miecz reżimu–STASI*	• *Wizjer View-Wnder* (4)
	Regime's shield and sword–	• *Fakty, ludzie, pieniądze (Facts,*
	STASI	*people, money)*
	• *Z plecakiem i walizką: With ruck-*	• *Kropka nad I (Point over i–no*
	sack and suitcase	*room for doubt)*
	• *Focus Magazine: "Swifter than*	• *Rozmowy w toku (Talks go on)*
	wind"	
	• *Agriculture on the World:*	
	Swedish Granary	
	• *Geezers 2000: Clochards from*	
	Poland	
	• *Exceptional Revision*	
	• *"Klonowanie skok w nieznane"*	
	Cloning–jump into unknown	
	• *Euroexpress*	
	• *Controversial documentary: "In*	
	the house of my father"	
	TVP2	
	• Europeans	

The Netherlands	*Public Channels (only)*

September NED 1
- *De Gevangenen van Buñuel / Prisoners of Buñuel*
- *Hoogtepunten van de Europese Kunst / Milestones in European Art*
- *Kruispunt / Crosspoint*
- *Ontbijt-TV / Breakfast Television*

TV2
- *Spel zonder Grenzen / Game Without Frontiers*
- *Correspondent in Avondland*

NED 2
- *Vrij zijn: Marco Borsato bezoekt Kosovo / Freedom: Marco Borsato visits Kosovo*
- *Rail Away*
- *Koude Oorlog: Kameraden 1917–1945 / Cold War: Mates 1917–1945*
- *2 Vandaag / 2 Today*

NED 3
- *Wereldgodsdiensten / Religions of the World*
- *Europa, de geschiedenis van de toekomst / Europe, History of the Future*
- *Kunst omdat het moet / Art because it is a must*
- *De leugen regeert / The lie rules*
- *Le mystère Anquetil / The mystery about Anquetil*
- *Een Engelse tragedie: Nick Drake / A skin too few: the days of Nick Drake 1948–1978*
- *Eutopia*
- *Noorderlicht / Northern Lights*
- *Parallel*
- *NOVA*

References

Anderson, B. (1983). *Imagined communities.* London: Verso.

Anderson, P. J., & Weymouth, A. (1999). *Insulting the Public? The British Press and the European Union.* UK: Longman.

Barker, C. (1999). *Television, globalization and cultural identities.* UK: Open University Press.

Bauböck, R. (1997). Citizenship and national identities in the European Union. Retrieved from *Working Papers Online,* Harvard Law School: http://www.law.harvard.edu/Programs/JeanMonnet/papers/97/97-04_.html

Blair, T. (1998, December 14). The papers miss the real story. Retrieved from *The Times* online: http://www.times.co.uk

Blumler, J. (Ed.). (1983). *Communicating to voters: Television in the first European parliamentary elections.* London: Sage.

Bogdanor, V. (1989). Direct elections, representative democracy and European integration. *Electoral Studies, 8*(3), 205–216.

Boxhoorn, B. (1996). European identity and the process of European unification: Compatible notions? In M. Wintle (Ed.), *Culture and identity in Europe* (pp. 133–145). UK: Ashgate.

Buonanno, M. (Ed.). (2000). *Continuity and change: Television Fiction in Europe* [Eurofiction third report]. UK: University of Luton Press.

Burley, A. M., & Mattli, W. (1993). Europe before the Court: A political theory of legal integration. *International Organisation, Winter,* 41–76.

Collins, R. (1994). *Broadcasting and audio-visual policy in the European single market.* London: Libbey.

Collins, R. (1998). *From Satellite to single market: New communication technology and European public service television.* London: Routledge.

Cozens, C. (2001, March 20). Brits come out top in TV watching league. Retrieved from *The Guardian* online: http://media.guardian.co.uk/newmedia/story/0,7496,459436,00.html

David Graham and Associates. (1999). *Building a global market: British television in overseas markets.* UK: DGA/Department of Media, Culture and Sport.

Davidson, F. M. (1997). Integration and disintegration; A political geography of the European Union. *Journal of Geography, 96*(2), 69–75.

de Búrca, G. (1999). *Re-appraising Subsidiarity's significance after Amsterdam.* Retrieved from Harvard Law School Jean Monnet Working Papers No.7/99, online: http://www.jeanmonnetprogram.org/papers99.html

189

de Mol, J. (2001). *The worldview address.* Guardian Edinburgh International Television Festival, 2001. Retrieved from: http://www.geitf.co.uk/speeches/worldview.php

Del Aguila, R., & Vallespín, F. (1996). Civic education and cosmopolitanism. In J. Timmer & R. Veldhuis (Eds.), *Political education towards a European Democracy, Maastricht, 1995* (conference proceedings; pp. 95–103). The Netherlands: Instituut voor Publiek en Politiek/ Bundeszentrale für politische Bildung.

Delanty, G. (1995). *Inventing Europe: Idea, identity, reality.* London: Macmillan.

Delfem, M., & Pampel, F. C. (1996, September). The myth of postnational identity: Popular support for European unification. *Social Forces, 75*(1), 119–143.

Eriksen, E. O., & Fossum, J. E. (2000). *Democracy in the European Union: Integration through deliberation?* London: Routledge.

European Audiovisual Observatory. (2000a). *Economy of European TV fiction market value and producer-broadcasters relations: Final report 2000.* Strasbourg: Author.

European Audiovisual Observatory. (2000b). *European Audiovisual Observatory Statistical Yearbook 2000.* Strasbourg: Author.

European Commission. (1996). *Eurostat,* N.31/96, May 1996. Brussels: DG X.

European Commission. (1998). *Facts and figures on the Europeans on holidays 1997–1998.* Eurobarometer survey for the European Commission, March 1998. Brussels: DG XXIII.

European Commission. (1999a). *Standard Eurobarometer 51.* Spring 1999. Brussels: DG X.

European Commission. (1999b). *Serving the European Union. A citizen's guide* (2nd ed.). Luxembourg: OPOCE. Retrieved from: http://wwwdb.europarl.eu.int/dors/oeil/docs/FR212_doc_en.htm

European Commission. (2000). *Socrates 2000 Evaluation Study Summary.* Study for the European Commission. Contract No 1999-0979/001-001 SOC 335BEV.

European Commission. (2001). *Eurobarometer 54 Special: Europeans and languages.* February 2001. Luxembourg: OPOCE.

European Marketing Surveys. (2000). *The EMS eligible: A pen portrait.* Retrieved from EMS online http://www.interview-nss.com/ems/docs/page_2000penportrait.htm

European Union. (1992). *Preamble to the Treaty Establishing the European Community as Amended by Subsequent Treaties.* Maastricht: European Union.

European Union. (1997). *The Amsterdam Treaty: a Comprehensive Guide.* Retrieved from: http://europa.eu.int/scadplus/leg/en/s50000.htm

Fiddick, P. (1990). Searching for the daily fix. *Intermedia 18*(2), 15–20.

Fischer, J. (1999, January 19). Bundesminister des Auswärtigen (German Minister for foreign affairs), speaking at 'Europa Wohin: Die Suche nach der europäischen Identität' (Where to for Europe: the search for a European identity), conference organised by Westdeutsch Rundfunk (WDR) Köln and the European Commission representation in Germany, Köln.

Foreign and Commonwealth Office. (2000, July 7). *The Europeanisation of South East Europe.* Keith Vaz, former UK minister for Europe. Retrieved from: http://www.fco.gov.uk

Fry, A. (1998). *Pan European media is attractive for its access to an upmarket business audience.* Retrieved from *The European Perspective* online: http://www.marketing.haynet.com/features/euromed/euromed.htm

Fundesco. (1997). *La Unión Europea en los medios de comunicación [The European union in the media].* Informes anuales de Fundesco, Madrid: Author.

Galtung, J. (1993). The role of communication in rethinking European identity. *Media Development, 4,* 3–7.

Gandy, O. (1982). *Beyond agenda setting: Information subsidies and public policy.* Norwood, NJ: Ablex.

Gardner, J. (1991). *Effective lobbying in the European Community.* The Netherlands: Kluwer.

Gehrke, G. (1998). *Europe without the Europeans: A Question of Communication?* Düsseldorf: European Institute for the Media.

Gellner, E. (1983). *Nations and nationalism.* Oxford: Blackwell.

Giddens, A. (1991). *Modernity and self-identity: Self and society in the Late Modern Age*. UK: Cambridge Polity Press.

Goff, P. (Ed.). (1999). *The Kosovo news and propaganda war*. Vienna: International Press Institute.

Greenwood, J., & Ronit, K. (1994). Interest groups in the European Community: Newly emerging dynamics and forms. *West European Politics, 17*(1), 31-52.

Haas, E. B. (1958). *The Uniting of Europe*. Stanford: Stanford University Press.

Habermas, J. (1989). *The structural transformation of the public sphere: An inquiry into a category of bourgeois society*. Cambridge: Polity Press. (Original work published 1962)

Habermas, J. (1992, April). Citizenship and national identity: Some reflections on the future of Europe. *Praxis International, 12*(1), 1-19.

Hamelink, C. J. (1993). Europe and the democratic deficit. *Media Development 4/*1993, 8-10.

Herman, E. S., & Chomsky, N. (1988). *Manufacturing consent: The political economy of the mass media*. New York: Pantheon Books.

Hoffman, S. (1982). Reflection on the Nation State in Europe today. *Journal of Common Market Studies, 21*, 21-37.

Inglehart, R. (1970). Cognitive mobilisation and European identity. *Comparative Politics, 3*, 45-70.

IP/CLT-UFA. (1999). *Television 1999: European key facts*. Germany: Author.

IP/CLT-UFA. (2000). *Television 2000: European key facts*. Germany: Author.

Janssen, J. (1991). Post-materialism, cognitive mobilisation and support for European integration. *British Journal of Political Science, 21*, 443-468.

Kevin, D. (1995). *Widening and deepening the European debate: Political communication in Denmark, Ireland and the United Kingdom*. Unpublished Dissertation, Dublin European Institute, University College Dublin.

Keohane, R., & Nye, J. S. (1971). *Power and interdependence: World politics in transition*. Boston: Little, Brown & Co.

Ladrech, R. (2002, July). Europeanization and political parties: Towards a framework for analysis. *Party Politics, 8*(4), 389-404.

Leonard, M. (1998). *Rediscovering Europe*. London: Demos.

Leroy, P., & Siune, K. (1994). The role of television in European elections: The cases of Belgium and Denmark. *European Journal of Communication, 9*, 47-69.

Luke, C. (2001, November 10). In *Proceedings of the 13th European Television and Film Forum 2001* (pp. 141-148). Düsseldorf: European Institute for the Media.

Machet, E., & Robillard, S. (1997). *Television and culture: Policies and regulations in Europe*. Düsseldorf: European Institute for the Media.

Machill, M. (1998). Euronews: The first European news channel as a case study for media development in Europe and for spectra of transnational journalism research. *Media, Culture and Society, 20*(3), 427-450.

Mair, P. (2000). The limited impact of Europe on national party systems. *West European Politics, 23*(4), 27-51.

Majone, G. (1996). *Regulating Europe*. London: Routledge.

Marks, G. (1995). *European integration and the state*. (RSC Working Paper, No. 95/07). Florence: European University Institute.

Mazey, S., & Richardson, J. (1993, September). Pressure groups and the EC. *Politics Review, 3*(1), 21-26.

McQuail, D. (1992). *Media performance: Mass communication and the public interest*. London: Sage.

Meyer, C. (1999). Political legitimacy and the invisibility of politics: Exploring the European Union's communication deficit. *Journal of Common Market Studies, 37*(4), 617-639.

Milward, A. S. (1992). *The European rescue of the nation-state*. Berkeley: University of California Press.

Miller, D., & Schlesinger, P. (2000). The changing shape of public relations in the European Union. In R. Heath (Ed.). *The handbook of public relations* (pp. 675–684). Newbury Park, CA: Sage.

Moravcsik, A. (1991). Negotiating the Single European Act: National interests and conventional statecraft in the European Community. *International Organisation, 45*(1), 19–56.

Morgan, D. (1995). British media and European Union news: The Brussels news beat and its problems. *European Journal of Communication, 10*(3), 321–343.

Morley, D., & Robins, K. (1995). *Spaces of identity: Global media, electronic landscapes and cultural boundaries.* London: Routledge.

Mundy, S. (1998). *Making it home: Europe and the politics of culture.* Amsterdam: European Cultural Foundation.

Newhouse, J. (1997). *Europe adrift.* New York: Pantheon Books.

Oreja, M. (1997, March 6). *Culture and European integration, foundations of the European Community's cultural activities* (Speech). Ferstel Palace, Vienna.

Palmer, J., Law, M., & Middleton, P. (2000). The press reporting of European Economic and Monetary Union in four countries. In B. Baerns & J. Raupp (Eds.), *Transnational communication in Europe* (pp. 88–100). Berlin: Vistas Verlag.

Philo, G. (Ed.). (1999). *Message received.* London: Longman.

Risse, T., Engelmann, D., Knopf, H., & Roscher K. (1998). *The "Euro" and identity politics in the European Union.* (RSC Working Paper, No 98/9). Florence: European University Institute.

Robertson, A. (2000). *Depictions of the European Union in 19 Swedish media.* Stockholm: The Media Group.

Russ-Mohl, S. (1992). *Regulating self-regulation: The neglected case of journalism policies. Securing quality in journalism and building media infrastructures on a European scale* (SPS Working paper No. 92/25). Florence: European University Institute.

Scharpf, F. W. (1997). *Balancing positive and negative integration: The regulatory options for Europe.* (Working Paper 97/8 Max Plank Institute for the Study of Society). Köln: Max Plank Institute.

Schlesinger, P. (1996). *Europeanisation and the media: National identity and the public sphere.* (ARENA–Working paper No. 7). Oslo: ARENA.

Schlesinger, P. (1997). From cultural defence to political culture: Media, politics and collective identity in the European Union. *Media, Culture, and Society, 19,* 369–391.

Schlesinger, P. (2001). Communications theories of nationalism. In A. S. Leoussi (Ed.), *Encyclopaedia of nationalism* (pp. 26–30). London: Transaction Publishers.

Schlesinger, P., & Kevin, D. (2000). Can the European Union become a sphere of publics? In E. O. Eriksen & J. E. Fossum (Eds.), *Democracy in the European Union: Integration through deliberation?* (pp. 206–229). London: Routledge.

Schmidt, V. A. (1997). Discourse and (dis)integration in Europe: The cases of France, Germany and Great Britain. *Daedalus, 126*(3), 167–197.

Shore, C. (1993). Inventing the People's Europe: Critical approaches to European Community cultural policy. *Man, 28,* 779–800.

Sinnot, R. (1994). *Integration theory, subsidiarity and the internationalisation of issues: The implication for legitimacy.* (RSC Working Paper no. 94/13). Florence: European University Institute.

Siune, K. (1993). The Danes said no to the Maastricht Treaty: The Danish referendum of June 1992. *Scandinavian Political Studies, 16*(1), 93–103.

Siune, K., Svennson, P., & Tonsgaard, O. (1994). The European Union: The Danes said 'no' in 1992 but 'yes' in 1993: How and why? *Electoral Studies, 13*(2), 107–116.

Slaata, T. (1998). *Europeanisation and the Norwegian news media* (Report No. 36, Series of the Department of Media and Communication). Oslo: University of Oslo.

Svennson, P. (1994). The Danes said yes to Maastricht and Edinburgh: The EC referendum of May 1993. *Scandinavian Political Studies, 17*(1), pp. 69–82.

Television Business International Yearbook 2001. London: InformaMedia Group.

Thomas, B., & Lopez, B. (1998, November). *Regional T.V. broadcasting: Political and cultural implications for European integration.* Paper presented at the Media Literacy as a Topic of Civic and Political Education in Europe conference, Granada.

Venturelli, S. (1993). The imagined transnational public sphere in the European Community's broadcast philosophy: Implications for democracy. *European Journal of Communication, 8,* 491–518.

Volkner, I. (1999). *News in the global sphere: A study of CNN and its impact on global communication.* UK: University of Luton Press.

Waisbord, S. (1998, August). When the cart of media is before the horse of identity: A critique of technology-centred views on globalization. *Communication Research, 25*(4), 377–398.

Ward, D. (2001). *The European Union democratic deficit: An evaluation of EU media policy.* Unpublished doctoral dissertation, University of Westminster, UK.

Weiler, J. H. H. (1993). Journey to an unknown destination: A retrospective and prospective of the European Court of Justice in the area of political integration. In *Journal of Common Market Studies, 31*(4), 417–446.

Weiler, J. H. H (1996). *The selling of Europe: The discourse of European citizenship in the IGC 1996.* Retrieved from Harvard Law School, Jean Monnet Papers Online: http://www.law.harvard.edu/Programs/jeanmonnet/papers/96/9603

Wheatley, M. (2000). Euronews: An EBU project starts to flourish. In *European Broadcasting Union Yearbook 2000* (pp. 44–45). Geneva: European Broadcasting Union.

Woldt, R., Dries, J., Gerber, A., & Konert, B. (1998). *Perspectives of public service television in Europe* (EIM Media Monograph No. 23). Düsseldorf: European Institute for the Media.

Author Index

Subject Index